David Eldridge

Plays: 1

Serving it Up, Summer Begins, Under the Blue Sky, M.A.D.

Serving it Up: 'all the verbal swagger, all the fine-tuned insight and all the confident theatricality of an established writer' *Daily Mail*

Summer Begins: 'Buoyant proof of the onward rise of a 23-year-old dramatist for whom great things clearly have only just begun' *Variety*

Under the Blue Sky: 'Like perfect blue skies, first-class new plays are few and far between, but when they appear they send your spirits soaring. Just such a heavenly piece of writing is the latest by David Eldridge' *Daily Telegraph*

M.A.D.: 'Beautifully written … a marvellous play' *Daily Telegraph*

David Eldridge was awarded the *Time Out* Live Award for Best New Play in the West End in 2001 for *Under the Blue Sky*. His full-length plays include *Serving it Up* (Bush, 1996), *A Week with Tony* (Finborough Theatre, 1996), *Summer Begins* (RNT Studio and Donmar Warehouse, 1997), *Falling* (Hampstead Theatre, 1999), *Under the Blue Sky* (Royal Court Theatre, 2000), *Festen* (Almeida and Lyric Theatre, 2004), and *M.A.D.* (Bush, 2004). *Festen* won the 2005 Theatregoers Choice Award for Best New Play.

also by David Eldridge

Festen
A Week with Tony

DAVID ELDRIDGE

Plays: 1

Serving it Up
Summer Begins
Under the Blue Sky
M.A.D.

with an introduction by David Eldridge

Bloomsbury Methuen Drama
An imprint of Bloomsbury Publishing Plc

B L O O M S B U R Y
LONDON · OXFORD · NEW YORK · NEW DELHI · SYDNEY

For Mum, Dad, Dennis & Faye

Bloomsbury Methuen Drama
An imprint of Bloomsbury Publishing Plc

Imprint previously known as Methuen Drama

50 Bedford Square	1385 Broadway
London	New York
WC1B 3DP	NY 10018
UK	USA

www.bloomsbury.com

BLOOMSBURY, METHUEN DRAMA and the Diana logo are trademarks
of Bloomsbury Publishing Plc

First published in 2005 by Methuen Drama

Introduction and collection © David Eldridge, 2005

Serving it Up © David Eldridge 1996, 2005
Summer Begins © David Eldridge 2005
Under the Blue Sky © David Eldridge 2000, 2005
M.A.D. © David Eldridge 2004, 2005

This collection contains revisions: these revisions replace those previously published in single editions

David Eldridge has asserted his right under the Copyright, Designs and Patents Act,
1988, to be identified as author of this work.

Applications for performance, including readings and excerpts, by amateurs in the English language throughout the world should be addressed to the Performing Rights Manager, Nick Hern Books, The Glasshouse, 49a Goldhawk Road, London W12 8QP, *tel* +44 (0)20 8749 4953,
email rights@nickhernbooks.co.uk, except as follows:
Australia: Dominie Drama, 8 Cross Street, Brookvale 2100, *tel* (2) 9938 8686, *fax* (2) 9938 8695,
email drama@dominie.com.au
New Zealand: Play Bureau, PO Box 9013, St Clair, Dunedin 9047, *tel* (3) 455 9959,
email info@playbureau.com
South Africa: DALRO (pty) Ltd, PO Box 31627, 2017 Braamfontein, *tel* (11) 712 8000,
fax (11) 403 9094, *email* theatricals@dalro.co.za
United States of America and Canada: Independent Talent Group

No rights in incidental music or songs contained in the work are hereby granted and performance rights for any performance/presentation whatsoever must be obtained from the respective copyright owners.

British Library Cataloguing-in-Publication Data
A catalogue record for this book is available from the British Library.

ISBN: PB: 978-0-413-77509-2

Library of Congress Cataloging-in-Publication Data
A catalog record for this book is available from the Library of Congress.

Series: Contemporary Dramatists

Typeset by SX Composing DTP, Rayleigh, Essex
Printed and bound in Great Britain

Contents

David Eldridge:
A Chronology

1995   *Cabbage for Tea, Tea, Tea!* (Exeter University)
Sideways Moving (Edinburgh Fringe)
Fighting for Breath (Finborough Theatre, London)

1996   *Serving It Up* (Bush Theatre)
Dirty (Stratford East Theatre, London)
A Week with Tony (Finborough Theatre, London)

1997   *Summer Begins* (Donmar Warehouse, London)

1998   *Thanks Mum* (Red Room; and Battersea Arts Centre,
London)

1999   *Falling* (Hampstead Theatre, London)

2000   *Under the Blue Sky* (Royal Court Theatre, London)
Killers (BBC Television)

2001   *Michael & Me* (BBC Radio Four)

2002   *The Nugget Run* (Short film)

2003   *Stratford, Ilford, Romford and All Stations to Shenfield* (BBC
Radio Four)

2004   *Festen* – adapted from the Dogme film (Almeida
Theatre, London)
M.A.D. (Bush Theatre, London)

2005   *Incomplete and Random Acts of Kindness* (Royal Court
Theatre, London)
The Wild Duck – a new version from Ibsen (Donmar
Warehouse, London)

Introduction

As a child I wasn't ever especially interested in creative writing, although I may well have had a talent for it, and I always imagined I'd be a history teacher. I didn't grow up in a theatre-going family and can't recall ever being taken to a pantomime. My father was a shoe maker and my mother stopped work as a book keeper to look after her three children. We were poor – often relying on the generosity of friends and relatives and the extra income occasionally provided by my dad's involvement with greyhound racing and as a sometime market trader.

Unlike Charlie and Val in *Serving it Up*, my mum and dad moved out of the East End, with thousands of others, and headed to Essex, with its promise of a new beginning. And I suppose much in the spirit of the times (I was five when Margaret Thatcher was elected) and in the passionate pursuit of wanting the best for their kids, I was put forward for public school and won a place.

I always imagined I'd work on a market stall when I was older, like the other boys who went to comprehensive schools in Romford. I loved going down to the market on a Saturday with my mum to visit Dad and to see Trevor, the market's first black trader, and manager of the stall. My dad's old friends Chris and Ray owned two ladies' shoe stalls in Romford Market and needed someone they trusted to keep an eye on the stalls on their busiest day – Saturday. When at twelve, and hating school, I started to play up, my dad got me a job there. He knew I needed to toughen up, he knew I liked it and that it would give me some pocket money and help me feel more grown up.

At school I did as much academic and extra-curricular work as I needed to get me by and as little as I could to remain unnoticed. What I lived for was Wednesday, Friday and Saturday which were market days, when I could help set up or pack in the stall, and the holidays when I could work all day serving the customers. Trevor, who used to give me some loose change for sweets as a kid, was as handsome as a prince, and part-Fagin, part-Don Juan, a father figure to all the boys who worked for him as they went through their teenage years. At school I got an academic education but on the market I learnt about sex and women, about making money, about criminality, racism, and the sickening nature of violence, about good jokes and wind-ups, about true friendship, utter loyalty and heart-breaking betrayal. I stayed at public school and on Romford Market until the week before I went to Exeter University – this weird double life that I lived largely informs the person I am and the plays I write.

Having so thoroughly loathed my schooling, and with the bottom falling out of the market at the beginning of a terrible recession, I turned in a different direction. In the sixth form I developed a political consciousness and became very angry about the obvious gap between rich and poor that I'd experienced first-hand. I despised the nauseous moral high ground the governing Tory classes contemptuously occupied and the often brutal lack of compassion with which they ruled Britain. I went along to the Historical and Debating Society meetings, heckled guests and fancied myself as something of a sixth-form Dennis Skinner.

A new teacher, Ruth Prior, had joined the school teaching English and introduced GCSE Drama to the curriculum. A friend of mine wanted to opt for Drama (the other two to sign up were girls) and persuaded me to take this as my subsidiary subject. I was, I suppose, very TV-literate and had an above-average interest in TV drama but I simply hadn't ever been to the theatre and I felt it wasn't for me. But Mrs Prior introduced us to improvisation and less conventional plays like Robert Patrick's *Kennedy's Children*, and very quickly I felt I had a way to express myself. I wanted to act, to write, to devise, but mostly to direct, as I wholeheartedly embraced making drama. It's important to emphasise just how quiet and inarticulate I was as a teenager – quite simply I felt I didn't have a voice or one that was worth anyone listening to anyway. I could role-play the cheeky market boy who could sell shoes by the gross and I could talk clubbing to try and impress girls, or be the angry politics student, but I simply didn't have a public identity and voice that was a true reflection of the whole person I was. Then within a few weeks I saw and experienced a way of having one – by making theatre. I went on every theatre trip I could and was knocked out by John Wood's RSC *King Lear* and when I saw Sam Mendes' productions of *The Alchemist* and *Richard III*, I felt I had found a hero whose career I wanted to emulate. I acted small parts in school plays but it was really in improvisations that I excelled. I applied to Exeter University to read English and Drama and worked extraordinarily hard to attain the A-level grades I needed to take up their offer of a place.

I adored my time in that Drama department – the learning, the laughter, and the passion with which everything was undertaken. Whether we were rolling around the floor devising rituals with pre-theatrical roots or erecting auditoria late at night for one showing or another, everyone was very committed. And no one more so than Professor Peter Thomson who more than anyone else has guided me towards the craft of making plays. I'd gone off the idea of directing quite fast as it was clear there wouldn't be much time to practice with a demanding degree programme, I couldn't find any plays which I wanted to direct, and rather naively I believed that being a director meant you had to be an arrogant bastard. As a first-year group we wrote a Brechtian version *of The Wind in the Willows*, which I loved. Not long afterwards, Peter took me to one side and stated bluntly that I couldn't act but I did have a real talent for writing and more importantly the right temperament for it. I didn't know quite what he meant but he gave me a crucial steer in the right direction when my sense of self and the sort of theatre I wanted to make was forming.

Serving it Up began as a doodle late at night: two lads, much like the market boys I knew, sitting on a park bench, talking. When I read it the next morning and got the approval of a friend on the way to a lecture, I decided to write a bit more each day. The characters were called A and

B to begin with, but eventually were given names – one, Sonny, an old-fashioned East End name – and I decided they were from families who had stayed behind on the council estates rather than moved out to Essex like we did. I didn't have a story, though, so I simply thought about what might come between two best mates, decided Nick was having an affair with Sonny's mum, and then I wrote. I was angry about the state of east London's council estates and the uncaring Tory government and I was stirred to react against some of my 'politically-correct' undergraduate contemporaries who would have displayed a similar lack of compassion or understanding where someone like Sonny was concerned and simply dismissed him as a racist.

Peter Thomson liked the play a lot and so did the playwright James MacDonald who was Research Fellow in the department. As I began my final year, both enthusiastically encouraged me to send the play to theatres in London. As I completed my degree I wrote a short, *Cabbage for Tea, Tea, Tea*, and I toyed with the idea of writing a big political play, influenced by writers like Griffiths, Edgar and Hare. I also thought about Ramsay MacDonald and even met a history tutor who was an expert, but really I was treading water and waiting to hear back from the London theatres. And gradually they replied – all positively except one. Mark Ravenhill, who was then reading plays and directing a bit for the Finborough Theatre, arranged a reading but it was Dominic Dromgoole at the Bush who said he might produce it and recommended that I got an agent. So I graduated, I got an agent, I waited and on my twenty-second birthday, the Bush Theatre rang to say they'd produce it as part of a 'London Fragments' season of plays early in 1996. I wrote my state-of-the-nation play *A Week with Tony* with the encouragement of Mark Ravenhill (who was to direct it later on) and I began work with Jonathan Lloyd on *Serving it Up*.

Jonathan was everything I had imagined a director wasn't – an unassuming thoughtful English graduate who was supremely respectful and polite. He had been assistant director at the Bush and Dominic impressed upon me that although he was barely older than me, Jon was brilliant and shared a love of the play. Jon and I got on well and so began the whole new process of putting on the professional production of a play. I took the casting seriously and I undertook conscientiously the odd rewrite Jon and Dominic encouraged – the most significant being the addition of Charlie to Act 2, Scene 5. Rehearsals seem distant now but I do recall being sent out to the colder kitchen area for making the actors giggle, getting a bit tetchy about the jeans Sonny had (I thought he'd be wearing Levi's 501s) and the stunning moment when the incendiary Eddie Marsan came in to the White City church hall having shaved off his curly hair for the role of Sonny. With his bullet head, awkward manner and slightly stiff-backed movements, his creation was both full of desolate sadness and quite thrilling violence. He simply electrified my play and the tiny Bush Theatre every night for five and a half weeks.

I was much less prepared for success than failure. Fortunately I was helped through the heady few weeks by Jack Bradley, Literary Manager at the National, who offered me a writing attachment to the Royal National Theatre Studio. The playwright Stephen Wakelam was my mentor and I read a lot of plays from the National's collection. I was beginning to find more and more in Robert Holman's beautiful writing and as I began work on my third full-length play, the out-and-out polemic of my second play already seemed out-of-date. I admired Robert's mode of placing a detailed poetic realism (and sometimes surrealism) in the context of history and society, and after two or three years of very angry urban plays which were clearly reacting to the selfish individualism of the Thatcher and Reagan years, many of us were searching for a new way of writing which resonated with the world we were living in. In the first nine months of 1996, when *Summer Begins* was written, it was clear John Major's government was on its last legs and Britain was changing remarkably and searching for a gentler, more understanding sense of self. Perhaps significantly the most disturbing acts of violence take place off-stage in this play. I decided to write a play that sought to capture something of what it was like to be in your mid-twenties at that point and thereby pick up on some of the winds of change blowing through the nation.

The narrative had come fairly simply once I'd decided upon the world of the play and I had a very strong image of a woman taking off and putting back on an engagement ring which is at the centre of *Summer Begins*. The RNT Studio were delighted with it and a co-production was arranged with the Donmar Warehouse as part of its New Writing season in spring 1997 with Jonathan Lloyd again directing. As rehearsals took place within the context of the run-up to the 1997 election, it seemed very much like an end-of-Thatcherism play as the character Dave's unrealistic dream of future happiness through the prosperity of enterprise and a small business is finally shattered by his intended Gina. But at its heart I think the play is more about the uncertainty of young adults beginning to assume responsibility as they find their way both in and out of love.

After leaving school I'd continued to stay in touch with my former Drama teacher Ruth Prior and had consequently got to know the world of teachers and teaching very well. I'd been trying to write about two teaching friends since 1997 but it wasn't until summer 1999 and a further writing attachment at the RNT Studio that I was really able to get down to it. I had lots of ideas that resonated off one another. There was something in the nature of unrequited love – and something in the nature of public service in teaching in an age when men no longer expect to be soldiers or women to nurse them that was intimately related in my mind but that wasn't fully formed either. There was also something forming from the tangential links teachers often made with each other as they gossiped about the schools they'd worked in, and from the theatrical conceits behind Schnitzler's *La Ronde* and Holman's wonderful triptych *Making Noise Quietly*. I liked the notion of writing my own geographical journey East End–Essex–Devon too. It was a potent brew and I knew that I needed this time to find a more certainly theatrical way of telling the stories of those ordinary

teaching lives and finding the extraordinary moments in
their encounters. I wrote *Under the Blue Sky* over eight weeks,
a happy time, and I felt as I finished it that I'd done
something important. I didn't dream the theatre that
commissioned the play would turn it down but they did.

In the nine months between that rejection and the Royal
Court Theatre picking up the play, I seriously considered
packing in writing. I applied for jobs to encourage other
writers and did more and more drama work in schools. The
BBC commissioned a TV play *Killers* which they committed
to make, which gave me a fillip, as did a commission for
Radio Four. The theatres I approached all liked *Under the
Blue Sky* but none went for it. Then Jack Bradley and
Jonathan Lloyd encouraged me to try the Royal Court
Theatre, even though the play didn't seem like an obvious
candidate for them. Nervously, then, I met the Court's
Literary Associate, Stephen Jeffreys, for a coffee in Soho to
talk to him and see if I might give him the play. Once again
I nervously waited. A few weeks later, Stephen showed the
play to others at the Court, and then I was in Artistic
Director Ian Rickson's office. He offered a production that
autumn and a commission, and after the hard year I'd had,
I virtually skipped along the Kings Road.

One director with a long association with the Court
claims all plays are either autobiography or journalism, but
actually it's almost always much more complex than that.
The relationship between my experience and the fiction is
perhaps easiest to delineate in *Under the Blue Sky*. My own
experiences of relationships when I'd behaved less well
informed Act One, my imagination took flight in the wild
drunken encounter between Michelle and Graham as she
retells her sexual history and he finally indulges in fascistic
blackmail and fantasy in Act Two, while Act Three was
partly inspired by two teaching friends who went on holiday
together. As Graham Whybrow, the Literary Manager at
the Court, suggested, raw experience, my imagination, and
observed experience informed the plays' three acts with
most emphasis in that order. Writing is almost always a
mixture of those three energies and where experience is

concerned it is shaped, morphed or thoroughly re-imagined as it is written.

Luckily for me, Ian Rickson, like Dominic Dromgoole before him, suggested a younger director I didn't know – Rufus Norris. I was captivated by his hunger for everything I could tell him about the play and the seriousness with which he approached his work. The five weeks' rehearsal and the production week with Rufus and a crack cast were the happiest I've had in the theatre. I don't know whether this is true, but someone told me my play had the first hopeful ending in Theatre Upstairs in fifteen years.

Under the Blue Sky was a success and it was as hard to deal with as it had been the first time around. I wasn't sure what to do next – I owed the Bush Theatre a play and now the Court a new play too. Two things helped me towards the final play in this volume – one a residency at a London advertising agency for the Soho Theatre and the other a commission to adapt the Dogme95 film *Festen*. But more than anything else it was the images of the burning towers I glimpsed through the windows of Dixons in Romford on 11 September 2001, and the epochal global shifts that gross act of terror brought about, which set me on a journey towards *M.A.D.* By Valentines Day 2003, when millions marched in London, I had a rough first draft, and a month later I gave a polished version to Mike Bradwell. He loved the play and said he'd produce it the following year and in the meantime we all worried whether we'd get a licence from the local authority for a thirteen-year-old actor to play the young John at the Bush. The wonderful Lewis Chase was permitted to appear, and Hettie's marvellously acted production was performed with such passion – Lee, Jo, Gerry, Danny and Lewis left audiences weeping in their seats.

Although some have attributed an autobiographical status to *M.A.D.*, the truth is it's no more directly based on my experience than any other work of mine for the stage. Certainly I used some of the anxiety I felt about leaving my friends in Romford to take up my place at public school. My brother thought there was something of Kelly's anger which was similar to my dad's, and the production evoked the sometimes chaotic and ill-decorated family home we had. But the play didn't come from a desire to make a sentimental tribute to my father (actually he's alive and well); rather it was a response to the world reshaped by 9/11. I felt it was wrong, even if it was understandable, for the Americans to seek revenge for 9/11 in Iraq and consequently I thought about someone displacing their own guilt in a less than admirable way on the eve of their father's funeral. I was inspired to look back at the early eighties as I felt some of the language of the Cold War was being revisited in Washington and London, and fears that a weapon of mass destruction might be used by a terrorist or in Iraq itself brought back memories of growing up with my brother and sister as children of the Cold War.

I'm not sure there's an overarching theme that links the plays in this collection, but certainly ideas and motifs crop up again and again: people trying to assume or avoid responsibility and its consequences; the family; society changed by the 'victory' of the West in the Cold War, and the legacy of Margaret Thatcher; sexual betrayal; Essex and the East End; class and classlessness; the redefinition of masculinity; and an affinity with the underdog (certainly something which drew me to adapt *Festen* too).

I've mentioned by name in this introduction many of those who have helped me, but I should also like to thank the following for their help and encouragement, witting and unwitting, which has helped me write these plays over the last ten years: Andrew Stevenson, Leslie Read, Leon Wilde, Emma Pallant, Julie Marshall, Alex Cross, Danny Edwards, Phil Skinner (Cameron), Verity Newman, David Carter, Jacki Tinsley, Deborah Aydon, Joanne Reardon, Sue Higginson, Diane Borger, Paul Sirett, Ben Jancovich, Jenny Topper, John Dove, Jonny Siddall, Roy Williams, Abi Morgan, Dawn Walton, Nicola Wilson, Matt Strevens, Sheila Hancock, Simon Stephens, Jonathan Harvey, Sally Avens, Mike Wadding, Rob West, Andrew Roughton, Anne-Louise Bye, Simon Bent, Paul Miller, Lucy Davies, Joe Penhall, Arbel Jones, Ruth Little, Sacha Wares, Ian Daly and Nicola Cattell.

I'd also like to thank Methuen for their loyalty. My first agent Alan Radcliffe and his successor Michael McCoy have also been constant sources of excellent advice and terrific advocates for my work and my friend David Marshall is a constant source of support and good jokes.

And finally thank you to my family to whom this volume is dedicated and to Caroline Finch, my partner and rock, who shares with me the joy that this collection of plays is published. The five of you know how much I love you and how much you mean to me.

Playwriting is a curious endeavour – partly the articulation of a singular vision and partly the product of several collaborative energies coming together at once. The act of publication asserts authorship and bestows a literary mantle. But at heart I'm a playwright because of the rare magic those energies together create with an audience. It's much more fun to have other people to work with too...

David Eldridge
February 2005

Serving it Up

for my dad
and Trevor
and the Romford Market boys, 1986–1992

Serving it Up was first performed at the Bush Theatre, London, on 14 February 1996. The cast was as follows:

Teresa	Kacey Ainsworth
Ben/Ryan	James Bannon
Charlie	Christopher Ettridge
Val	Arbel Jones
Sonny	Eddie Marsan
Wendy	Melissa Wilson
Nick	Jake Wood

Directed by Jonathan Lloyd
Designed by Nick Sargent
Lighting by Paul Russell
Sound by Seb Lee-Delisle

Characters

Sonny
Nick
Val
Charlie
Wendy
Teresa
Ben *and* **Ryan**
(*who should be played by the same actor*)

Setting
1990s east London.

'Serving up' is a slang term for drug-dealing in parts of east London.

Act One

Scene One

A park bench somewhere in east London. **Sonny** *is a skinhead. Both boys are hard-faced and look out at the audience most of the time.*

Nick It's the environment.

Sonny Do what?

Nick Environment, we did it at school, didn't we?

Sonny Mr Swindler?

Nick Yeah, that's right.

Sonny He was a tit.

Nick I liked him. He told jokes.

Sonny Went on about whales all the time.

Nick He wasn't from Wales?

Sonny No. Whales – the big fish in the sea, you turd. Had a Save The Planet badge.

Nick I reckon they've got to do something about the environment.

Sonny What?

Nick The sun will burn the shit out of us.

Sonny Load of bollocks put about by the government. Give us a fag.

Nick That salmon you are going to light up is contributing to the ozone.

Sonny Will you shut up? Haven't you got anything better to say? What about the bird down at the chip shop?

Nick Piss off.

Sonny Big knockers.

Nick   Leave it out.

Sonny   Good shag?

Nick   I didn't shag her.

Sonny   Bullshit!

Nick   Wouldn't let me do it.

Sonny   No way!

Nick   Didn't have a wet suit, did I? Gave me a blow job though.

Sonny   You should've put her in her place. You could have shot it all over her stomach.

Nick   She might've had a dose of crabs.

Sonny   Got a right fit mum she has. Wouldn't mind fucking a mum, eh, Nicky-boy? Nice old piece of roughage to teach you a lesson or two.

Nick   Yeah.

Sonny   Know something about her sister an' all.

Nick   Oh yeah?

Sonny   Got Aids

Nick   No way!

Sonny   Straight up. HGV positive, mate. Wears one of them red ribbons an' all.

Nick   I'm not going to that chip shop any more. You know I've had a saveloy and chips every week for the last year. I thought it had started to smell funny. Must've been contaminated.

Sonny   Have to get a blood test now.

They laugh. Silence.

Nick   Picking up my motor tomorrow, Sonny. Lovely. Escort mark two. Red it is. Some rust on the doors and wheel-arches but it's superb. Danny's old man reckons I'll get ninety out of it.

Sonny   Ninety my arse. Where? Downhill?

Nick   No, it's proper.

Sonny   Boy-racer now, Nicky-boy. Down on the circuit. On the front at Southend?

Nick   We'll go to the countryside.

Sonny   Yeah, Kent.

Nick   Yeah, do a couple of pills and drive. We'll fly. Excellent.

Sonny   Kent. (*A beat.*) My dad's always going on about Kent. He used to go hopping when he was a kid.

Nick   Hopping?

Sonny   Picking hops, to make beer. They used to do it in the old days, before tractors. My dad used to go in the summer.

Nick   Sounds really shit to me.

Sonny   I reckon they had a real laugh. Sleeping out. Rabbiting and all that. My dad reckons he did his cherry hopping. Said her fanny smelt soapy. The old git still thinks he's Tom Jones.

Nick   I like your dad.

Sonny   You don't have to live with him.

Nick   He's all right.

Sonny   He gets right on my tits.

Nick   First time I got pissed, in the pub with your dad and you. Mine wouldn't drink with me. Wanker.

Pause. **Sonny** *notices something in the distance and smiles.*

Sonny   Oi, Nick, look at that, look at that! Oi – get your tits out!

Pause. **Nick** *laughs.*

Same to you an' all!

Sonny *gestures with two fingers.*

Nick   You're knocked

Pause.

Sonny   Nick.

Nick   What?

Sonny   Remember your birthday?

Nick   What a night.

Sonny   It was brilliant.

Nick   The pub was packed . . .

Sonny   I was fucked on gear and drink, I puked out of me arse.

Nick   What? You shit yourself?

Sonny   No – it was puke. Brilliant night, Nicky-boy. I fucked Vikki that night. Cunt like a Big Mac.

Pause.

I wouldn't mind a regular bird as it goes, Nicky-boy.

Nick   You!

Sonny   Yeah, me. I know how to show a girl a good time.

Nick   The last bird you took out threw her kebab on your head.

Sonny   Her way of saying she loved me.

Nick   Chilli sauce an' all.

Sonny   Didn't half sting.

Nick   You'd just asked her if she took it up the arse.

Sonny   Bullshit. No, not me.

Pause.

I reckon Wendy would be a good lass to take out.

Nick   She's fit.

Sonny   Not just that. She's got a bit of noddle. I like Wendy.

Nick   Known her a few years, ain't you?

Sonny   Since we were kids.

Pause.

Nick   I've been thinking about some mad stuff lately. When I'm bored, I just think about – space, Sonny.

Sonny   Space?

Nick   I've been reading a book.

Sonny   You nob.

Nick   It's not posh. No long words.

Sonny   Words bollocks. Didn't you have enough of books at school?

Nick   It's about a geezer who's pissed off. Everyone he knows walks all over him. His bird, the blokes at work, his mates . . . Well, he gets up one morning and kills them. Kills them all, takes a machine-gun to work and blows them away.

Sonny   Sounds all right.

Nick   It is.

Sonny   Is it out on video?

Nick   No. I've been thinking about loads lately. I've got itchy feet.

Sonny   You want to go to a chirpodist.

Nick   I want to do something.

Sonny   You going funny?

Nick   No, I just . . . I just get fucked off sometimes, Sonny. I get up in the morning and I walk about . . . I want something to do . . .

Sonny   Stay in bed, you tit . . .

Nick   I can't . . . I need to do something, Sonny.

Pause.

Chirpodist? Chiropodist, you plonker. Didn't anyone teach you anything?

Sonny (*thinks about it*)   No.

Pause.

Nick   This environment is heavy shit. The ice-poles melting and the ozone is bad news.

Sonny   Skin up, Nicky-boy.

Nick   I haven't got any.

Sonny   Where did you get all this environment shit?

Nick   On the telly, in the morning, *Open University*.

Sonny   What were you watching that shit for?

Nick   I was tripping. The programme really freaked me out. I thought the sun was going to explode. We'll be in the shit, Sonny. The whole world will be flooded. The bits still in the sun will fry, the ultraviolet there, Sonny.

Sonny   What?

Nick   The blue stuff coming out of sunbeds.

Sonny   Oh right! I know. It makes everything glow in the dark.

Nick   That's the one. That stuff is in the sun.

Sonny   Good on a trip that blue stuff.

Nick   Right.

Sonny   How come's the sun ain't blue?

Nick   Don't know.

Sonny   You've got all the mouth.

Nick   Well, it's not blue – it's fucking orange! (*A beat.*)
That stuff, though, it fucks your skin.

Sonny   They've been saying that for years. Listen, I've
been to Majorca, mate, and there's nothing wrong with me.

Nick   When did you go again?

Sonny   Last year – I went last year, didn't I? Got the job
to pay for it, an' all.

Nick   I've never been abroad.

Sonny   It was brilliant. On the piss every night, loads of
birds, the sun and the sea. Had a couple of good rumbles
an' all with the spics. Joined up with some geordies and beat
the shit out of them. Got a great tan!

Nick   Did you use cream?

Sonny   Queers use cream.

Nick   You need the cream. What was I saying about the
environment?

Sonny   Cream bollocks!

Nick   That ozone blocks out some of the shit in the sun,
that you get cancer from. My mum says that only the
darkies will survive on account of the skin being used to it
all.

Sonny   No!

Nick   If we don't turn Sambo, we're dead.

Sonny   Sod that, I've been smoking since I was twelve. Already booked my appointment with the big 'C', Nicky-boy. Forty, I'm kicking the bucket.

Nick   You're not going to die then.

Sonny   Yes I am. I've planned it since I was ten. In a pub. A fight. I do this bloke over with a pool cue, fuck him right up. Just as I walk away, his mate says something, I turn, a gun. The cunt shoots me . . . in the stomach. The prick. Second bullet right between the eyes, no mistake that time, just like the Krays.

Nick   You might not last that long. You watch, a great big coon's going to cut your throat.

Sonny   How are you dying, Nick?

Nick   Nothing as good as that. I'm at home on my bed having a wank. There's a siren, it's the Russians, thousands of nukes five minutes away. They've had enough of McDonalds and Pizza Hut.

Pause.

Fuck them all, I just hope I come in time.

Sonny *laughs.*

Scene Two

A flat somewhere in east London. **Sonny***'s parents,* **Val** *and* **Charlie***, are sitting on the sofa. There's also an armchair.* **Charlie** *reads the* Sun *and* **Val** *knits.*

Val   Do you want some cake? I've got victoria sponge.

Charlie   I don't like it.

Val   You always used to like it.

Charlie   I didn't.

Val   I always used to make it specially.

Charlie   No you didn't.

He puts down his paper.

Val   I did. I made it listening to Tony Blackburn.

Charlie   That's it.

Val   What?

Charlie   I liked it when you made it. Now you buy it – out of a packet. I don't like it out of a packet.

Val   If I make it tomorrow will you eat it?

Charlie   I will if you put cream in it. Extra cream and I'll eat it.

Val   I'll buy some after work.

Charlie *returns to the paper. Pause. He looks up again.*

Charlie   Will you put some flake on top?

Val   Chocolate on a victoria sponge? That's a bit queer.

Charlie   No it's not. I like it. Put chocolate on it.

He returns to the paper.

Val   Viv's baby's due.

Pause.

Be nice to hear the sound of a baby in the flat again. Remember when Sonny was a baby, Charlie? He was a lovely kid.

Charlie *looks up.*

Charlie   No he wasn't. He was bloody awful.

Val   Not our Sonny.

Charlie   Up all night screaming. (*A beat.*) I knew he was a wrong'un when he first spoke. Did he say mum or dad? No, not our Sonny. Tit! – That was his first word.

Val   That was your sodding fault!

Charlie   I haven't got any tits! And you were the one here all day with him. I was at work.

Val   Work! You must be joking. When Sonny was born you were in Mile End Road knocking out a suitcase full of watches.

Charlie   It fed us, Val, it fed us.

Val   Get out of it! You're a lazy bugger. Look at you. You haven't moved in the last two hours.

Charlie   I'm studying the form.

Val   Pity you don't study those rebate forms.

Charlie   Leave off, Val.

Pause. **Charlie** *looks at the paper.*

Val   Are you going over the track later?

Charlie   I might.

Pause.

Val   Sonny was a lovely kid. I had high hopes for Sonny. Could've been anything that boy, anything he wanted. If only he'd stayed on at school. Didn't I tell him, Charlie. He got off to a good start with me. He had everything he wanted.

Charlie (*finally folding his paper*)   You spoilt him, that's what. What he needed was discipline. Show 'em your strap – that's what my father always said.

Val   You can't treat children like that. You have to teach them, and talk to them . . .

Charlie   Rubbish. Round here? Get off. People from round here only go one way – down. It's all about keeping your head above water, getting one bastard before he gets you. I tried to make the boy a bit streetwise. Some lookout.

Val   Streetwise? Is that all you wanted for our boy?

Charlie   I had ideas for him all right. He could've been a great footballer, but he wanted to play cricket. Cricket! Who ever heard of a cricketer from Hackney! He could've been over at Upton Park by now. Gets my goat it does, Val.

Long pause. **Charlie** *again returns to his paper.* **Val** *lifts her knitting.*

Val   What do you think of this pink?

Charlie *mumbles.*

Val   I like this pink. They're going to call it Alexandria.

Charlie (*looking up*)   How does Viv know it's a girl?

Val   She had a scan. I told you before. They put jelly all over her belly.

Charlie   What flavour?

Val   No, not that jelly.

Charlie   I'm pulling your leg – I'm pulling your leg!

Pause.

Alexandria – what sort of a name is that?

Val   It's nice, a bit sophisticated. It's time we had something sophisticated in this family.

Charlie   Was it John's idea?

Val   I think so.

Charlie   Bloody ponce.

Val   He's all right.

Charlie   Looks down his ruddy great nose at us. Your Viv hasn't been the same since she shacked up with him.

Val   You can't blame her for doing better for herself. John's all right.

Charlie   He's a ponce – And if he wasn't seeing your Viv I'd swear he was a bandit.

Val   Never! He's been good to us. He offered Sonny a job. You heard him, Charlie.

Charlie   Exactly . . .

Val   All Sonny had to do was a year at college, and there it was for him. Eight thousand a year as well.

Charlie   Sonny's got enough money.

Val   Computers are the future, Charlie.

Charlie   Gets on my wick. People like John ponce about in the city, taking us all for a ride, fiddling millions and I'm the one who gets done for having a few quid off the social!

Val   It's your bloody fault. You better just hope they don't start following you over the dogs. No wonder Sonny's turned out like he has.

Charlie   He's all right.

Val   But where does he get his money? He doesn't work. He's going to end up in prison just like you are.

Pause.

Charlie   Where is Sonny?

Val   He's out with Nick.

Charlie   Good boy that Nick.

Val   He is a nice boy.

Charlie *turns again to his paper.*

Val   Nick is a nice boy. Came round this morning for a cup of tea. Ever so polite, Charlie. Made the tea as well. Makes a lovely cup of tea. Had a big slice of victoria sponge an' all.

Val *continues with her knitting. Pause.*

Charlie   Did you screw him, Val?

Val   Charlie! I wouldn't! You know I wouldn't!

Charlie   What you said before.

Val   When. When, Charlie?

Charlie *puts down his paper.*

Charlie   You know who, Sonny's mate – the boy from cricket.

Val   Never!

Charlie   You know who I mean.

Val   No!

Charlie   Don't insult me, Val! Pretty boy, bit older than Sonny. The boy who run the cricket team. What's-his-name – Ryan. That's it, Ryan . . .

Val   Once, I did it once.

Pause.

Why did you say it, Charlie! Why! You know I don't . . .

Charlie   What? Fuck boys! No, course you don't, Val. Course you don't. You just stay away from Sonny's mates. You just leave Sonny alone . . .

Val   How dare you, Charlie!

Charlie   Don't worry, Val, I don't think you fucked your own son, but just let him get on . . .

Val   What are you saying?

Charlie   You know what I'm saying . . . The pissing boy can't move without you asking where he's going. Everything anyone does you have to have your two penn'orth! It's like being watched – you can't move – you smother him, like you try to smother me!

Val   Smother you? – You, you're never here . . .

Charlie   Oh, leave it out . . .

Val   You set up home, fifteen year ago in that bloody pub. How dare you lecture me on being a mother! Hark at you mister-fucking-wonderful. The dad who changed all Sonny's nappies, who always got up in the night, who always sat down and helped him read! Father! Father, Christ, it's a fucking joke!

Charlie   Val!

Val   Where were you when I give birth? Twelve pissing hours I was in labour and you –

Charlie   Val!

Val   And when my mother died. I had Sonny, he was a baby, and you? Where the fucking hell were you, eh, super-dad? Eh? – My husband. At the dogs! At the pissing dogs. You couldn't even get yourself home from the dogs when me mother was lying dead in her bed! How dare you say I smother you!

Charlie   Shut up! Just shut up, just shut up, just shut up!

Pause.

You just keep quiet about your stupid poxy men and I don't give a monkey's, all right! You just make the dinner and bake the fucking cake. That's how it is.

Pause.

Scene Three

Wendy *and* **Teresa** *sit on the park bench where we saw* **Sonny** *and* **Nick** *earlier. They both smoke.*

Wendy   I've given up on a real tan. (*A beat.*) I've got to get on me mum's sunbed, Trese.

Teresa   You don't need it. Sunbed just gives you wrinkles.

Wendy   White legs. Look at them, Trese – like a milk bottle!

Teresa   Get some tanning lotion.

Wendy   It goes all streaky.

Teresa   Your legs are all right.

Wendy   This country. Sun – we've had sun all summer and the week I'm off for a weekend on the beach it's been pissing down. (*A beat.*) Mary's not coming any more. Fucking bitch. She's not getting her deposit back.

Teresa   What are you going to do?

Wendy   Well, you're not doing anything this weekend.

Teresa   I can't afford it, Wend.

Wendy   Come on – what do you reckon?

Teresa   I don't know.

Wendy   It'll be a laugh.

Teresa   A caravan in Bognor?

Wendy   You're just a snob.

Teresa   I'm not. I just draw the line at Bognor, that's all.

A beat.

Wendy   Well, if you're not going to go I'll just have to pull tonight.

Teresa   Where are we going?

Wendy   Don't know.

Teresa   I'm not going to the Red Fox again.

Wendy   Options?

Teresa   I'd rather get food poisoning at the Red Fox.

Wendy   They've changed the music now, Trese . . .

Teresa   My idea of a night out does not involve five hundred sixteen-year-olds bobbing up and down on their first fucking E.

Wendy   They don't play hardcore any more.

Teresa   What is it? Load of metallers and a trip-head shagging a weirdo in the corner?

Wendy   I thought you liked Indie?

Teresa   Will you just leave it, Wend.

Wendy   Sorry!

Teresa   Look, there is more to life than a Friday night and a weekend in Bognor, right.

Wendy   Why don't you just leave the PMT routine, Trese.

Pause.

Teresa   I'm a week late.

Wendy   I thought you stopped seeing Freddie?

Teresa   Yeah – well.

Wendy   Forget it, darling. Talk to me about it in a week's time and you'll wonder what you were worrying about. (*A beat.*) Tell you what. Wouldn't mind a dirty weekend with that Nick.

Teresa   You're a nympho!

They laugh.

Nick's all right. His mate Sonny's a prat though.

Pause.

Wendy   I used to fancy Sonny.

Teresa   He looks like an ape.

Wendy   He's not that bad.

Teresa   Sonny's just like the other blokes round here. If you want to meet someone decent you've got to look up west.

Wendy   I haven't got West End money.

Teresa   And most of them are wankers. I met this city bloke once, Wend. Honestly – he stroked his mobile like it was his prick. And I said to him – I don't care where you're from or how much money you've got, if you try and touch my tits again I'll knee you in the bollocks –

Pause.

I don't know why you bother with blokes so much.

Wendy   You're just a feminist.

Teresa   I'm not a feminist!

Wendy   You are! Always saying it about men. Next thing you'll be shaving your head and shagging a lesbo.

Teresa   Bloody cheek. I just don't let blokes take liberties with me.

Wendy   I like a bloke who takes a few liberties. At least it's a bit of excitement.

Teresa   It's not. They crap all over you. I'm not getting married.

Wendy (*nodding somewhere in the audience*)   Look at him over there walking his dog. I bet he ain't a piss-taker.

Teresa   He must be thirty-odd.

Wendy   I wouldn't mind an older man. Someone to look out for you. Someone to listen to, talk to.

Teresa   No. Look at his face. I've seen that look before. My dad had it. I bet he's just been with a bird, and not his wife either . . .

Wendy   No! Not him – he looks like Richard Gere.

Teresa   He's a shit – just like the rest.

Wendy   He's lovely in *Pretty Woman*. Anyway, Cindy Crawford wouldn't go with a bastard.

Teresa   They split up, you silly tart.

Pause.

Wendy   What will you do, then? You can't live on your own . . .

Teresa   I'm not going to live under the thumb.

Wendy   What about when you fall in love?

Teresa   No way!

Wendy   I believe in love.

Teresa   You still believe in Father Christmas.

Pause.

It's all rubbish, Wend. You'll wake up one morning and think – I'm forty, I'm fourteen stone and I don't know what I'm doing. But before it pisses you off, you look at your old man and you ask him for a cuddle. What does he do? He rolls over, farts, and tells you to go and make him a cup of tea. I don't want that.

Wendy   You've got to have love. You've got to have love, Teresa.

Pause.

I've been in love – I know what it's like. I was in love with Jason.

Teresa   Jason?

Teresa *laughs.*

Wendy   Yes.

Teresa   That plonker? You could hit him with a hammer and that fuckwit would still grin.

Wendy   He had a nice smile.

Teresa   He was born with that. His mum dropped him on his head.

Wendy   Don't take the piss.

Teresa   And he had a twitch. We used to call him Shakin' Stevens at school!

Wendy   You always take the piss.

Teresa   Bloody hell. That's your romance? What was that? Hand up your skirt and make your fanny wet?

Wendy   Fuck off.

Teresa   Wend . . .

Wendy *goes to leave.*

Teresa   No, wait. Wait, please, Wendy.

Wendy *stops and turns.*

Teresa   You know what I believe, Wend? Sometimes I can see it when I'm here at the park. I look at the kids with their mums and dads, and I know that I shouldn't feel it, because I look at the faces of the mums and they're so heavy and drawn – But I look at the kids and there I see it – life.

Pause.

This place, the park, the playground – You remember, Wend, when we were kids, on the swings. Swinging higher and higher, faster and faster, so you could almost feel, you could jump off and you would fly – but you don't. You hold on tight. We lop off each year backwards and forwards on that swing, and it gets slower and slower and when you finally want to jump – you really want to jump – you're going nowhere, you're stuck.

Pause.

I'm not saying I'm going to fly, but I can't be tied to a bloke who doesn't give a shit and I can't be tied here for the rest of my life.

Wendy   Are you saying you're leaving?

Teresa   No, no – but I have to be free. I have to have a choice when something comes along.

Wendy   What's coming along? What's going to turn up round here?

Scene Four

The flat. **Nick** *and* **Sonny** *sit on the sofa getting stoned.*

Sonny   Good smoke, Nick.

Nick   Lovely.

Sonny   What is it?

Nick   Afghan. I got it from Tony.

Sonny   You took a chance.

Nick   He wouldn't knock me.

Val *enters carrying two bags of shopping.*

Val   Put the kettle on, Sonny.

Sonny   I've just sat down.

Val   You're on that funny stuff again. No wonder you can't get off your arse. Makes your brain go funny. Why everyone slurred their speech in the seventies, years of taking that stuff. Mark my words, Sonny, you'll be a cabbage by the time you're forty.

Sonny *laughs.* **Val** *goes into the kitchen offstage.*

Sonny   I'll be dead then, right, Nicky-boy?

Val *wanders back in.*

Val   Hello there, Nick. I didn't see you when I came in. Do you want some tea?

Nick   Lovely.

Val   Do you want some cake? Don't be shy, there's plenty of it. Sonny'll only stuff it all. It's a victoria sponge.

Nick   Just a small bit.

Val   I'll give you a nice big slice.

She goes out but we can hear her.

How's your mum, Nick?

Nick   She's all right.

Pause. **Val** *begins to hum 'Love Me Do'.*

Sonny   She fucking gets on my tits. Here, take this.

Nick   Cheers. Can you get any more?

Sonny   Reckon I can. Fancy some weed though. Nice bit of skunk.

Nick   Ages since we've had a bit of skunk.

Sonny   Can't beat it. Reckon I might be able to rustle up a couple of deals of whizz an' all. Bobby owes me.

Nick   I can't lug any more of that shit up me nose.

Sonny   Bomb it!

Nick   I'm not taking any more of that shit . . .

Sonny   Stop fucking moaning. It'll do you good. You'll be on your toes and ready to fight the fucking world.

Nick   My prick will shrink up into my stomach.

Sonny   Hark at the stud – Works the other way an' all, you nobber. Get the horn and the old boy'll be up for the week.

Pause. **Val** *enters with a tray. There are three mugs of tea and a sponge cake on the plate.* **Val** *cuts the cake into three and passes the tea and cake round, still humming the song.*

Val   What've you been up to, Nick? Still after a job?

Sonny *grins.*

Val   At least he's looking. More than you. You're going to end up in prison – like your dad if he's not careful.

Sonny   I'm going to the top me.

Val   You're going to bloody prison.

Sonny   Piss off.

Val   I've told you. I bet you don't speak to your mother like that, Nick. Not like him – bloody animal.

Sonny   Fuck off.

Val   I've fucking told you!

She tries to stand, but can't – the tray is on her lap. So she throws her cake at **Sonny**, *but it misses.* **Sonny** *throws his cake at* **Val** *and it hits her in the face.* **Sonny** *laughs.* **Val** *wants to laugh, suppresses it, but laughs eventually.*

Val   You sod. Wait till your father comes home.

Sonny   Who, Elvis? – Bollocks!

Pause.

Nick   Have you got a snout?

Sonny   No, last one went in the spliff.

Nick   Shit.

Val   Charlie might have some?

Sonny   No, we just finished his Bensons. I'll get some. Come on, Nick.

Nick   No. I want to stay here. I'm too stoned.

Val   Where are you going?

Sonny   I'm going to get some fags. Do you want anything?

Val   No.

Sonny *gives* **Nick** *the joint and exits. Pause.* **Val** *takes the tray from her lap and moves over to* **Nick** *on the sofa. They kiss tenderly, lovingly.*

Nick   Lovely eyes. Beautiful.

Val *smiles and kisses* **Nick** *passionately. She clambers on top of him and starts to undo his shirt.*

Nick   Leave off a minute, Val.

Nick *moves himself from under her.*

Val   I didn't know you were coming today.

Nick   Sonny'll be back in a minute.

Val   I want you, Nick. Come on, now.

Nick   Leave off.

Val   Give me that.

Val *takes the joint.*

Nick   You don't smoke this.

Val   Yes I do. I need to calm down. You've got me going.

Pause. **Val** *smokes.*

Nick   Give us it back.

Val   I've got an apple pie in the fridge.

Nick   No.

Val   Do you want a slice? Made it for Charlie. Hasn't touched a bit.

Nick   No – really . . .

Val   Are you coming back later on?

Nick   I can't. I've got to sign on.

Pause.

What's that knitting for, Val?

Val   It's for me sister Viv. She's having a baby.

Nick   How old is she?

Val   A bit younger than me – And don't ask.

Nick   I didn't know Sonny had an aunt?

Val   He's got two. Me other sis's called Violet.

Nick   Val, Viv and Violet?

Val   The three Vs. Always used to do 'Bubbles' at the end of the karaoke. See, I'm not such an old biddy.

Nick *smiles.*

Val   Used to go karaoke every week with me sisters. Until Viv met John. Computers, Nick. He works in the city.

Nick   Don't you like him?

Val   No, I like him. It's Charlie who don't like him.

Nick   Bit flash is he?

Val   Well, I think he's all right – But we went to the curry house a couple of years ago when Viv first started going out with him and Charlie didn't take a liking to him. It was awful – I didn't know where to put me eyes. Charlie kept making jokes about the Pakistanis. And he wouldn't drink any wine. Said he might as well write ponce across his head. It weren't too bad till the end. John said he'd treat us but Charlie wouldn't let him. He kept going on about not being bought by a little prick from Highbury. I wouldn't mind but he didn't have any money! And he ripped up John's cheque book!

Nick *grins.*

Val   Don't laugh, Nick. That was a week's wages I had to pay. And he had a fight on the bus home. Some Sikh boys broke his arm in two places.

Nick   Good old Charlie.

Val   Serves him right.

Nick   What about the other one?

Val   Violet? No – I don't get on with Violet.

Pause.

Nick   Can – can I ask you something?

Val   You dirty bugger.

Nick   No. Something else. I've been thinking.

Val   Have you now?

Nick   See – I like Charlie.

Val   I like Charlie. He's just a lazy bastard.

Nick   You know – This, Val.

Val   What?

Nick   It's out of order – and what about Sonny?

Pause.

I just . . .

Val   You want to know? Because you've got a nice bum and I wanted a little comfort.

Nick   Charlie's a better man than my dad'll ever be and I'm hardly . . .

Val   You've got a cheek. Don't you dare compare yourself to my Charlie. You? You're a boy and you'll never be in the same league as my Charles. I know you, Nick – you're all the same with your grinny look. What do you want me to say? We row, we've got separate beds? No, not good enough. What you want is a fantasy, a real story to toss over . . .

Nick   No, Val . . .

Val   I know men. I know them too well. I'll tell you what you want. He can't get it up. How do you like that, Nick? Impotent.

Nick   I'm sorry, Val.

Val   Don't make me laugh.

Pause.

The cleaners all talk about their comforts. What a funny thought – a room full of scrubbers sharing their comforts.

She picks her way round the room clearing up the bits of cake.

I love my tea break. We have such a laugh – fall over laughing. Some of the things Daisy told us this morning about me in the war.

Nick   Are you all at it then?

Val   Don't say it like that. Makes it sound so sleazy. No. But we all enjoy the stories. Some of them lie sometimes. You can tell – there just isn't that spark in their eyes.

Pause.

What about you, Nick?

Nick   What?

Val   I mean, you must be able to do better than me? I've heard you're a right little tart.

Nick   I don't know . . .

Val   Of course you know. It's up there in that little brain of yours.

Nick   You're different.

Val   I'm old.

Nick   You're all right.

Pause.

At home. My mum . . . It's not like here. You and Charlie, friendly and . . . well, Sonny. We're a bit different . . .

Val   You can say that again . . .

Nick   He's been my best ever mate, Val. Before I met Sonny, I was always the kid who got beaten up at school. I had things straight up here . . . (*Points to his head.*) . . . but I . . . was a fuck-up. My dad. He'd hit me and then he'd buy me stuff, loads of stuff, stuff he couldn't afford . . .

A door slams offstage. Pause. **Sonny** *enters.*

Sonny   Oh, Nick!

Nick   What?

Sonny   Guess who I've just seen down the road. Wendy and Teresa – and guess what, Nicky-boy – they've asked 'us' to meet 'them' for a drink.

Nick   Right, great.

Sonny   Red Fox. Seven o'clock. Well, for fuck's sake put a smile on your face.

Val   He's shy, Sonny. Doesn't want to say much in front of your mum. Not an uncouth sod like you. Don't worry, boys, I'm going into the kitchen.

Val *exits.*

Sonny   Let's go down the pub.

Nick   I've got to sign on yet.

Sonny   So?

Nick   Look, I can't afford it – and anyway, if we go now we'll be well pissed by seven.

Sonny   Don't worry, Nick, I've got fifty knicker.

Nick   Where did you . . .

Sonny   I've sold Tim five Es.

Nick   What?

Sonny   Well, they weren't E, were they. Anadin. Dipped them in some food colour. Told Tim blue Es were new in straight in from Amsterdam. One hundred per cent MDMA.

Nick   He'll do you for that.

Sonny   If he comes anywhere near me I'll cut him – he knows that.

Pause.

Nick   Still, if we go now, we'll be fucked. Wendy and Teresa won't sit there with us rolling around, will they?

Sonny   I don' know . . .

Nick   What if they do? You know Wendy.

Sonny   What?

Nick   She comes on – on heat.

Sonny   On heat?

Nick   You won't be able to get it up, too pissed. She'll laugh at you, Sonny.

Sonny   Don't know about that, Nicky-boy. You know me – ten pints and I could still shaft an elephant.

Pause.

These birds are hot though. Better stick to the spliffs.

Nick   Yeah.

Sonny   Yeah.

Scene Five

A pub somewhere in east London. Opening music fades into a continuous juke-box soundtrack. **Nick** *and* **Sonny** *stand smoking, and* **Charlie** *enters with three pints.*

Sonny Cheers, Dad.

Nick Cheers, Charlie.

Charlie Get that down, boys. Lovely. So what time are the ladies turning up?

Sonny Seven.

Charlie Fuck. You're bloody keen. It's not half past yet.

Sonny These birds are quality, Dad.

Charlie Are they?

Sonny Not like the other scrubbers round here. Bit of class.

Charlie Well, boys, let me give you a bit of advice. If you've not got your hands inside their knickers by closing time, forget it, class or not.

Sonny Go on then, Casanova.

Charlie I tell you, when I was your age the birds knew where they stood with me – and they respected me for it. But, then I always was a bit of a smoothie when I was younger. Should've seen me on my bike. Parker and Fred Perry T-shirt down at Brighton beach.

Sonny I thought you was a rocker.

Charlie Piss off! Rocker! Your mother was the one who liked Elvis. The king – there was only one king, Pete Townshend was the king.

Nick I've seen him on the Woodstock video.

Charlie *breaks into 'My Generation' which* **Sonny** *tries to interrupt.*

Sonny Fucking hell, Dad!

Charlie *continues.*

Sonny Shut up . . .

Charlie *still continues.*

Sonny   If you don't shut up I'm gonna kick your head in!

Charlie *breaks off.*

Charlie   You know, I was told, Roger Daltrey once pissed on my Lambretta.

Sonny   Dad.

Wendy *and* **Teresa** *arrive.* **Charlie** *doesn't notice.*

Charlie   Now, boys, tell me when the girls come in and I'll scarper. But you know, Sonny, I've always had a silver tongue. You could do a lot worse than get me in on the act – their knickers will fall off.

Wendy   Who's the old prick, Sonny?

Charlie   Sonny, you didn't tell me the young ladies had arrived. Hello there, my love.

Wendy *and* **Teresa** *laugh.*

Charlie   Here, look – what did I tell you boys. Now listen, ladies. I was a snake-charmer in a previous life.

Sonny   Fuck off, Dad.

Charlie   It's all under control, boy, leave it to me. Do you like to dance? They used to say I moved like Tom Jones.

Sonny   Oh, shit . . .

Charlie   Now, dear, what's your name?

Wendy   Madonna.

They all laugh except **Sonny**.

Charlie   Sense of humour! I like a sense of humour in a lady. You know I once knew the Two Ronnies. Painted the town red we did. They autographed a pair of their glasses for me! Shame I can't wear them – right eye seeing the black squiggle, see.

He laughs.

Now, darling, that is a very becoming top you're wearing there. Now what does that say?

He ogles **Wendy**'s *tight top.*

Wendy   Never you mind . . .

Sonny   For fuck's sake!

Charlie   Well, ladies . . . Listen, I've got to go and have a tinkle – but I'll see you later on.

Sonny   Go, Dad, go!

Charlie   Ta-ta, girls.

Charlie *exits.*

Teresa   Who was that?

Nick   Sonny's dad.

Wendy *and* **Teresa** *laugh.*

Sonny   No, no – I'll do you, Nick – no because, that bloke ain't my dad. He's my uncle – you know the type – had his last erection when the telly was black and white.

A beat.

So . . . Nick, this is Wendy and this is Teresa . . .

Wendy/Teresa   All right.

Nick   All right.

Wendy   I ain't met you before, have I?

Nick   No, I've seen you about.

Wendy   Yeah.

Sonny   Yeah. So what have you been up to then?

Teresa   Not much.

Sonny   Yeah?

Wendy   Not much – we went down Edgware Road.

Sonny   Oh right. Yeah, sounds great. Me and Nick have been at work. You were lucky you caught me at the corner. I was just on my way back to the site.

Nick   How comes you weren't at work?

Wendy   I get Friday afternoon off of the salon.

Teresa   I heard you and Nick got laid off?

Sonny   No, no – who told you that? That was ages ago. This is a different firm – and it's more dosh.

Wendy   Yeah?

Nick   Oh yeah, that's right . . .

Sonny   No darkies either.

Pause.

Would you two like a drink while I go to the bar?

Teresa   No, we can't stop long.

Wendy   Yes we will. I'll have a double Tia Maria and Coke and Teresa'll have a double vodka and lime . . .

Nick   Doubles!

Sonny   D'you want crisps? I know you like prawn cocktail, Wend.

Teresa   No.

Sonny   Give us a hand with the drinks, Nick.

Sonny *and* **Nick** *exit. Pause.*

Teresa   Fucking hell, Wendy . . .

Wendy   They're all right.

Teresa   Jesus, they're like Pinky and Perky.

Wendy   We're not going. I want to talk to Nick.

Pause.

I know you used to fancy Sonny, whatever you say.

Teresa   That was before I had a brain. I thought Simon
Bates was sexy and I still listened to Bros.

Wendy *laughs.*

Teresa   I preferred it when the old boy was here. At least
I was having a laugh.

Wendy   We'll have the drink and we can say you're
feeling sick. I can't stay that late anyway, I'm up at six for
Bognor tomorrow.

Teresa   Listen. I'm not saying I'm sick. I'm fed up with
getting you out of shit. You can explain to them.

Wendy   Getting me out of shit? I don't want to go.

Pause.

Have you come on yet?

Teresa *shakes her head.*

Wendy   What you going to do?

Teresa   I don't know.

Wendy   Get rid of it . . .

Teresa   Don't say it like that. It's a baby.

Wendy   No it's not. It's just a load of . . .

Teresa   What?

Wendy   I don't know. But it's not a baby.

Pause.

I can't wait to get away from that pissing salon.

Teresa   I don't know how you put up with it.

Wendy   And I always wanted to be a hairdresser.

Teresa   You're not serious?

Wendy   After air stewardess, Trese, then nurse – oh, and a nun. Course I'm not serious! Dandruff, scabby, leering old men and the blue-rinse brigade are not my idea of fun.

Teresa   Get out then.

Wendy   I need the money.

Teresa   We all need the money.

Pause.

Wendy   I wanted to be a secretary.

Teresa *laughs.*

Wendy   I would've an' all if college hadn't chucked me out.

Teresa   You can't even spell let alone type.

Wendy   What I need is to meet someone very rich to take me to Hollywood. Nice big stretch limo, house in Beverly Hills, and a fucking great tit job. Oh yes, I could do with meeting a bloke who could give me that . . .

Sonny *and* **Nick** *enter with the drinks.*

Sonny   They didn't have any prawn cocktail, Wend.

Nick   There you go.

Wendy   Cheers.

Teresa   Cheers.

Teresa *downs her drink.*

Sonny   Do you always swallow that fast?

Teresa   Are you trying to be funny?

Sonny   Don't get your knickers in a twist, Trese.

Teresa   Have you always been running on just the two brain cells or are you down to the one?

Wendy   Trese!

Sonny   Just joking – a joke, Trese!

Pause.

Guess what, girls – If you fancy it – We can go back to
Nick's flat.

Nick   Sonny . . .

Sonny   No one'll be in – and I've got a bottle of Jack
Daniel's in Nick's motor.

Wendy   Sounds great.

Teresa   You're leaving early tomorrow, Wend.

Wendy   No, not that early.

Sonny   Never know, Trese, if you're game for a laugh,
Nick might let you swallow it all in one.

Teresa   What did you say?

Sonny   Just having a giggle.

Teresa   Fuck off, Sonny. You just can fuck off! Come on,
Wend . . .

Sonny   Do what?

Teresa   Drink up, we're going.

Wendy   Trese . . .

Sonny   We just . . .

Nick   It's all right, Sonny . . .

Wendy   Wait a minute . . .

Teresa   I'm going.

Sonny   You can't go.

Teresa   Well, we are. I could have a better time with a
couple of stiffs down Manor Park cemetery.

Sonny   You've only been here five minutes.

Wendy   Teresa . . .

Teresa   Come on, Wend!

Nick   Go on, piss off!

Wendy *and* **Teresa** *exit.*

Sonny   Nick, you prat! They can't do that.

Shouting after them.

You fucking slags, come back here!

Pause.

Well, fuck off then! Go on, piss off you old-doers!

Nick   Shut up, Sonny, we'll be barred.

Sonny   You wait. When I see that Teresa I'm going to give her a slap. Fucking bitch.

Pause. **Charlie** *enters.*

Charlie   All right there. Hello? Where's the totty gone? I've been gone five minutes and they've left – What did you say to them?

Sonny   Nothing.

Charlie   Nothing? Well, it's a crying shame, boy – I didn't half fancy a Donald.

Pause.

Sonny   Anyway, they're dykes.

Charlie   Never!

Sonny   Everyone knows – 'strap it on' merchants.

Charlie   Well, you never can tell. I knew a dyke once. Lovely she was – what I would've done to give her one. Still, a man can't have every woman.

Sonny   Course you can. If you got the spondooli anything's possible. Thirty quid and your train fare to King's Cross – you've got a low-life with a dose. Thirty million and a yacht and Fergie will be sucking your cock.

Charlie *thinks about it.*

Charlie   I don't like Fergie. She's ginger. There are some things you can't buy, boys. A dyke's a dyke. But, look at me and your mother, Sonny. Now you can't buy that twenty-five year's worth.

Sonny   Shut up, Dad. You were probably the reason why they left early.

Nick   Don't worry, Sonny.

Sonny   You silly old tosser . . .

Charlie   Sonny . . .

Nick   Like you never said a fucking word, Sonny . . .

Pause.

Come on – you've still got the nifty.

A beat.

Let's get really pissed.

Sonny   Yeah . . . Yeah, let's get really pissed.

Scene Six

Nick *and* **Sonny** *wait for a bus on the street. They are very drunk.*

Sonny   Nicky-boy.

Nick   Sonny-boy.

Sonny   How long's the bus? I'm going to puke.

Nick   No, no – you don't want to do that.

Sonny   Deep breaths.

He takes in gulps of air.

That's better.

Nick Does it work?

Sonny Yeah.

Nick *takes in gulps of air.*

Nick I feel sick.

Sonny No, no. You're not doing it right. Like this –

He shows him and **Nick** *copies.*

That's it. That's it.

Nick This country's shit, Sonny. Look at it. Fucking shit everywhere. All over the floor. They can't even empty the bins. All the shit blowing around.

Sonny No. That was me. You've got to do the bins on the way home. Wouldn't be a night out without doing the bins – and the aerials – we'll do the aerials an' all. Tell you what, Nicky-boy, if you do a Porsche I'll give you a hundred quid.

Nick Yeah?

Sonny Yeah. I will an' all.

Nick This country is shit.

Sonny No. No it's not. Greatest country in the world, England. We won the war, didn't we? And the fucking Argies. And them fucking Arab-cunts.

He starts to sing 'Rule Britannia' drunkenly.

Ben, *a young bloke a bit older than* **Sonny** *and* **Nick**, *enters eating some chips.*

Sonny Oi, oi. All right, mate! We've been singing, haven't we, Nicky-boy – 'Rule Britannia'. Had a night out, have you? We have. We're pissed.

Ben Yeah, mate, nice.

Sonny   Yeah, nice.

Ben   All right there, mate? Look like you're going to fall over –

Sonny (*laughing*)   Not me, cocker . . .

Pause.

Oi, mate – you got a fag?

Ben   No, mate.

Sonny   Go on – give us a fag.

Ben   No, mate – I don't smoke.

Sonny   Oi, Nicky-boy. He don't smoke . . .

A beat.

Oi, mate, give us a chip.

Ben (*laughing – to* **Nick**)   Oi, is your mate taking the piss?

Pause.

Sonny   Am I black or what? Oi, give us a chip.

Ben   Leave off, mate . . .

Nick   Sonny . . .

Sonny   Give us a chip . . .

Ben   Leave it out, mate . . .

Sonny   Give us a fucking chip . . .

Ben   Piss off . . .

Sonny   You tight cunt . . .

Sonny *tries to grab some.*

Ben   Piss off you wanker . . .

Sonny   You fucking tight cunt . . .

Nick   No, Sonny . . .

Ben   Oh yeah . . .

Sonny   You cunt . . .

Ben (*pulling a knife*)   Fuck off before I cut you.

He throws the chips and frees his other hand.

I mean it, you prick!

Nick   Sonny . . .

Sonny   Silly boy . . . Silly boy . . .

Sonny and **Ben** *square up to each other at a safe distance, then the stand-off begins. Each moves waiting to pick his moment.* **Sonny** *lunges at* **Ben** *and catches him off balance. They struggle and fall to the ground.* **Sonny** *gets the upper hand.* **Ben** *drops the knife which* **Sonny** *takes hold of as he takes control. The lights begin to fade.*

Sonny   Silly boy . . . Silly boy . . . I'm going to cut you up, you cunt.

Ben   No . . . No . . . No . . . No . . .!

Blackout. **Ben** *screams.*

Scene Seven

Police sirens wail and flashing blue lights bathe the stage. **Charlie** *stands alone and eats a kebab. He is very drunk.*

Charlie   Oi, copper! Copper! I hope you're going to catch the bastard who did that! Hey – copper! (*Pause.*) Cunt . . . Fucking shit . . . (*Pause.*) Law . . . Not my fucking law, you bastards! (*Pause.*) You want my dole . . . Have it . . . Fucking have it, you bastards . . .

He unsteadily reaches with his free hand into a pocket and then tosses out his change and a crumpled-up note.

Have it . . . (*Pause.*) I'd rather have the shit off your shoes, copper . . . You wait . . . There will be the day when I hold the keys to your fucking cell, copper! And, copper – you won't get any grub either! (*Pause.*) I remember you . . . I seen you at the dogs with your missis . . . you ain't so proud then . . .

Pause. He reflects drunkenly.

Poor kid . . . Could've been my Sonny. (*Pause.*) Blood on the streets . . . That's what they said . . . (*Pause.*) Blood like shit on my hands, copper . . . (*Throws his kebab.*)

Look at 'em . . . Wank, wank, wank, wank, wank . . . Val . . . Val . . . Fuck her . . .

He laughs loudly at himself.

Can't even manage a fucking toss . . . Charlie Jaffa, right, copper . . . Charlie Jaffa, but I dances like Tom Jones . . .

He stumbles around stupidly, but then starts to spin, faster and faster, till he falls. Pause. He doesn't move and he moans with pain.

Help, copper, help . . . I hurt my leg.

He cries with terrible, searing pain – from the gut.

Fucked it now . . . Fuck, fuck, fuck . . . (*Pause.*) God! Someone listen to me! Just a hand . . . I hurt!

He is drowned out by a wailing siren which at first offers hope, but gradually fades into nothing.

Act Two

Scene One

Nick *and* **Val** *sit on the park bench.*

Val Just fancied some fresh air. You know.

Nick Yeah.

Val On my way to see Charlie.

Nick Is he all right? Sonny said it was a broken ankle.

Val Fracture.

A beat.

He can be a miserable bastard when he's ill.

Nick How long is he in for?

Val Just a couple of days. It's a nasty break.

Nick I'll get him a card.

Val Don't you bloody dare! It serves the bugger right! He won't be going to the pub for a while, I can tell you that for sure.

Nick Is he all right?

Val He's bloody loving it, Nick. And don't ask me why – but the nurses are like flies round shit. I went in to see him yesterday morning and the soppy sod was singing 'Love Me Tender' to a little group of them. He followed it with his two favourite Ronnie Barker jokes, and the dirty sod asked them if they wanted to draw straws for the first bed bath! And he didn't notice me standing there. I don't know what's wrong with them. They've all signed his plaster.

Pause.

Are you coming over tomorrow?

Nick I don't know, Val.

Val   Right.

Nick   I mean, I don't know what I'm doing yet. I'll try to get over.

Pause.

Val   Is it someone else?

Nick   What?

Val   Have you met someone? Look, you don't have to lie . . .

Nick   I haven't.

Val   Hark at me. Stupid, jealous old woman.

Nick   No, Val.

Pause.

Val   You're my greatest pleasure and my greatest curse. Do you know that, Nick?

Nick   I don't understand.

Val   Being with you. It sends a shiver of excitement up my back, you make me laugh, you listen to me, you make me feel . . . I don't have any words for how you make me feel, Nick, but when I look in the mirror doing me hair I think about you and I smile.

Pause.

I see the wrinkles and I think of you . . .

Pause.

I'm old, Nick. I have grey hairs in my head, and the vanity of believing that you could love me, the things I think of. Leaving Charlie, Jesus, Charlie, he couldn't survive . . . I don't know where I am or where I'm going, Nick, but every time I'm with you, I can't help thinking – How many times will I see you again and is this the last time and it's driving me mad, Nick, because as the evenings draw in, and the days go by I think, is this the last time I'll be with a man, and is this the last time I'll love someone. It doesn't matter to me whether you care a jot for me, but the day I stop loving, the day I stop caring . . . The day I don't want to care . . . That frightens me, Nick. Because I will have become one of them.

Nick   Who, Val?

Val   Out there. Like the rest that go on and on and on, day after day . . . I used to think . . . I mean, I thought that my men, my boys, were the sparkle. The thing that put the twinkle in my eye.

Pause.

But this morning when I was going through cupboards looking for a puzzle for Charlie, I found something. Ages, years ago I had a boyfriend who worked in London Zoo, I didn't see him for long, but he was such a laugh, such fun. We even screwed in the giraffe enclosure one night. He bought me a present, a tiger bear, and I kept it.

Pause.

When I saw that bear this morning, it made me cry. The memories, things I hadn't thought of for years . . . I felt the way you make me feel.

Pause .

I realised then, that what I have been doing, year after year is fooling myself – kidding myself. With every bloke there comes new promise, and I do work at it, I give them everything I have here. And they . . . They come and go. They go, Nick. Just like you will . . .

Nick   I won't, Val . . .

Val   But I still dream, I still . . . Christ. It's so stupid, so stupid. You're twenty, for God's sake, and you haven't been the first young one either.

Long pause.

Nick   What's in the brown bag, Val?

Val   Just some cake.

Nick   Oh.

Val   Made it for Charlie. Put bloody cream and chocolate on it as well. Still didn't eat it. Had his fall, didn't he? It's gone stale, Nick.

Pause.

I'm going to feed it to the birds.

Nick   I used to feed the birds when I was a kid with me mum. Remember, they used to have lovely great swans then, Val.

Val   All gone now.

Nick   Like the bandstand. Used to play soldiers in the bandstand.

Val   Still got the playground.

Nick   Kids still play, Val.

Val   Mums still watch them.

Pause.

Did anything happen on Friday night, Nick?

Nick   No, Val.

Val   It's just Sonny's jeans . . .

Nick   No – nothing.

Val   And what with Charlie . . .

Nick   Nothing happened.

Pause.

Val   Did you know it's my birthday tomorrow, Nick?

Nick   No, Sonny hasn't said.

Val Suppose it's why I'm being so . . . I haven't enjoyed a birthday in years.

Nick I'll come over . . .

Val You don't have to.

Nick It'll be great. We'll have a laugh. I've got some money left from me giro. I'll get a bottle of plonk. Anyway, reckon I might be able to get some work. Council are taking on at the tip.

Val I've got to go. Charlie will wonder where I am.

She stands.

Tomorrow then.

Nick Yeah.

Val *bends down to kiss his cheek, but* **Nick** *directs his mouth towards hers. Pause.* **Val** *exits.*

Scene Two

Nick *and* **Sonny** *sit on the park bench.*

Sonny I've been thinking, Nicky-boy.

Nick When did that happen, then?

Sonny No. I'm serious. They should make me Prime Minister.

Nick You!

Sonny Yeah, I'd be great.

Nick You'd make Hitler look like the Tooth Fairy.

Sonny I'd be the bollocks. You wait and see. Be brilliant. Holidays in Spain for everyone except the posh people – they're going to Blackpool. Legalise hash, 'n big newspapers and satellite telly in every house. If you don't have a dish you get your nuts chopped off and if you're a bird you lose one tit.

Nick *laughs.*

Sonny   Excellent. Imagine everyone in the country all able to watch the cricket series. I'll tell you one thing, Nicky-boy, the darkies can't half play cricket. Viv Richards – what a player he was! Black as the ace of spades though.

Nick   Why do you hate the blacks so much?

Sonny   Just do. Always have. Hate the Pakis more though.

Nick   No – Why?

Sonny   What do you mean, why? Hark at Ken Livingstone!

Nick   No, but why?

Sonny   What? Piss off, Nick. Don't give me that lefty shit . . .

Nick   What shit?

Sonny   The only reason they're any good at cricket is because they've got more monkey in them than us – Makes them bowl faster.

Nick   I'm not a fucking lefty.

Sonny   You sound like it.

Nick   So what are you, Sonny?

Pause.

Sonny   Stoned.

Nick   Don't fuck about.

Sonny   I'm not talking about this.

Nick   Why?

Sonny   Politics is crap.

Nick   No, Sonny. What are you? Who the fuck are you, Sonny?

Sonny   You know what I'd do? I'd sling all the darkies and Pakis out, the Kurds can go, and the fucking Greeks. There are enough of them around.

Nick   So?

Sonny   There must be millions of blacks here now, Nicky-boy. We should have England just like it used to be. This country's going down the swanny. We should be the best – For fuck's sake, we didn't even qualify for the World Cup!

Nick   It'll never change, Sonny.

Sonny   Yes it will. You know it will, Nick, just a matter of time. Just think, Nicky-boy. The more foreigners I do, the more I scare, the more they're off back to jumba-jumba land. It's simple. The loony-lefties down the council are just interested in looking after the coons. My dad's told me about Enoch Powell. He'd've slung them all out.

Nick   It's not that easy, Sonny.

Sonny   Yes it is. If they are going to stay here we should give them a couple of sheets of corrugated iron and a packet of nails and let them build their shanty towns down the road.

Nick   But, Sonny . . .

Sonny   They'll be all right. What happens if you lose a dog. It doesn't suddenly die, does it? It survives and gets a bit here and there. The foreigners will do the same. They live like animals anyway. People can look after themselves. White people do it as well. I'm all right, I've never worked proper – and I don't want to either. Charlie's been in and out of work all his life, we're sweet. Come on, Nick – I can go on to the estate, get two ounces of resin on tick and by five o'clock I've earnt a ton and got a deal for myself. Dad gets a few quid on the side down at the dogs. Don't need a job. Got the dole. I can live. If I knock someone every now and again, then who gives a shit. You've got to look after number one, mate.

Pause.

Nick   Sonny.

Sonny   Yeah.

Pause.

Well, spit it out.

Nick   I . . .

Sonny   What?

Nick   I need a change.

Sonny   What do you mean?

Nick   What do we do?

Sonny   Don't know.

Nick   Sit about.

Sonny   Not all the time.

Nick   Get stoned.

Sonny   It's all right. We have a grin.

Nick   Yeah.

Pause.

Last Friday. The bloke at the bus stop.

Sonny   That prick with the chips?

Sonny *laughs.*

Nick   Yeah.

Sonny   What about him?

Nick   You didn't have to cut him, Sonny.

Sonny   Yes I did. I always cut them.

Nick No.

Sonny What the fuck's the matter with you?

Nick It just pisses me off, that's all.

Sonny Don't get moody on me, Nick. He was an arsehole. He pulled the blade on me. He deserved it.

Nick He was all right.

Sonny No way.

Nick It weren't about that . . . That, that was about enjoying it, seeing the blood.

Sonny Don't give me this shit.

Nick He was screaming like a baby, Sonny, like a baby. All that blood pissing out of his mouth. You enjoyed it.

Sonny No.

Nick Yes you did, you loved it, you always do. You always do. That . . . That was . . .

Sonny Fuck you, Nick!

Nick That was shit, Sonny, that was shit! And we always do it. We always do it, Sonny! I do it, you do it – it's bad, Sonny, it's bad.

Sonny Yeah, we do it. We do it, Nick. So fucking what? You should think about where you stand. Who your mates are.

Pause.

Nick Yeah. Like I said, I'm pissed off.

Long pause.

They want someone down the tip to do a bit of refuse collection. I'm thinking of going after it.

Sonny You don't want that . . .

Nick Get some work, have a bit of money.

Sonny   You're all right.

Nick   I want to do some normal stuff for a while.

Pause.

Sonny   It's down to you.

A beat.

You're a mug if you do though.

Nick   I ain't had me car a week, Sonny. I don't want to sell it, but I can't afford it.

Sonny   You've got things sorted as it is. Bits of pocket money. Live at home, what d'you want to spend your life clearing up shit for?

Nick   I don't know.

Pause.

Sonny   You . . . You're my mate, Nick.

Nick   I know, Sonny.

Pause.

Sonny   Let's go down the pub.

Nick   No, Sonny.

Sonny   Look, if you're a bit hard up, I know a geezer who's got five hundred trips he wants to knock out. I mean that stuff got your car in the first place. You know the new under-eighteen night in Ilford? – Well, I've heard they're crying out for some acid down there.

Nick   Yeah?

Sonny   Yeah. Little kids having their experiments – you'll make a bomb. The only reason I haven't been down there is because they won't let me in.

Nick   You're twenty as it is.

Sonny It's because of my barnet. Get down there. Gap in the market, Nicky-boy. Use your noddle, mate, make your own luck. Stay on the trips for a couple of months. If it's all going all right start taking a few Es with you. That Escort will be a Porsche by the time you're twenty-one. Gap in the market – serve it up and knock it out, Nicky-boy. Sweet as a nut.

Nick *looks at his feet.*

Sonny You're my mate, Nick.

Scene Three

Sonny *sits on the sofa in the flat reading the* Sun. *Pause. A door slams offstage and* **Val** *enters with* **Ryan**. *He's a few years older than* **Sonny** *and carries some of* **Val**'s *shopping.*

Val Look who I bumped into, Sonny.

Sonny *turns.*

Sonny Jesus! All right, Ryan, mate.

Val I saw him coming out of Tesco's. And I said to him – you must come back for some tea and a slice of cake.

She takes the bags from **Ryan**.

Tea, Ryan? Sonny?

Ryan Yes please, Val.

Val *exits.*

Sonny Jesus – Look at you . . .

Ryan You all right, Sonny?

Sonny Yeah – I can't believe it. You haven't changed.

Ryan Neither have you.

Pause. He sits down on the sofa.

So are you working?

Sonny   No – Did a bit on the side a couple of months ago. But that's it. Nothing for ages. What you up to?

Ryan   Not much. Bit of voluntary work for Mencap.

Sonny   Bloody hell! All right, Mother Teresa?

Ryan *smiles.*

Sonny   Still down there are you?

Ryan   Where?

Sonny   Uni-ver-sity. That's where you went, weren't it.

Ryan   No, I finished a couple of years ago. But I decided to stay on and live there, like . . .

Sonny   Wolverhampton? That's a bit of a shit-hole, ain't it?

Ryan *laughs.* **Sonny** *grins.*

Sonny   Mind you, you always had a nut and bolt missing.

Ryan   Yeah?

Sonny   Well, I mean if it's a trial for Middlesex, or . . . What did you do?

Ryan   Sociology and economics . . .

Sonny   Or that at fucking Wolverhampton, what would you do?

Ryan   I'd do the same again, Sonny . . .

Sonny   Well, I mean doing a bit for a few dribblers ain't all that, is it?

Pause.

Mad you was, Ryan. I would have given my right bollock for a trial at Middlesex . . .

Ryan   I know.

Sonny   Yeah . . .

Ryan   I wanted to get away from London, Sonny.

Pause.

Sonny   Five years is a long time, mate.

Pause.

Ryan   I went over the park earlier.

Sonny   Yeah?

Ryan   When I think of all the time I spent over there with you lot I can't believe it . . .

Sonny   Who ever heard of a cricket team from Hackney – What my dad always said.

Pause.

Ryan   How is Charlie?

Sonny   You know Charlie, West Ham, the dog track and a bottle of cheap Scotch. That's my old man. Soppy sod's gone and fractured his ankle . . .

Ryan   I wondered if I'd see him over there . . .

Sonny   The dogs? No – he ain't over there much now.

Ryan   I had a wander round all the old places this morning. They were running some trials, Sonny. I saw the porter sweeping up in the stand still the same. The old sod used to give me fifty pee for a bet when I was a kid.

Pause.

Saw a weird thing. They was getting ready for the first heat and I was buzzing – well, I ain't been the dogs since I left. The hare, right, it shot up the track, but as it turned the corner it slowed and slowed, Sonny. Something must've been wrong with the power. But the dogs – they caught up – and they caught it. They ripped it apart, Sonny.

Pause.

Sonny   Well, it weren't a real rabbit, was it? You want to see a greyhound get hold of a cat . . .

Ryan   It stuck right in my head. I was thinking about it when I went over the park. I sat down on a bench next to the playground and had a fag. I was thinking over the cricket an' that – the kids' team, you know, Sonny?

Sonny   We wasn't kids . . .

Ryan   I used to dream that one day I'd be Ian Botham or Viv Richards. But your dad's right, Sonny. Kids round here don't play cricket. They shovel shit.

Pause.

Something else I noticed – and it took me ages to work it out cos I knew I was in a funny mood and I didn't know if it was me. But it weren't. It was the playground, Sonny – a playground. No children in it.

Val *enters with a tray with three mugs of tea and cake cut in three bits.*

Val   You could've done the washing up, Sonny.

Sonny *and* **Ryan** *take a mug and a piece of cake each.* **Val** *sits down with the tray.*

Ryan   Cheers, Val.

Val   I thought you'd come back all posh, Ryan . . .

Ryan   You've only got to be back here a day and the accent comes right back.

Val   Still playing cricket, are you, Ryan?

Ryan   Just an odd Sunday morning . . .

Val   I used to enjoy our chats, Ryan. I missed your company when you left – and I was worried, wasn't I, Sonny? You did so well in your O levels . . .

Ryan   A levels, Val . . .

Val And we didn't see you any more.

Pause.

You used to bring Sonny home from cricket practice and I'd make you sausage and chips.

Ryan That's right – rice pudding for afters . . .

Sonny Flake on top an' all . . .

Ryan I don't eat sausages any more.

Val Neither do I. All the mad cow stuff . . .

Ryan Good old British beef – rotten to the core. It's me other half actually. She's a vegetarian.

Sonny You're knocking off a veggie!

Val Shut up, Sonny. You've got a girlfriend, Ryan?

Ryan It's a bit more than that now. We're getting married.

Pause.

Why I came back. You know, doing the rounds . . .

Sonny You should've brought her over, Ry, I bet she's a right stunner, eh, Mum? Ryan always got the birds . . .

Ryan *grins.*

Sonny What's her name then?

Ryan Sharman.

Sonny Sharman? That's a funny name. Sounds like a bloody wog.

Ryan *looks at his feet embarrassed.*

Sonny Get on – you've not shacked up with a fucking jungle bunny?

Val Will you shut up your foul mouth!

Long pause.

Ryan   Still have a knockabout with a bat, Sonny?

Sonny   No.

Ryan   Right.

Sonny   Don't play no more. Still like to watch it on the telly though . . .

Ryan   Yeah?

Sonny   Hang about with Nick now.

Ryan   He wasn't in the cricket team?

Sonny   No – you know him though. His dad had the chippie in Mare Street.

Ryan   That bloke. He was crazy!

Sonny   Still is. Knocks his missis about, and Nick.

Val   I don't know how she puts up with it. She was black and blue when I saw her in Dalston last week.

Sonny   I've said to Nick, if he wants me to have a word, a few of the lads'll go and pay a visit.

Val   I've told you, Sonny . . .

Sonny   He'll piss himself.

Val   She should go to the social.

Sonny   You can't go beating up women. You've got to have a few principles.

Ryan   You haven't changed, Sonny.

Sonny   I mean, if he wants to crack a few soots' heads together . . .

Pause.

Ryan   So what's this Nick like, then?

Val   He's a lovely boy. Sonny's best mate. And he's not sitting about on his arse like Sonny. He wants to get out and about and do things – like you, Ryan . . .

Sonny   Yeah. He's got some brains – and he's a good laugh, like.

Val   He's a bit like you, Ryan.

Sonny   Most of the time he's there and right bang on for you but sometimes it's like coming up against a brick wall. You just can't talk to him.

Ryan   S'pose it's the old man?

Sonny   Yeah.

Pause.

Ryan   Have you still got the David Gower gloves?

Sonny   I wouldn't part with them for the world.

Ryan   I had to queue two hours to get them signed for you.

Sonny   They're in me room. Shall I get them?

Ryan   Yeah.

Val   They're not there any more.

Sonny   What?

Val   They're not there.

Sonny   Where are they?

Val   Your dad took them down the car boot sale a couple of years ago.

Sonny   No –

Val   You said he could take them. He got a fiver –

Sonny   That's all the cricket stuff I had left. Oh no! I wouldn't have let him sell them. They were my David Gower gloves. I wouldn't . . .

Val   Yes you did. I remember – there were some records, the gloves, some Lego bricks and a Darth Vader . . .

Sonny   I don't believe it.

Pause.

I loved those gloves. They were the best thing I ever had. You remember?

Ryan   Yeah.

Sonny   Always scored sixes with my David Gowers.

Pause.

You're fucking lying!

Val   Sonny!

Ryan   Sonny . . .

Sonny*'s up on his feet and facing* **Val***.*

Sonny   You fucking bitch! You fucking lying bitch!

He grabs **Val***'s mug which he throws down on to the floor and smashes.*

You always do this to me! Take my things! You didn't ask me, you didn't!

Val   Sonny, I promise you . . .

Ryan   Come on, Sonny – They were just gloves.

Sonny   They were my David Gowers.

Ryan   Come on, Sonny. Leave it . . .

Sonny   Oh piss off!

Sonny *turns and exits fast.* **Ryan** *goes to follow, but stops. Pause.*

Val   I'm sorry about Sonny.

Ryan *nods.*

Ryan   I should go.

Val *nods. Pause.*

Ryan   I'll be off then.

Val   I missed you, Ryan. You could've got in touch . . .

Ryan   I couldn't. Charlie . . .

Val   When are you going home?

Ryan   Next week.

Val   You can come over in the week if you like? I'll bake something. Give us a ring and I'll stick the kettle on . . .

Ryan   No, Val.

Pause.

See you then, Val.

Ryan *turns and exits.* **Val** *stands and puts the tray on the floor. She gets on her knees and scoops some of the broken crockery with her hand. She looks at a piece.*

Val   Shit.

She discards the piece and reaches for her slice of half-eaten cake.

Scene Four

Wendy *and* **Teresa** *sit on the park bench.*

Wendy   Look, don't tell Freddie – You don't know yet, Trese . . .

Teresa   Well, if I'm not pregnant it won't matter anyway – will it?

Pause.

I'm not getting rid of it, Wend.

Wendy   But if you tell Freddie he might want you to get rid of it . . .

Teresa   Well, then he can fuck off!

Pause.

Wendy   I don't think that bloke I met in Bognor was up to much, eh, Trese? He's a bouncer for a club in Peckham, Trese . . .

Teresa   I know. You told me already.

Pause.

Wendy   Bloody bastard tried to stick his hands in me knickers soon as I grabbed hold of him. I said to him – you fucking dare and I'll have your bollocks, mate . . .

Teresa (*smiling*)   You never told me that.

Wendy   Well . . . You were death-warmed-up all weekend and I've never heard anyone moan like it . . .

Teresa   Don't rub it in.

Sonny *enters. He has a cheap bunch of flowers. He pauses as he notices* **Teresa**.

Sonny   All right.

Wendy   She's going in a minute . . .

Teresa   You didn't tell me you were meeting Sonny . . .

Sonny   Yeah – well. We're going to the pub, like.

Pause.

Well, go on, then – Piss off, Trese . . .

Wendy   Sonny!

Teresa   It's all right. I'll leave you to it, Wendy – I know when I'm not wanted . . .

She gets up.

Better offer than boring – Wend . . .

Wendy   No . . .

Teresa   I don't need it.

Teresa *exits.*

Wendy   Teresa!

Pause. **Sonny** *wanders over to the park bench and sits down. Pause.*

Sonny   Cheers for coming, Wend.

Wendy   Don't call me Wend. My name's Wendy.

Sonny   Wendy – I'm sorry.

Wendy   What do you want?

Sonny   The pub – I'm sorry. The bloke who turned up.

Wendy   Who, your uncle?

Sonny   Yeah. Well, no. He's not my uncle. He's my dad.

Wendy   So?

Sonny   Well, I know he embarrassed you and Trese.

Wendy   Oh yeah?

Sonny   We were all right till he turned up.

Wendy   Was that it?

Sonny   What, Wendy? I'm trying to say sorry.

Wendy   I don't care if he's your dad.

Sonny   I brought you some flowers.

Pause.

Wendy   Who told you to do that?

Sonny   I thought of them.

Wendy   Great imagination.

Sonny   Don't take the piss. I thought you would like them.

Wendy   Like I said, great imagination.

Sonny   Why did you come here if you just want to take the piss?

Wendy   Because I'm as fucking sad as you are.

Pause.

Sonny   You met me at the pub.

Wendy   My whole life revolves around washing hair for one-fifty an hour. For a minute the thought of going out for a drink sounded exciting.

Pause.

Sonny   You went Bognor, didn't you?

Wendy   Fucking shit that was. Pissed down all day Saturday and all day Sunday and Teresa didn't stop moaning.

Sonny   I don't know why you hang about with her, Wend . . .

Wendy   Silly bitch thinks she's pregnant.

Sonny   Teresa? I thought she was right frigid.

Wendy   Yeah – well . . . She just pisses me off sometimes, that's all . . .

Pause.

Sonny   Me Aunt Viv had her baby yesterday. They're calling it Alexandria.

Wendy   Alexandria?

Sonny   Shit, innit?

Pause.

I reckon that – that you would feel better about things if you had someone.

Wendy   What?

Sonny   A bloke, like.

Wendy *laughs.*

Sonny   I can't say this very good. But – I think you're – beautiful.

Wendy   Shit. You just don't give up.

Sonny   I well fancy you, Wend . . .

Wendy *laughs.*

Sonny   Don't fucking laugh at me! I mean it!

Pause.

Wendy   You're unreal.

Sonny   I mean it, Wend. I've always liked you.

Wendy   No, Sonny.

Sonny   Come on, Wend, give us a go.

Wendy   I'm not a piece of meat, Sonny.

Sonny   I really mean it, Wendy.

Pause.

I've got some dough on me now. We could go up west, go to the pictures in Leicester Square, it'll be great.

Wendy   If I wanted to be bought I'd be knocking about down Commercial Road.

Sonny   I would pay anything in the world to have you.

Pause. **Sonny** *takes out a packet of cigarettes, gives one to* **Wendy**, *puts one in his own mouth and then takes out a box of matches. He shakes it. No sound – it's empty.*

You got a match, Wend?

Wendy   My arse, your face.

Sonny *grins and* **Wendy** *lights the cigarette with her Zippo.*

Sonny   Look at the kids over there, Wend. I used to be like that. Used to stand on top of the slide, look all around me at London. All them flats.

Pause. **Sonny** *pulls out his hanky and blows his nose making a disgusting noise.*

Wendy   Sonny, that's disgusting. You're just like my brother.

Sonny   Jimmy? Thought you'd disowned him.

Wendy   No.

Sonny   He's a fucking disgrace.

Wendy   You've got a cheek. He's not gay. He's just confused.

Sonny   That's what they all say. Just you keep him away from the school gates . . .

Wendy   Piss off!

Pause.

Sonny   I didn't want to upset you, Wend – just a joke.

Wendy   No more jokes, Sonny.

Pause.

If anyone's queer you are. Stuck to Nick like glue you are. Like his arse, do you? Don't blame you. He's got a great arse.

Sonny   What?

Wendy   Got a great arse Nick.

Sonny   You fancy him . . .

Wendy   So?

Sonny   You're after Nick. The cunt, he knows I . . .

Wendy   What?

Sonny   Bastard, all that shit about the bird at the chip shop and it was you.

Wendy   So what are you trying to say, Sonny?

Sonny   Cunt, I'll have him for this.

Wendy   You lay a finger on Nick . . .

Pause.

Sonny   Good in the sack, was he? Got a big prick, has he?

Wendy   Leave off, Sonny.

Sonny   Come on, Wend, don't get all shy on me. You've never been one to hold it all in before, I've heard your filth in the pub.

Wendy   I really want to fuck Nick. I wank over him in the bath. I want to suck him off and I want him to fuck me till I cry. Are you satisfied now, Sonny!

Pause.

Don't try and look upset, Sonny, you don't give a shit about Nick. I know you too well.

Pause.

It's been up there in your little brain for at least a year, hasn't it, Sonny?

Sonny   Leave it alone now, Wend –

Wendy   No, Sonny, I've never liked you. You think everyone's against you, betraying you, using you, Sonny, just like you think Nick is. But you use people – and when you've had enough of them you just smash them in. I know you, Sonny.

Sonny   No – you don't know me. No one knows me!

Pause.

I came here to say what I meant. Feel.

Wendy   Don't give me this, Sonny.

Sonny   One thing I know is, I've known you all my life. I always thought . . .

Wendy   Don't flatter yourself . . .

Sonny   I don't need this!

Wendy   Yes you do!

Sonny   You're no better than me!

Pause.

Wendy   Today I was washing this bloke's hair. He reached up and squeezed my tit. My right . . . Not hard – just a squeeze. I didn't do anything. He abused me, but I – I wasn't . . .

Sonny   Who is he? Tell me who he is – I'll kill him.

Wendy   You abuse me.

Sonny   I've never laid a finger on you.

Wendy   The way you talk to me, the way you look at me . . . I don't know why I came here, Sonny. I pretend I care what Teresa says. I pretend that my mum hates me. I pretend like a fucking kid!

A beat.

When I picked up the phone I thought – Shit, go to the pub, get out – have a laugh. No. With you, Sonny? I must be thick. I must have been in a right sodding dream.

Scene Five

Val *and* **Nick** *sit on the sofa in the flat.* **Val** *has a wrapped present.*

Val   You didn't have to, Nick.

Nick   It's all right. My treat. Plonk's in the fridge.

Val   Never had a birthday like it.

Nick   Go on, open it.

Val *opens the present. She takes out a pink jumper.*

Val   Oh, it's lovely, Nick.

She kisses him.

Oh, look, you've only gone and left the price tag on, you berk!

Nick   I haven't.

Val   You have. Look. Nine ninety-nine.

Nick   Show us?

Val   I thought I was worth more than that to you, you dirty bugger!

Nick *kisses* **Val** *on the cheek.*

Nick   Course you are.

Val   Thanks, Nick.

Nick   So where's the cake and candles?

Val   You must be joking. The day my Charlie and Sonny manage to get me a birthday cake I'll run up and down the block naked. I'll tell you something, Nick. I love a sponge, or a gateau, or a fruit pie, or cream, but the day I bake my own bloody birthday cake is the day I pack it in.

Charlie (*offstage*)   Val!

Nick   Christ . . .

Charlie (*offstage*)   Val! Val – make us a cup of tea, love! I'm gasping . . .

Pause.

Nick   I didn't know Charlie was here . .

Val   He came out this morning . . .

Nick   You could've said. We could've been . . . doing anything . . .

Val   It's all right, Nick – Can't get out of bed unless I help him . . .

Charlie (*offstage*)   Val! Are you making that tea? Val!

A beat.

I don't know. I'm in hospital in agony. I'm putting up with all the geriatrics and the nurses.

Nick *and* **Val** *smile.*

Charlie (*offstage*)   Not a smiling face on that ward in all the time I'm in there. And you look forward to the comfort of being in your own home – and you get out and your own wife can't even be bothered to make you a cup of tea . . . Val . . . Val!

Val   All right, Charlie!

Pause.

Nick   Where's Sonny?

Val   Don't know – but I think he must have gone to meet a girl because he stank of Charlie's Old Spice.

Pause.

Charlie's mate's bringing a wheelchair round tomorrow so he can take him over the park. If that lift's out of order I'll go spare, Nick. He's driving me up the bloody wall.

Charlie (*offstage*)   Val!

Val   If you don't shut up, Charlie, I'm going to stick that crutch you've got in there right up your bloody arse!

Nick *grins and sits up a bit on the sofa.*

Nick   I feel a bit uncomfortable here, Val. I think I'm sitting on something.

He reaches behind his backside and pulls out a crumpled card.

It's a birthday card – I'm sorry, Val. It's a bit creased.

Val   Give us it here. It's Sonny's card.

Nick   Can I read it?

Val   If you want.

Nick (*reads aloud*)   Dear Mum. Have a really pucker day and get pissed.

Val   I don't know why he said get pissed. Even when Charlie's here he doesn't take me anywhere.

Nick   Love from Sonny. Kiss, kiss, kiss. He's spelt love wrong!

Val   He may not be able to spell it but he means it.

Nick   Thought you had problems with Sonny?

Val   He's a bloody sod but he's never hurt me.

Nick   The way he talks to you?

Val   His way of carrying on. Doesn't mean it – just does it. His protection I think. There are only two things in the world Sonny really cares about – his cricket and his mum. I worry about Sonny.

Pause.

Last Friday, Nick . . . It's not the first time he's come home with blood . . .

Nick   I told you, Val.

Pause.

Sonny can take care of himself.

Val   Can he?

A beat.

I see him looking out of the window across London. I just think it would take so little to make him push it open and jump.

Nick   Not Sonny.

Val   I know, Nick. I know.

Pause.

I know.

Pause.

You know the council have painted some of the prefab squares on the blocks red and blue.

Pause.

Nick   You're all right. You've got Sonny and Charlie.

Val   Liberal council that is. Looks like bloody Lego. Looks like it could fall apart so easily.

Nick   You've got some money coming in. Could be a lot worse.

Val   Funny. Things can always be worse. It's just how much you can stand.

Pause.

You know, Nick, however big or small a slice of cake I have, I still feel sick. If I stuff myself silly it's too sickly and I'm bloated. If I just take a bite I feel hungrier and hungrier till I feel mad.

Nick (*laughing*)   P'raps you should stop eating cake?

Val *laughs and reaches over for a kiss.*

Val   P'raps I should.

Val *and* **Nick** *kiss, easily, lovingly.* **Charlie** *appears in the entrance into the room. He's dressed only in a dirty old vest and Y-front underpants. He hobbles forward and goes to speak but notices* **Nick** *and* **Val** *kissing, who don't notice him.* **Charlie** *turns away.*

Scene Six

Sonny *sits on the sofa in the flat reading a copy of the* Sun. *A doorbell rings offstage.* **Sonny** *gets up and goes out to answer it. Pause.* **Sonny** *and* **Nick** *enter.* **Sonny** *sits downs and picks up the paper again.*

Nick   I got it, Sonny. I fucking got it, didn't I!

Sonny   When do you start?

Nick   Monday. Got to be at the depot by six o'clock though. Jesus, last time I was up that early I was tripping my tits off.

Sonny   Won't be doing that any more then, now you're working.

Nick   Oh no. I might not be out as much but I'm still going to trip out. Never know, Sonny – might be able to get some Charlie now I'm earning. You watch, we'll soon be doing lines of coke through fifty-pound notes.

Sonny   Off bin-money?

Nick   It's a start, Sonny.

Sonny   Yeah, great.

Nick   Do what?

Sonny   I said great.

Nick   You sound fucked off. What's up?

Sonny   Nothing.

Nick   No, come on, we're mates.

Sonny   Are we?

Nick   What's that supposed to mean?

Sonny   What do you think it means?

Nick   I don't know. What's the mater? Look, Sonny . . .

Pause.

For fuck's sake, Sonny, tell me what's wrong?

No reply.

Just leave this shit out, Sonny!

Sonny (*showing him page three*)   Tits on that.

Nick (*ripping the paper away*)   Don't fuck with me, Sonny. What is this moody bollocks?

Sonny   Nothing.

Nick   You ain't fucking jealous, are you?

Sonny   Piss off, Nick.

Nick   What's is it then?

Pause.

Sonny   I know you've been seeing her.

Nick   What . . .

Sonny   Tell me the truth.

Nick   I don't . . .

Sonny   I'll kill you.

Nick   Sonny . . .

Sonny   She reckons you haven't but I know you've been fucking her.

Nick   I couldn't help it.

Sonny   Oh yeah . . .

Nick   Val's always so nice . . .

Sonny   What?

Nick   Val . . .

Sonny   Val?

Nick   I . . .

Sonny   My mum?

Pause.

Wendy's told me . . .

Nick   But I thought – Val . . .

Sonny   No. No.

He sits in stunned silence.

The jumper and card. From you – the jumper and card. I thought it was strange.

Nick   I'm sorry . . .

Sonny   Shit, you still left the price tag on. Nine fucking ninety-nine – is that what she was worth?

Nick   I didn't mean it.

Sonny   What, leave the tag on? You've been fucking my mum, you cunt! Aaaaarrrrgh – I could fucking kill you now! You bastard!

Nick   Sonny.

Sonny (*on his feet*)   Don't fucking speak to me. I don't want to hear it!

Pause. He continues less angrily.

We're meant to be mates. I trusted you. I don't trust anyone. I trusted you. Shit, I would die for you, you cunt. I would die for you!

Long pause.

So, Nicky-boy, how long's it been going on?

Nick   It's only happened twice.

Sonny   Only! What's the matter, sack of shit, was she?

Pause.

Nick   No.

Sonny   Aaaah you cunt!

He lunges at **Nick** *and throttles him. They fall onto the floor and* **Nick** *gasps for breath. They struggle.* **Sonny** *slaps* **Nick** *around the face.*

Sonny   Don't fucking cry!

He gets up.

Fucking bollocks, bollocks! Get up, get out! Go on, fuck off!

Nick *exits quickly. Long pause.* **Sonny** *picks up the* Sun *and sits down on the sofa. Pause as he reads.* **Val** *enters with two bags of shopping.*

Val   All right, Sonny. Put the kettle on for me, would you, love.

She goes offstage into the kitchen. We hear her voice.

I saw Nick on his way downstairs. He ran straight past me. You haven't been on that funny stuff, have you? Nick didn't look very well.

She wanders back in.

D'you want some cake, Sonny? It's a victoria sponge – I know you like victoria sponge. I got two in Tesco's. Special discount. Sonny? I don't know, you and your moods.

She goes back into the kitchen.

I know where you get your moods. It's your father's side of the family. Your uncle's just the same. I saw Nick's mum in Tesco's. She said Nick got a job at the depot.

She comes back in with a tray, two mugs of tea and the cake cut in two.

Here you are, love. I cut you a bit of cake anyway. I know you like your victoria sponge. Are you all right, Sonny? Sonny? Sod you – I'll eat it then.

She eats half of the cake very quickly punctuated by gulps of tea. Her mouth is half full.

Are you sure you don't want any cake?

She carries on chewing.

I don't know if I can manage all this, eyes bigger than my belly. I saw Nick's mum in Tesco's . . .

Sonny Yeah, I know.

Val She said Nick's got a job at the rubbish tip. You didn't say anything about it, Sonny.

Sonny No.

Val You are in a funny mood. Too much of that pot makes your brains go funny.

Pause.

I like Nick. You should try and take after him a bit more, Sonny. It's a wonder you hadn't thought of going down that rubbish tip. Whatever else, people always have rubbish to get rid of. Now there is a business that's never out of work and I bet there are some good bits and pieces thrown out that you can pick up. You know your Aunt Vi. Well, she knew a bloke who was on the dustbins. When she was courting with him you'll never guess what he found – a solid diamond ring! Amongst all that filth and muck – a diamond ring. He had it valued – guess how much it was worth? Two thousand quid, in 1969! Didn't tell anyone he'd found a ring. He told them all he'd won the pools. He paid everyone in his block of flats a week's rent and treated your Aunt Vi to a weekend in Blackpool. I don't think your Aunt Vi was very grateful. I think she thought she was off to sunny Spain.

Pause. She starts to hum 'Viva España' then laughs at herself.

Bloody hell, Charlie never has any of that luck. And I'll tell you, Sonny – I wouldn't mind Blackpool. I'd like to see the lights.

Pause.

I've got a new cleaning job, Sonny – you'll never guess where. Harrods! Oh, you should see it, Sonny, it's beautiful. Beautiful – and the toilets, you've never seen anything like it in your life, Sonny. Lovely tiles. I don't expect to say this about any other lav, but I would have those tiles in my kitchen.

Pause.

Pokey little thing that kitchen is. Can't swing a cat.

Pause.

Two of us who've got jobs today. Me and Nick. You see, you can get a job if you really want one, Sonny. You should do what what's-his-name said. Erm . . . You know, Norman . . . Looks like a bit of a skeleton with a bald head. Anyway, you should get on your bike. Go out and look. There's nothing wrong with good honest hard work. We've done it in the past and we'll do it again. Now I'll you what's wrong with this country, Sonny. We have become mollycoddled. The immigrants are the only people used to hard work. Now whatever you say about the Pakistanis, they know how to work. What do I get for my cleaning? One-fifty, two quid an hour. Not much. But it gets me by. I'm not proud. I don't mind not having much. People like us have always been poor. But I know I'm honest and I've never needed to take drugs. You lot have got it made, Sonny, sitting on your backside claiming the dole and going out thieving. Now I know you do it. I don't know how you've got the cheek sometimes. D'you know, Sonny, that a pair of jeans you put in the laundry bag last week still had the labels all over it. And it was a size forty-two, so I know it wasn't yours. Anyhow, I know you haven't got the money to afford to buy them.

Pause.

I don't know what's the matter with you, Sonny. I did my best for you and look how you've turned out – and the temper sometimes. It's like putting up with a bloody kid. And that mug you smashed in the week – that was my royal wedding souvenir that was, and I only got it out cos there wasn't a clean one in the kitchen to be had. You don't lift a finger – and the habits . . . That was my favourite mug. The only thing I had, Sonny. Your bloody father chucked the scrapbook out with the rubbish. That wedding was beautiful – beautiful, Sonny. Charles and Di. That beautiful dress, beautiful. Didn't I cry – Didn't I cry, Sonny . . .

Sonny *stands.*

Val   Where are you going?

Sonny   To the pub.

Val   What for?

Sonny   I'm going to get arseholed.

Val   Funny mood you're in.

Sonny   I want to see Nick.

Scene Seven

Wendy *and* **Teresa** *sit on the park bench in one stage area.* **Val** *and* **Charlie** *sit on the sofa in the other stage area.* **Val** *has a tray with a cake and* **Charlie** *has his foot in plaster and reads the* Sun.

Teresa   I can't believe it.

Wendy   Neither can I.

Val   There's some cake here, Charlie.

Pause.

Wendy   I feel sick thinking about it.

Pause.

Charlie   I'm not hungry.

Wendy   And now to top it all off that wanker at the salon has sacked me. Two days off, Trese – that's all I had. When do I ever have a day off?

Val   When are we going to see the baby?

Pause.

Teresa   It's hard to take in, Wendy.

Val   The baby's been born four days, Charlie . . .

Wendy   I know.

Val   She's my sister.

Pause.

Wendy   I feel numb. It's my fault – I know it's my fault, Trese.

Val   Are you going to eat any of this cake?

Charlie   No.

Val   I made it specially. It's got cream on it – and flake. Flake on top as well . . .

Charlie   I don't want your fucking cake!

Pause.

Wendy   He cut that poor bastard's face to pieces.

Pause.

Teresa   I've come on, Wend . . .

Val   I'll eat it then – I'll eat it.

Teresa   I've come on . . . No more worries, eh, Wend . . . Wendy?

Val   Cake.

Teresa   They're all monsters, Wendy . . .

Val   Cake.

Teresa   Sonny's a fucking monster . . .

Val *breaks off handfuls of the cake which she disturbingly stuffs in her mouth. The tears roll down her face.*

Wendy   We're all monsters, Trese.

Val   I want to eat cake.

Summer Begins

We are on a perilous margin when we begin to look passively at our future selves, and see our own figures led with dull consent into insipid misdoing and shabby achievement . . .

George Eliot, *Middlemarch*, Chapter 79

Good morrow, masters, put your torches out.
The wolves have prey'd, and look, the gentle day
Before the wheels of Phoebus round about
Dapples the drowsy east with spots of grey.

William Shakespeare, *Much Ado About Nothing*, Act 5 Scene 3

Summer Begins was first performed at the Royal National Theatre Studio on 26 March 1997. The cast was as follows:

Gina   Beatie Edney
Sherry Elizabeth Chadwick
Dave   Gary Webster
Lee   Darren Tighe
Beth   Heather Tobias

Directed by Jonathan Lloyd
Designed by Conor Murphy
Lighting by David Plater
Sound by Sebastian Frost

Characters

Gina Killick, *aged twenty-four*
Sherry Killick, *aged twenty-three*
Dave Stams, *aged twenty-eight*
Lee Hulse, *aged twenty-three*
Beth Killick, *aged forty-two*

All the characters have east London/Essex accents.

Setting
Spring and summer 1996. Except for two scenes, the play is set in Barking, suburban east London.

Act One

Scene One

Tuesday evening, nine o'clock. A pub in Barking, east London.
Sherry *and* **Gina** *enter drinking, respectively, a glass of white wine and a bottled beer.* **Sherry** *is dressed casually in jeans and a baggy, summery shirt and* **Gina** *wears a supermarket uniform.*

Gina   He just sat in front of the telly, Shell – and didn't move a muscle . . . I mean – I don't expect him to fuckin' kiss me feet but I spent all afternoon in the kitchen gettin' it ready . . .

Sherry *indicates a table.*

Sherry   Here . . .

They sit down. **Sherry** *lights up a cigarette.*

Gina   Don't, Shell!

Sherry   Strugglin' are ya, darlin'?

Gina   It's only been two days. Look at the state of my nails.

Sherry *looks at* **Gina***'s hands.*

Gina   An' that's another thing!

Sherry   What?

Gina   Has Dave made any attempt to give up?

Sherry *(laughs)*   Has he fuck – He's smoking another ten a day just to rub it in – I'm sure he is.

Pause. **Sherry** *has a sip of her wine and* **Gina** *swigs from her bottle.*

Gina   How's Mum?

Sherry   Awful.

Pause. **Gina** *takes another swig.*

Gina   Look at the state of these nails. I used to really look after my nails and look at the state of 'em now.

A slight pause.

Well, I dunno where Dave is – If he's pissin' it up down the road I'll kill him . . .

A slight pause.

Sherry   What a ya gonna do?

Gina   I dunno . . .

A slight pause.

Sherry   What did you say to him?

Gina   I said I'd think about it.

A slight pause.

The fucking prat got on his knees as they were serving up the poppadums, Sherry, so all the waiters got wind of it an' before I knew it the whole bloody tandoori was waiting for me to say yes.

Sherry   So what did you do?

Gina   Well, what did Mr Del Monte do? I put the ring on me finger an' had a serenade from three dodgy-toothed waiters while the whole bloody restaurant clapped.

Sherry   So what did you do then?

Gina   I told him I'd changed me mind when we got back to the flat an' kicked him up the arse for making me feel such a prat.

Sherry   Gina! He'd just proposed to you!

Gina   Well, at least we got the curry on the house . . .

Sherry *gasps and raises her eyebrows.*

Gina   What?

Sherry   I can't believe you just said that! Dave had just proposed to you.

Gina   What's a matter with you?

Sherry   Well, Dave was tryin' to be romantic.

Gina   Hark at Barbara Cartland!

Sherry *grins. A slight pause.*

Sherry   So what a ya gonna do?

Gina   I dunno, Sherry, but it's gettin' me right down . . .

Pause. **Gina** *takes a swig.*

Gina   I wanna finish it, Sherry – I wanna finish it for good – an' shit-for-brains goes an' proposes.

Sherry   Where ya gonna go?

Gina   Well, he can go somewhere – He's got plenty a mates . . .

Sherry   I s'pose you could always have your old room back at home?

Gina   You must be joking, Sherry? No – he's the man, he can find somewhere.

Pause.

Eh – I'll tell you what has cheered me up, Shell . . . We've got a lovely new boy started last week. Martin he's called. He's on cold meats.

Sherry   Yeah?

Gina   Fucking gorgeous. We are talking Brad Pitt and Gary Barlow in one bod, darlin'.

Sherry *laughs.*

Sherry   I thought I'd converted you to dark-haired men!

Gina   I can't take me eyes off him, Sherry. I nearly fainted when I saw him slicin' a salami this morning. Fit as you like an' he's only seventeen, Sherry. I look at him an' I feel like a total falidomide . . .

A slight pause. **Sherry** *doesn't know what she means.*

Y'know – Perverts who fancy children.

Sherry   Gina . . .

Gina   What?

Sherry *laughs and shakes her head.* **Gina** *smiles and takes a swig and* **Sherry** *takes a sip.*

Sherry   Mum's been terrible. I don't know what to do.

Gina *tuts. A slight pause.*

Gina   Well what d'you want me to say?

Sherry   I don't know – It wouldn't hurt you to come round a bit more.

Gina   Is that what you want?

Sherry   Yeah.

Gina   I can do it, I can come over – I can come over every night of the week but it's not gonna change anythin'.

Sherry   Well it'd help.

Gina   It won't help Mum.

Sherry   It'd help me.

Gina   She's gotta start making a new life for herself, Sherry – You're not gonna be there forever – are ya?

Sherry *smiles and shakes her head. Pause.*

Gina   You've not touched your wine.

Sherry   I've had a mouthful – It's gross.

Gina   Hark at you! Is this the same Lambrusco queen of Loxford Park speaking?

Sherry   Piss off!

Gina   I remember you! – Litre an' half down ya neck every Thursday, then stagger up Woodlands to the Palais . . .

Sherry   An' you!

Gina   It was a good laugh – eh, Shell? It was a good laugh them Thursday nights. I used to feel so good about meself then . . .

A slight pause.

D'you remember me blue dress? The one with the tassels? (**Sherry** *smiles and nods.*) I used to love that dress. Remember where I got it, Shell? Roman Road. Fifty quid it cost me.

Sherry   Yeah. What about when you shagged Darren Yems in the bogs?

Gina   How could I forget?

Sherry   I can't believe I was bangin' on the door – but I thought it was an epileptic fit . . . (**Gina** *laughs.*) You old slapper . . .

A slight pause. **Gina** *smiles.*

Gina   Don't call me that.

Sherry   Alright.

Pause.

Did you bring me the tape a *Speed*?

Gina   Oh shit – sorry . . . I forgot it.

Sherry   It's alright – I've got another one for you to borrow at home – I dunno if you'll like it . . .

Gina   What is it?

Sherry   It's about a Buddha.

Gina   Is it?

Sherry   Well, you can borrow it if you want.

Gina   Alright.

Sherry   Eh – I'm goin' up to head office tomorrow.

Gina   What for?

Sherry   To talk about my future. I'll've finished me year trainin' in August.

Gina   I wanna know when I'm gonna get me free drawers . . . (**Sherry** *laughs.*) Two bloody years you've worked for Marks and Sparks an' have I seen a free pair of knickers? I've told ya, Shell – I don't mind samples and try-outs – as long as they haven't been worn.

Sherry   You wanna see the state of some of the underwear they bring back – it's disgusting.

Gina   Oh – don't tell me! Skid marks?

Sherry   I don't know how they've got the cheek.

Gina   Some people make you sick, don't they? (**Sherry** *nods.*) You know this morning this total arsehole picked his nose and wiped it on the checkout.

Sherry   No!

Gina   I said to him – 'Picked us a winner, mate' and the tit only told us to get on with me job. I'll tell ya – I came this close to smackin' him on the nose with a tin of his fuckin' Winalot.

A slight pause.

It gets me down on that bloody till sometimes.

Long pause. **Gina** *has a swig.*

I saw Dad last night.

Sherry   Yeah?

Gina   He asked after ya, Sherry.

A slight pause.

Well?

Sherry   Well what?

Gina   Well, he asked after you – he's ya father.

Sherry   Don't start on this now.

Gina   I'm not startin' anything, Sherry.

Sherry   I don't wanna know, alright.

Gina   It's alright for you to start on at me about Mum.

Sherry   Please . . .

Gina   Please what?

Sherry   We're just havin' a drink.

Long pause. **Sherry** *sips her wine and* **Gina** *finishes her bottle.*
Dave *enters. He wears jeans, a West Ham shirt, trainers, and his*
wet hair is neatly parted in the middle. He carries a sports bag.

Dave   Hello, Sherry.

Sherry *smiles.* **Gina** *doesn't.*

Dave   What've you done to your sister? She's got a face
like a turkey week before Christmas.

Gina   Why are you late, Dave?

Dave   Sortin' out who's helpin' set up on Saturday night
. . . I said I'll deejay.

Gina   Very funny.

Dave (*bursting into song*)   Don't you want me baby – Don't
you want me – whoooaahhh!

Gina   Prat.

Dave   Nah – not really . . . I'm the bouncer . . . What
d'you reckon, eh, Shell? – If your name's not on the list
you're not comin' in . . .

Sherry *laughs.* **Gina** *shakes her head.*

Dave   Still, it's not as though anyone's gonna know I'm the bouncer what with the togs.

Gina   It's a football do – not a rave!

Dave   I dunno – few pills, bit a wizz, bit a charlie, have a spliff . . .

Gina   Go and get me another drink, Dave.

Dave   Alright, alright . . .

Gina   Rolling Rock – an' if they haven't got that – Molson.

Dave   Alright, Sherry?

Sherry   Yeah . . . Last trainin' of the season, Dave?

Dave   Yeah – just the do on Saturday then that's it – we've not even got together a five-a-side tournament this year . . . (**Gina** *tuts*.) I'm talkin', babe –

Gina *pulls a face. So does* **Dave**. **Gina** *half-smiles and* **Dave** *plants a kiss on her lips and sits down.* **Lee** *enters. He wears a trendy jogging tracksuit, has a smart over-the-shoulder sports bag and carries two pints of lager.*

Dave   Alright, geeze.

Gina   Hello . . .

Dave   Sit down, mate – This is me girlfriend Gina . . .

Gina   Alright.

Lee   Alright.

Gina   This is my sister Sherry.

Sherry   Hi.

Lee   Alright.

Gina   Lee an' Dave are decorating a house out in Essex.

Dave   Sit down.

Lee *sits down and* **Dave** *takes his pint.*

Dave   Your balls still hurt?

Gina   Dave!

Dave   Alright! – He got one in the nuts when he was in the wall!

Gina   One of these days I'm gonna stick a football in your fuckin' gob!

Dave   You should've lamped that little Scottish cunt. He hit it into the wall on purpose.

Gina   An' what've I told you about that word?

Pause.

Dave   You haven't got a fag I can sponge, have ya, Sherry?

Gina *tuts.* **Sherry** *passes* **Dave** *her cigarettes and lighter and he lights up. Pause.*

Gina   You do know that every time you smoke a cigarette . . .

Dave   I love it.

Sherry *laughs. A slight pause.*

Lee   Given up, Gina?

Gina   Yes.

Lee   How long –

Gina   Two days!

Sherry *(offering the cigarettes)*   Oh, I'm sorry . . .

Lee   No, no, honestly, I don't smoke.

Sherry   So where're you from, Lee?

Lee   Dagenham originally – I'm living off of Longbridge Road now.

Dave   From the 'Nam to Barking? Out a the fryin' pan, eh?

Sherry   Your own place?

Lee   Yeah. What about you?

Gina   Still livin' with Mum, ain't ya, Shell?

Sherry   Yeah.

Lee   I'm sure I know you?

Gina   I don't know how, Lee.

Lee   Did you used to go Ilford Palais on a Thursday night?

Gina   She don't go Ilford Palais!

Lee   About seven, eight years ago – it must be now – You'd've still been at school probably.

Sherry   Yeah.

Lee   Did you get off with a bloke called Tony Clive one night?

Sherry   Yeah – You've got a good memory.

Lee   I knew it – I knew I knew you when I walked in! – I was at school with him – we used to knock about together . . .

Sherry   It used to be such a cattle market down there – an' everyone under-age an' pissed out of their minds.

Lee   You might know another mate of mine – Darren Yems? Yemsy?

Dave   Do I know him?

Sherry   Yeah – I know Darren.

Gina   I remember Darren – He used to get off with someone different every week – I fancied him for ages.

Lee   You weren't there the night he got hold of that little slapper. They were virtually a side show for the whole club up against the wall. You must remember her. Everyone knew her – she used to go every week – the one with peroxide hair who used to trot about in the same electric blue dress with these – tacky tassels.

Sherry   I don't think so.

Lee   He only ended up shagging her in the ladies' toilets!

Sherry   I don't think . . .

Lee   Yemsy told me she was making such a racket they were banging on the cubicle door!

Dave   Didn't you get suspended from school for dying your hair blond, Gina? Wasn't you, was it?

Lee and **Dave** *laugh loudly.*

Gina   Well, that's a nice thing to say about your girlfriend!

Pause. They all drink.

Sherry   You goin' the end-of-season do on Saturday night, Lee?

Lee   Yeah.

A slight pause.

Gina   It's gonna be really smart, Sherry – All the fellas have gotta wear tuxedos and all the gels have to wear smart dresses – I've got a lovely yella cocktail dress . . .

Dave   Bollocks idea if you ask me.

Gina   If it was left to you it'd be jeans and T-shirts.

Dave   There's nothing wrong with that.

Gina   It's a nice change – I bet you look dead smart in your tuxedo, Lee? You hirin' an' all?

Lee   Me dad's got one I can borrow.

Dave   I dunno – Goin' to an end-of-season football do in a tuxedo an' bow-tie! I've never heard of anything like it. It's

Barking Juventus for fuck's sake! Eleven blokes hungover on a Sunday morning an' a manager with a wank-mag an' a thermos!

Gina   It's smart.

Dave   Smart my arse. It's not bein' held at the bloody Hilton!

Gina   Well, you're not the only club team.

Dave   You know, the last time I was in the youth club re-plasterin' the gents I caught three glue-sniffers with a pot a Evo – An' they told me to piss off!

Gina   I think it'll make a nice change.

Dave *shakes his head, drains the rest of his pint and stands.*

Dave   Who's up for another one?

Gina   Rolling Rock.

Dave   Or a Molson. Lee?

Lee   No.

Sherry   No thanks, Dave.

Gina   You taking your girlfriend, Lee?

Dave *laughs.* **Gina** *and* **Sherry** *give* **Dave** *a look.*

Dave   Dumped him for someone her own age, eh, Lee?

Sherry   Dave . . .

Dave   Sixteen, Gina.

Gina   You cradle-snatcher!

Dave   Fuckin' paedophile, ain't he?

Gina   No, Dave – you dick-head – it's falidomide.

Lee   It's not.

Gina Don't make excuses for him. He comes out with these big long words thinking he can impress us all and he's as thick as two planks.

Dave If you say so, Gina.

Pause. **Sherry** *checks her watch.*

Sherry I should go, Geenie . . . Nice to meet you, Lee.

Sherry *stands up.*

Lee Yeah – I'll see you around.

Gina Here – why don't you come on Saturday night?

Sherry No – I can't.

Gina Why?

Sherry I said I'd keep Mum company.

Dave You could go with Lee.

Gina Go on, Sherry – When was the last time we went out?

Dave You don't mind, do ya, Lee?

Lee Well – No, course not . . .

Sherry You're just being polite.

Lee No . . .

Sherry I don't know – I'll speak to Mum – I'll see . . . (*A slight pause.*) I'll see you, Dave, Gina . . . (*Offers* **Lee** *her hand.*) Nice to meet you, Lee . . .

Lee Yeah – Saturday maybe . . .

Dave Here, Sherry – before you go . . . (*A slight pause as* **Dave** *reaches into his sports bag and pulls out a video tape.*) You left her video in the kitchen.

Lee *has a look as he passes it on to* **Sherry**.

Gina We love Keanu –

Sherry *laughs and exits.* **Dave** *shrugs his shoulders.*

Dave   I don't know what they see in him.

Gina   Best you go get the drinks in, Dave.

Dave *nods, exits and* **Lee** *smiles politely at* **Gina**.

Scene Two

Saturday, seven o'clock. Living room of a terraced house in Barking, east London. The house belongs to **Sherry** *and* **Gina**'s *mum,* **Beth**. *The living room door opens and* **Beth** *enters with an ironing board under her arm which she erects. We can hear a hairdryer offstage which gets a bit louder as* **Beth** *enters and fades again as the door is closed.*

Beth   Sherry! Move yerself! They're going to be round here in a minute!

Sherry (*off*)   Alright!

Beth   Ya gonna to be late!

Sherry (*off*)   Alright for fuck's sake!

Beth   Don't swear!

Beth *exits back through the living room door. We hear* **Beth** *off, too.*

You've not even dried your hair yet!

Sherry (*off*)   I'm doing it now!

A slight pause.

You're driving me up the fucking wall!

Beth (*off*)   Don't swear! Well if they're all round here and you're still fart-arsing around in your birthday suit you'll be the one who'll be making a fool of yerself – not me!

Beth *re-enters with a long Laura Ashley-type dress over her arm and an iron and extension lead in her hand.* **Beth** *uncoils the extension lead which she attaches to the plug on the iron. The hairdryer stops.*

Sherry (*off*)   What a ya doing?

Beth   Ironing your dress.

Sherry (*off*)   I said I'd iron it!

Beth   Just get on with what you're doing!

As **Beth** *waits for the iron to warm up she lights a cigarette. Pause. Off we hear faint music start playing as* **Sherry** *puts on her hi-fi.*

Turn that down!

Pause.

Turn that down, Sherry!

Pause. **Beth** *stubs out her cigarette, licks a finger and tests the temperature of the iron, then opens out the dress across the ironing board. The faint music gets a bit louder and* **Sherry** *enters. She has a towel wrapped around herself.*

Sherry   I can iron my own dress . . .

Beth   Look, don't start, Sherry! I'm tryin' a do you a favour.

Sherry   Well, you're not – you're just pissing me off . . . (**Beth** *starts to iron the dress.*) Why don't you just let me get on with it?

Beth   Go and get yourself dry.

Sherry   I can iron my own fucking dress.

Beth   If you use that language again I'm goin' a give you what for, madam.

Sherry   Don't call me madam – I'm not just some little teenager you can boss around.

Beth   Just go and get ready, Sherry.

Sherry   Just go and sit down and just let me get on.

Beth *continues to iron the dress and* **Sherry** *makes a grab for the iron.*

Beth   Get off!

Sherry   I said . . .

Beth   You silly cow!

Sherry   I said to just let me get on.

Beth   Sherry!

Beth *and* **Sherry** *each have a hand round the handle as they both try to get the upper hand. They fall into the ironing board which crashes to the floor. The iron catches* **Sherry**'s *arm and she screams.*

Beth   Look!

Sherry *looks at her arm and sobs.* **Beth** *looks around, pulls the plug out and places the iron carefully on the floor.*

Beth   That's your bloody fault! I was trying to help you and you have to go and cause an argument!

Sherry   Why can't you just let me get on?

Beth   You bloody pig-headed cow!

Sherry   You can't just let me get on with my life!

Beth   I was just trying to help you.

Sherry   You have to interfere!

Beth   I have just about had enough of you, young lady!

Sherry   I'm twenty-three years of age, for Christ's sake!

Beth   And you treat this place like a hotel.

Sherry   Well, why don't you fucking throw me out then?

Beth   Well, why don't you just pack your bags and go then?

Sherry   Well, I will cos I've just about had enough of you an' the way you try an' treat me like a kid!

Beth   And I've had enough of the way you think you can walk all over me! Well, my girl – this is my house –

Sherry   Don't I fucking know it!

Beth   And while you're in my house you can just do what I say!

Sherry   This isn't your house!

A slight pause.

Beth   What?

Sherry   What have you ever paid towards this house?

Beth   You better just watch it . . .

Sherry   If this is anyone's house, this is Dad's house!

Beth   After all I've done . . .

Sherry   When he was here you never so much as spent –

Beth   After all the money I've spent on you . . .

Sherry   You never so much as spent a penny on this house.

Beth   How dare you!

Sherry   No wonder Dad left you!

Beth   He left because of that slut!

Sherry   No wonder he found someone else – You never loved him!

Beth   You spiteful bitch!

Sherry   You just took him for every penny he had!

Beth   You spiteful, mean . . .

Sherry   And you spent every penny you had on gin and fags.

Beth   You!

Sherry's *anger starts to dissolve into tears.*

Sherry   He never had a life with you – All he had was work – working his fingers to the bone so you could have everything you wanted at home – and go down the pub an' hang off any Tom, Dick or Harry's shoulder who'd keep your glass full for the night!

Beth *slaps* **Sherry** *around the face hard – so hard she knocks* **Sherry** *to the floor. Pause.*

Beth   Work? What d'you think I've done all my life but to work – and spoil you and Gina rotten so you can treat me like this and begrudge me a packet of fags an' a drink on a Friday night? How dare you, Sherry? After all I've done for you, Sherry – Who's seen you through university while your father's pissed off and left? Who's put a tenner in your pocket so you can have a drink with your mates? Who's put a roof over your head while you studied and this is the gratitude you show me?

Sherry   I didn't wanna stay here . . .

Beth   Well, you should've pissed off out of it then.

Sherry   I wanted to get out.

Beth   You should've pissed off to Manchester then.

Sherry   An' I had to look after you . . .

Beth   You never had to look after me.

Sherry   I didn't wanna go university round here – I wanted to go away.

Beth   I've had enough of this.

Sherry   I wanted to get out an' live my own life an' all you could do from the minute Dad left was to pack your job in.

Beth   I got the sack.

Sherry   And sit in your poxy chair with a bottle and a packet of fags feelin' sorry for yaself!

Beth   You're pushin' me, Sherry . . .

Sherry   You push me . . . You push me!

Long pause. **Beth** *tries to go and help* **Sherry** *up off the floor.*

Sherry   Get off . . .

A slight pause. **Beth** *sits down in the armchair and lights another cigarette.*

Beth   When your father left, Sherry, it was like someone took half of me away.

Pause.

It was like he'd taken all the laughter and life I had right out of my body there and then, an' it's not got much better, Sherry.

Pause.

It's the hardest thing, Sherry. It's the hardest thing.

Pause.

Get up, Sherry – please.

A slight pause.

Gina an' the boys'll be here in a minute.

Pause.

Sherry   I'm sorry.

Beth   It's alright, love.

Sherry   I'm really sorry but you've just got to let me get on.

Beth   I know, love.

Sherry   I can't cope with you tryin' to control what I do all the time.

Beth   I don't mean to, love.

Sherry   I'm twenty-three, I'm a grown woman, Mum.

Beth   Are you, Sherry?

Long pause.

I don't mean to, Sherry, but it's hard . . . I don't want you to go, Sherry . . .

A slight pause.

You can stay here as long as you want – You know that, darlin'.

Sherry   I know.

Pause.

Beth   I loved your dad, Sherry. I loved him with all my heart.

A slight pause.

I was never unfaithful to your dad, Sherry . . . I've never.

A slight pause. **Beth** *is tearful but she doesn't cry.*

He was the one, Sherry. He was the one who went off . . . I've always stuck by you girls – I've always tried to do the best for you girls. I've gone to work before now with holes in me shoes so you girls and your dad had dinner on the table. We've had the good days and the bad but I've always tried to do good by my family an' if you'd gone to Manchester I wouldn't have minded, Sherry – honest I wouldn't.

Sherry   Please, Mum . . .

Beth   You stand by your family, Sherry.

The doorbell rings. **Beth** *gets up to get it and exits.* **Sherry** *stands the ironing board back up and holds her dress up as we hear a door open and* **Lee**, **Dave** *and* **Gina**'s *voices.*

Beth (*off*)   Hello.

Dave (*off*)   Alright, Beth.

Lee (*off*)   Hiya.

Beth (*off*)   You must be Lee.

Gina (*off*)   Hasn't Sherry got herself a gorgeous date, Ma?

Gina *enters wearing a bright canary-yellow cocktail dress, followed by* **Lee** *in a single-breasted dinner jacket, holding some flowers.*

Gina   Hello . . . You better get your skates on.

A slight pause as **Gina** *and* **Lee** *sense something's up.*

Gina   Shell?

Dave *enters wearing a double-breasted dinner jacket and bright bow-tie with a full carrier bag over his wrist. He grins broadly and lets a party popper go, watching the streamers fall on* **Sherry**'s *head.* **Beth** *enters. The next section of dialogue overlaps.*

Beth   What was that?

Dave   Sorry, Beth, but I had to let one go . . .

Beth   What?

Gina   Are you alright, Sherry?

Sherry   Yeah.

Gina   Ignore him, Mum. He's being a total prat.

Lee *offers the flowers to* **Beth**.

Lee   I got these for you.

Gina   Sherry?

Beth   Please – call me Beth.

Sherry   Yeah – I just need to get ready.

Dave   Here look at this . . .

They all turn their attention to **Dave** *who undoes his jacket to reveal the loudest waistcoat possible to imagine.*

Top banana, eh?

Sherry   I didn't think you wore a waistcoat with double-breasted?

Dave   Dunno . . .

Gina   Only an extra fiver, Shell . . .

Beth   Here, give us that iron – Go and get yourself ready.

Dave   You look like you're goin' to a fancy dress – Sheik of Bath, Shell.

Sherry *exits followed by* **Gina** *who tuts at* **Dave** *on the way out.* **Dave** *reaches into the bag and pulls out two cans of lager and gives one to* **Lee**. **Beth** *places the flowers on the armchair and crouches down to plug in the lead from the iron at the same time.*

Lee   Cheers.

Dave   You alright, Beth?

Beth   Coping, love.

Dave   Fancy dress an idea for next year, eh, Lee?

Lee *nods.*

Dave   Me Batman, you Robin . . .

Beth   You look more like Hale an' Pace.

Dave   That's funny – I'm on the door tonight.

Beth   Well I hope there's no trouble . . .

Beth *licks her finger and tests the iron's temperature.*

Lee   There won't be no trouble tonight . . .

Dave   Well, if there is I know where it'll be coming from . . .

Lee   Who?

Dave   McNeill.

Lee   He won't cause no trouble – There'll be a load a kids there.

Dave   He better not cause any trouble, mate . . .

Lee   You heard what he's wearing tonight?

Dave   One of them funny skirts.

Lee   An' one of them funny hairy pouches.

Dave   Little Scottish dick-head.

Beth   Oh – A kilt an' sporan?

Dave   Yeah – something like that.

Beth   They're smart.

A slight pause. **Dave** *looks at* **Lee** *and then back at* **Beth**.

Dave   Yeah, but they let it all hang out.

Lee *grins and takes a picture from the sideboard.*

Dave   Well, he's not going behind me in the conga.

Beth *smiles as she again tests the temperature and starts to iron* **Sherry**'s *dress.* **Dave** *lifts the flowers.*

Dave   Alright if I take a pew, Beth?

Beth   Yeah.

A slight pause. **Dave** *sits down and takes a long swig from his can.*

Beth   That was taken at Land's End, Lee . . . (**Lee** *smiles.*) We got a couple from Newcastle to take it for us . . . Gina an' Sherry were pretty little girls, weren't they?

Lee   Yeah . . . Pigtails an' matching dresses – look . . .

Dave   Oi – Watch it, you.

Lee *grins.*

Beth   Always the same they had . . . Never one more spoilt than the other . . .

Lee   I've never been to Land's End . . .

Beth   That was a lovely holiday – And their dad was ever so good with them . . . All over Cornwall we went – Penzance an' Falmouth, Truro – Oh an' we had a lovely day in St Ives . . . The girls spent all day playin' on the

beach an' me an' their father had two big bottles of
Scrumpy an' was so pissed we had to get a cab back to the
campsite an' pick the car up the next day . . . (**Dave** *and*
Lee *smile.*) You know when their father went back for the
car the next day – He found two boys asleep in there. I
dunno – we must've forgot to lock it up when we was pissed
– but the two boys had got in cos they said they'd been
chucked out of home an' had been sleepin' on the beach but
it was cold. Soft bugger gave them fifty quid . . .

Beth *smiles. A slight pause.* **Beth** *lifts* **Sherry**'s *dress which she's
made short work of.*

Dave   Professional job you done there.

Beth   That's a lifetime of ironing for ya . . . It's very kind
of you to bring those flowers for me, Lee.

Lee   No problem.

Gina *enters, annoyed.*

Gina   Have you got Sherry's dress?

Beth   Yeah.

A slight pause as **Gina** *takes it and exits.* **Dave** *glances at* **Lee**.
Beth *collapses the ironing board.*

Dave   Got a right beer-head on now, boy.

Lee   Yeah?

Dave   Yeah.

Beth   You make sure you have a pint of water before you
go to bed.

Dave   I always reckon a good fry-up, two mugs of tea, an'
a bloody mary's the best hangover cure.

Lee   I hope you don't get sick.

Dave   Me? Asbestos guts, mate!

Lee   Any chunder on the suit an' you'll have to cough up extra.

Beth   That's right.

Dave   I'm not gonna chunder!

Lee *grins and* **Beth** *leans the ironing board against the wall. Off,* **Sherry** *'s music stops.*

Beth   So what is it you do, Lee?

Lee   Not much at the moment . . . I'm helping Dave decorate this place out in Prittlewell . . .

Dave   I've said to the boy – we should start in business . . .

Beth   Well I wish you the best a luck – it's difficult startin' up yourself these days.

Lee   I haven't got a trade.

Dave   It's just hard work. That's what you need. No muckin' about – just get down to some hard work.

Gina *enters, followed by* **Sherry**. *The two sisters are a real contrast:* **Gina** *dolled up to the nines and* **Sherry** *with hardly any make-up and a long dress.*

Dave   Ah – You look lovely, gels.

Gina   Come on, then, get yourself up.

Lee   You look nice.

Sherry   Thanks.

Gina   Come on – the cab's booked.

Beth   Let me get me camera.

Sherry   No, Mum.

Gina   There'll be loads a pictures taken later.

Beth   But you'll all be pissed – let me get one now.

Lee   I don't mind . . .

Dave   Only a couple, Gina.

Gina *tuts as* **Beth** *rushes out and* **Sherry** *sits down. Pause.*

Dave   Well this is a happy gatherin' . . .

Gina   You better watch yourself tonight, mate . . .

Dave   What?

Gina   I'm warning you. You overdo the sherbets an' make a tit a yerself I'll swing for you.

Dave *laughs and blows a raspberry.*

I mean it – You said you were gonna go to Texas early tomorrow an' fix the shower – so just you remember.

Dave   Listen, love – I can fix the fuckin' shower with a headache.

Gina   Don't swear!

Beth *enters with her camera.*

Beth   Quick! I think the taxi's here!

Gina, **Sherry**, **Lee** *and* **Dave** *form a bunched huddle.*

Beth   Get in a line . . .

They form the line with **Dave** *and* **Gina** *in the middle.*

Beth   Now smile . . .

A slight pause.

Dave   Lee sniffs little girls' bicycle seats.

Dave *grins broadly as* **Lee** *and* **Sherry** *look at him and* **Gina** *shouts.*

Gina   Dave!

The flash goes, the doorbell rings and they break and start to exit.

Gina   Come on!

Dave   See you, Beth.

Lee Bye.

Sherry Bye.

Beth Have a good time. Don't get too drunk!

Beth *follows them out of the living room.*

Beth *(off)* Bye.

Pause. **Beth** *re-enters with a vase which she puts the flowers in and she sits in the armchair and lights a cigarette. She picks up the framed photo which* **Lee** *left on the arm of the chair and stares at it. A slight pause. Her eyes well up as she fights back the tears.*

Scene Three

Saturday, ten o'clock. Car park of a Barking youth club. Off, the sound of faint party music. A door bangs open and for a few moments before it's shut a full-party chorus of Human League's Don't You Want Me Baby *is audible. Footsteps stagger towards us and* **Dave** *enters. He is very drunk, has no jacket on, his waistcoat is undone, top shirt buttons are open, there is a long puke stain on his right trouser leg and he clutches his bow-tie. His nose is also bloodied and his mouth is full. He stumbles over to a corner by a bush and is violently sick. Pause.*

Dave Ah . . .

Dave *kneels, takes off his waistcoat and crumples it up for a pillow and lies down next to the vomit in his dingy corner. Long pause.* **Sherry** *wanders in from another direction and doesn't notice* **Dave***. She's got* **Lee***'s dinner jacket over her shoulders and smokes.* **Lee** *enters drinking lager from a half-full plastic pint glass.*

Sherry Gina's gonna kill him.

Lee I know.

Pause.

I think he must've got a cab home.

Sherry Why?

Lee   He's done it before when he's been out with the boys . . .

Sherry *tuts like her sister.*

Did you see what happened? (**Sherry** *shakes her head.*) Dave challenged Sam to a drinking competition.

Sherry *tuts.*

It was sad, Sherry. Tone told me they had six pints an' six double bacardis, an' I saw them finish Gina's jug a Malibu an' pineapple.

Sherry   No wonder she's pissed off.

Lee   He was shit-faced, Shell. He saw McNeil head for the bar an' he saw red. He took a swing, missed the geezer and smacked his hooter on a stall. Then the soppy sod only tried to pull McNeil's kilt down from the floor.

Sherry   Did Gina see this?

Lee   No. She was doing the *Birdy Song* with Alison an' the kids. McNeil's missis accosted her in the toilets an' told her to sort her fella out but Dave had gone.

A slight pause.

I tried to stop him drinkin' so much – I tried to stop him goin' after McNeil but I couldn't, Sherry.

Pause.

Sherry   It's so tacky.

A slight pause.

I knew it'd be like this – I knew it . . . People round here, they get a drink in them and they're fucking awful.

A slight pause.

If I ever have kids I don't wanna bring them up round here.

Pause. **Sherry** *offers* **Lee** *a drag on the cigarette, which he accepts.*

Lee   I don't know if I want kids.

Sherry   Don't ya?

Lee   I don't know.

Sherry   I'd've thought you were exactly the type.

Lee   What type's that?

Sherry   I dunno.

Lee *smiles.*

Lee   Do I look like a father?

Sherry   I dunno. Say – 'Get up to your bedroom now'.

Lee *grins and does a Frank Butcher impression.*

Lee   'Ricky'!

Sherry *laughs. A slight pause.*

Lee   You're right about round here. It's gettin' worse. Me dad says it used to be like a trip into the country coming out here – Dagenham, Ilford an' them places.

Sherry   The east end's spreading out.

Lee   Yeah.

Sherry   You see loads a boarded-up windows in little parades a shops, loads of charity shops now, don't ya?

Lee   You see that bloke sellin' *Big Issue* on Longbridge Road?

Sherry   Yeah. You been to Ilford lately?

Lee   Yeah.

Sherry   You seen the new shopping centre? Half the units haven't got new shops in yet.

A slight pause.

Lee   Eh, Sherry?

Sherry   What?

Lee   There's an Englishman, an' Irishman, an' a Scottishman . . .

Sherry   Lee . . .

Lee   What?

Sherry *tuts.*

Lee   I was only gonna tell a shit joke.

Sherry   Well, if it's shit, why tell it?

Lee   I was just tryin' to make you laugh. That's what we're meant to do, ain't it?

Sherry   What?

Lee   Fellas – in the company of ladies. Tell jokes. Try to be funny.

Sherry   Not really.

Lee   Don't tell me. You look for someone you can talk to . . .

Sherry   Well, this has moved on.

A slight pause.

I don't know what I want, Lee. I don't want to be patronised, I know that. What do you look for? A school uniform?

Lee *laughs.*

Lee   Not that old one – Gina's been calling me a trainer-bra all night.

Sherry   Not thalidomide any more then?

Lee   I showed her in the dictionary round at their flat.

Sherry   They've got a dictionary?

Lee *and* **Sherry** *laugh. Pause.*

Sherry   That's a terrible thing what happened to those women with thalidomide, ain't it?

A slight pause.

Imagine having a baby growing inside you an' then giving birth an' it's like that. Arms an' legs missing an' deformed.

Lee   I'd still love it – if it was me kid.

Sherry   If those women had got pregnant a few years earlier they wouldn't've gone through all that pain.

Lee   It happened.

Sherry   It's just being in the wrong place at the wrong time, Lee. So much of life's like that. It's not fair.

Lee   Works the other way. My old man won the lottery.

Sherry   You're joking.

Lee   Straight up.

Sherry   You're winding me up.

Lee   Honest. Five numbers and a bonus ball. Hundred an' twenty grand he got.

Sherry   Really?

Lee   Yeah . . . Fuckin' hypocrite. He's been goin' on about how the country's goin' to the dogs with no one goin' to work an' waitin' for their numbers to come up – an' then he gets a ticket in a birthday card, he gets lucky, an' he's saying the lottery's the best thing since sliced bread.

A slight pause. **Lee** *smiles.*

Still – who am I to moan? He got me me flat.

Sherry   An' I thought it was all hard work.

Pause.

Lee   D'you think I'm a prick?

Sherry   No. Why did you say that?

A slight pause.

Lee   I don't know.

A slight pause.

Sherry   D'you think I'm serious?

A slight pause.

You do!

Lee   You're alright . . .

Sherry *laughs.*

Lee   You're nice . . .

Sherry *laughs more. Long pause.* **Lee** *looks up at the sky.*

Lee   Here, Sherry – Look at the stars.

Sherry *looks up.*

Lee   Nice, ain't they?

Sherry *nods. Pause.*

Lee   The stars make you feel small, don't they?

Sherry   Yeah.

A slight pause.

I always feel thick when I look at the stars. I can never pick out the signs an' stuff.

Lee   I don't know them.

Sherry   Gina knows them.

Lee   So does Russell Grant an' he's a right pillock.

Sherry *laughs.*

Sherry   When I was little I used to imagine if you looked up at the stars hard enough for long enough it might rain chocolate.

Lee   Milky Way?

Sherry *nods and laughs.*

Lee   It's nice being out here, ain't it?

Sherry   Yeah – it's warm.

Lee   We've had good weather this spring.

Lee *very tentatively moves his hand towards* **Sherry***'s, about two feet away. Just as he's about to touch he loses his bottle and slowly withdraws his hand.*

Sherry   Lee . . .

Lee   Yeah?

Sherry   Did Gina get you to ring me?

Lee *looks straight at* **Sherry***.* **Sherry***, too, turns her gaze from the sky.*

Lee   No.

A slight pause.

Sherry   Good.

Sherry *puts an arm around* **Lee***'s waist and nestles her head on his chest.*

I think it's gonna be a good summer this year.

Lee   Yeah?

Sherry   Yeah.

Sherry *playfully snatches a peck on* **Lee***'s lips and he responds by kissing her on her forehead. They both smile. Just as they're about to have a proper snog* **Dave** *sits bolt upright and retches furiously.*

Lee   Who's that?

Lee *wanders over to the source of the noise.*

Dave!

Dave   Leave me alone.

Lee   Dave, you twat! Shell – it's Dave . . . He's here.

Sherry *advances.*

Lee   You stink.

Sherry   You alright?

Dave   I feel like fucking shit.

Lee   Look – he's parked a tiger!

Sherry   Lee!

Lee   He's got chunder all over his suit!

Sherry   You alright? Your nose . . .

Lee   Oi, oi! Look at you, chunder-bunny!

Dave   Don't be so fuckin' immature.

Lee *and* **Sherry** *fall about laughing.*

Dave   Look – just fuck off, alright.

Dave *starts to cry.*

Sherry   Dave . . .

Lee   Eh, eh, what's a matter with ya?

Dave   I fucking shit meself.

Lee   Oh no.

Sherry   You haven't?

Dave   I'm a wanker.

Sherry   No . . .

Dave   Yes, I am.

Lee   Come on, mate.

Dave   I'm the biggest wanker in Barking.

Dave *really cries as* **Lee** *and* **Sherry** *take an arm each and try to pull him up.*

Lee   Come on.

Sherry That's it.

Lee Fuck, he's got puke on me now – Watch it, Dave.

Dave I can't help it.

Lee Well, you can pay the dry-cleaning.

Sherry Lee!

Lee What?

Lee *spots* **Dave**'s *puke stain rubbing against his trousers and he lets his arm slip.*

Dave Fuck!

Sherry Lee, you dick-head!

A slight pause.

Lee Eh, Dave – Squashed a turd?

Lee *laughs and so does* **Sherry** *and* **Dave** *slowly puts his head in his hands. Off a door opens and for a few seconds we get a burst of Bobby Vinton's* Blue Velvet *before it shuts again. Footsteps come towards us and then pause.*

Gina (*off*) David Stams, are you out here?

Sherry Fuck – it's Gina.

Dave Don't let her know I'm here.

Gina (*off*) Dave!

Lee This is stupid.

Gina *enters. She's very drunk and in a bit of a state as she clutches her handbag and a bottle of alcoholic lemonade.*

Gina There you are!

Sherry Gina . . .

Gina There you are, you no-good fucking bastard!

Dave Gina.

Sherry   Geenie.

Gina   You stay out of this, Sherry.

Dave   I'm sorry.

Gina   Don't you sorry me, ya sad bastard! Sick all over ya, blood all over ya nose and ya. (**Gina** *notices the smell*.) Ya smell as if you've fell in a pile a dog shite!

Lee   No, he's . . .

Sherry   Yeah – I think I trod in it as well, Gina.

A slight pause. **Sherry** *glances at* **Lee**, *who grins.*

Gina   An' you can wipe that smirk off your mouth an' all . . . If you were a turd, Dave, I'd kick you in the fuckin' gutter! An' you want me to marry you!

Dave   I love you, Sherry.

Gina   Don't think you can fuckin' talk your way out of this, shit-for-brains, because you can't.

A slight pause.

Look at you – you're a disgrace . . . Pissed out of your mind cos one or two drinks ain't enough for you. Oh no! Big-bollocks-get-the-beers-in-prat-face over there has to have a skinful! And does he make any effort with me? It's always the fuckin' same!

A slight pause.

Where does he take me, does he make me feel nice and look after me? I'm lucky to get a fucking prawn cocktail at the Harvester! You're just a no-good fat fucking bastard who sits on his arse an' eats the cupboards bare!

A slight pause.

An' d'you know what, Lee? D'you know what? We hardly even fuck any more!

Sherry   Gina . . .

Gina It's true. The only pleasure I've got runs on two
Duracell an' . . . an' . . . it's not bad – but I . . . I . . . You
never think about me, you selfish bastard, Dave! (**Lee** *looks
at his feet both suppressing a laugh and embarrassed.*) So you can
fucking well forget any idea of me putting a ring on my
finger until you get your finger outta your arse with me, my
boy! An' I tell you this now, David Stams, as these two are
my witness. If you don't get the shower fixed tomorrow you
can pack ya bags and park your lazy arse somewhere else!

Gina *takes a swig of her bottle and staggers off. A slight pause. The
door opens off and we get a burst of George Michael's* Careless
Whisper *before she shuts the door.*

Dave Help me up.

Lee *has* **Dave**'s *hand and pulls him up.* **Lee** *passes* **Dave** *his
crumpled waistcoat.*

Dave I'm sorry.

Sherry Don't worry.

Dave I am sorry.

Sherry I know.

Lee D'you want me to get you a cab?

Dave No. I'll walk.

A slight pause. **Dave** *turns and starts to go out, but pauses before he
exits.*

Dave I know I do stupid things, Sherry. But I don't mean
to be a wanker.

A slight pause.

I love your sister.

Sherry I know.

Dave An' if she'll have me I'll be the best husband in the
world. I'll change – I really will change.

Sherry   I know you will.

Dave *turns back and exits. A slight pause.* **Lee** *wanders over to* **Sherry** *and takes her hand.* **Sherry** *again leans her head on his chest.*

Sherry   You smell of sick now.

Lee   It's not very romantic smelling of sick is it? (**Sherry** *nods.*) The first time I got off with a girl she'd just been sick after two cans of Tennents Super. I was only twelve.

Sherry   I snogged a bloke whose breath smelt a barbecue beef crisps once.

Lee *smiles. A slight pause.*

Sherry   Were you really goin' out with a girl who was sixteen?

Lee *nods.*

Sherry   Did you like her?

Lee *nods.*

Lee   She was in love with East 17, though. What about you?

Sherry   What?

Lee   You been seein' anyone?

Sherry   No – Not for a while.

A slight pause.

I was seeing this lecturer guy for a while.

Lee   Ain't that against the rules?

Sherry   He didn't teach me. He taught politics. Turned out to be a real arsehole.

Lee   What did you do?

Sherry   I dumped him.

Lee (*smiles*)   No, your course . . .

Sherry   Oh. Business Studies. It's got me quite a good job. Graduate position at Marks an' Sparks.

Lee   Plenty of free underwear, eh?

Sherry   Why does everyone say that?

Lee   Dunno. S'pose you always think about the perks on a job?

Sherry   Yeah. But it's a job, really, just work at the end of the day.

Lee   At least you got a good job.

Sherry   Yeah. Loads of my mates are stuck at home on the dole. They wanna leave home an' they can't. It's stupid. All these clever people with qualifications up to their eyeballs and not much work.

A slight pause.

I can't help thinking sometimes – I've got another fifty or sixty years in me maybe, and if I'm lucky, half a that time I'll be working. If I'm lucky.

A slight pause.

I wanna do things, Lee – I wanna travel an' I'm only twenty-three and I can see the years stretchin' out in front of me just of work, and work, and work.

A slight pause.

Still, nothing's for certain any more, is it? You gotta just work while you can.

Lee   I can tell ya. I've done the sitting in me flat, an' there's only so much time you can spend watching videos an' orderin' pizzas, sweetheart.

A slight pause.

You just have to wait an' see what comes along an' what you feel's right . . . If you wanna drop everything, fine, if you wanna work, that's fine.

Sherry   It's not that easy, Lee.

A slight pause.

Me mum's so difficult . . . It's stupid. If I'd gone up to Manchester to study, I'd've made the break – but I haven't, an' it's hard.

A slight pause. **Sherry** *smiles.*

Come here.

Sherry *pulls* **Lee** *close and they kiss, very lovingly.*

Lee   Do I still smell a puke?

Sherry   A little bit. It's not as bad as barbecue beef crisps.

Lee   Come on – I'll call a cab.

Sherry   Lee, I'm not sure if I . . .

Lee   What? (*A slight pause.*) I'll go and call a cab an' we'll drop you off first an' then me. Alright? (**Sherry** *nods.*) Come on.

Sherry   Call it . . . I just want a bit a quiet out here for the minute.

Lee *nods and turns to exit.*

Sherry   Eh, Lee?

Lee   What?

Sherry   What d'you think a Keanu Reeves?

Lee *smiles.*

Lee   Dunno.

Sherry   Any better than East 17?

Lee   Loads.

Sherry *laughs and* **Lee** *exits.* **Sherry** *looks up at the sky. A slight pause. Then she looks over where* **Dave** *was and back to look at her feet. She finally returns her gaze to the stars.*

Sherry   Cheers.

Scene Four

Monday morning, nine o'clock. A bedroom in a house in Prittlewell, Essex. **Lee** *fixes the plug on a power drill and* **Dave** *plasters the wall.* **Dave** *does this for the whole scene, but it only takes* **Lee** *a few minutes to complete his job.* **Dave** *works with real skill and artistry, each movement sure and fine, as he talks and listens to* **Lee***. They both wear work overalls and* **Dave** *has a plaster across the bridge of his nose. A slight pause.*

Dave   Did you shag her then?

Lee *grins.*

Dave   You dirty sod!

Lee   No – I didn't.

Dave   D' you get hold of her, then?

Lee   Yeah.

Dave   Any smelly finger?

Lee   Dave!

Dave   What?

Lee   How old are you?

Dave   Twenty-eight.

Lee   Well then.

Dave   What?

Lee   You're acting like a fifteen-year-old!

Dave   No I'm not.

Lee   You are – You're like a bloody teenager.

Dave   I'd just like to know, that's all.

Lee   I got hold of her after you went an' after the cab dropped us off – that's all.

Dave   At her house?

Lee   Yeah.

Dave   Hoping for the old coffee on the sofa an' hand up her skirt, eh?

Lee   No. I walked home from hers when her mum let her in.

Pause.

Dave   I bet you're gutted?

Lee   No.

Pause.

Dave   You seein' her again?

Lee   Yeah.

Dave   That's alright – get your leg over then . . .

Lee   Well, I dunno.

Dave   Why not?

Lee   Because . . . She might not want to.

Dave   You do, though?

Lee   What?

Dave   Wanna give her one.

Lee   Well, course I'd like to give her one.

Dave   Well then . . .

Lee   Well what?

Dave   It's only human.

Lee   Yeah.

Dave   She's an attractive girl.

Lee   What are you talking about?

Dave   You and Sherry.

Pause.

Got a great pair, Sherry . . .

Lee   Dave!

Dave   What?

Lee   She's Gina's sister!

Dave   Yeah?

Dave *laughs. A slight pause.*

An' I tell you another thing – if she's anything like her sister I bet she can suck a golf ball through a hose pipe.

Lee *shakes his head. A slight pause.*

You're a bit uptight, ain't ya? Must be that erection you've been stiflin' all weekend.

A slight pause.

I've got some quality porn you can borrow at home.

Lee   No – it's alright.

Pause.

You fix Gina's shower alright?

Dave   Yeah.

A slight pause.

Lee   Is your nose broken?

Dave   Just a cut.

Pause.

I tell ya what I have realised working out here, Lee.

Lee   What's that?

Dave   When me an' Gina get married I'd like to have a place like this.

Lee   In the country?

Dave   Well, Barking's getting worse. You've only gotta go a couple a miles down the road into West Ham an' it's like the black hole a Calcutta. It won't be long before it's the same round our way.

A slight pause.

You gotta make sure you leave everything locked up, an' it's not often you'll see me out late without a screwdriver in me pocket. An' I mean I can handle meself, right? (**Lee** *smirks.*) Eh!

Lee   What?

Dave   I was pissed on Saturday!

Lee   What?

Dave (*grins*)   You know what, you cheeky cunt.

A slight pause.

Lee   Sherry was sayin' if she has kids she wouldn't wanna bring 'em up round here.

Dave   An' just think – you could be the father a those kids.

Lee   Don't say that!

Dave   Why?

Lee   I've only got hold of her on Saturday.

Dave   You never know how things are gonna turn out.

Lee   Well . . .

Dave   Four years down the road you could well be in exactly the same position as me. You've gotta think about the future.

Lee   Yeah – So what a ya saying? Get a good job, save up, get a pension – it's all bollocks.

Dave   It's not.

Lee   There's no good jobs any more – Even if you've got a trade, even if you've got a education – you should've heard what Sherry said about some of her university mates.

Dave   Well – you work for yourself, don't ya?

Lee   But it don't matter if you're working for yourself if there's no work to be had.

Dave   Well you generate it yourself – Work hard – Market yourself right . . .

Lee   But if there's no work there . . .

Dave   There's always work.

Lee   There's not, Dave. What a you doing when we finish here at the end of the month?

Dave   I've got one or two things in the pipe-line.

Lee   Like what – mini-cabbing?

A slight pause.

Dave   It's all about havin' bit a confidence, Lee.

A slight pause.

I tell ya – you should come in with me.

Lee   Do what?

Dave   You should come in with me – An' go legit . . . A proper business. We could get a van an' start up together proper, like.

Lee   But I can't do anything, can I? I can't plaster, I'm not a brickie, I'm not a spark, an' I don't know any plumbing. Fuckin' hell, Dave, I can just about paper a wall.

Dave   I'll teach ya.

Lee   It's a different kettle a fish me becomin' your partner to me helping out.

A long pause.

It's weird, ain't it?

Dave   What?

Lee   How things a different to what you expect they're gonna be.

Dave   Like what?

Lee   I remember at school we all done these geography projects about how in the future we'd have all this time, like – for leisure. Should've seen me, Dave – outside Dagenham swimming pool gettin' these people to fill in me questionnaires.

A slight pause.

Yeah. Everyone'd be on part-time, but the wages'd be good enough to do what you wanted, an' the work wouldn't be, like, factories – it'd be shops, an' fixing things.

Dave   What we're doin', ain't it?

Lee   An' all, like, this time – for leisure. That's where I thought I'd work – in a leisure centre. So the rest a the time, you'd be like, going . . . dry-skiing an' stuff.

Dave   Dry-skiing?

Lee   Yeah.

Dave   I bet there's a million out there on the dole livin' a life a leisure an' signin' on . . .

Lee   You're signin' on.

Dave   Yeah – but I'm workin' – I'm not sittin' on me arse.

Lee *grins. Pause.*

I wanna place like this. It'll be great for the kids. Have a coupl'a dogs. Nice big garden. Lovely countryside. Nice big kitchen for Gina.

A slight pause.

If I won the lottery I'd have a place like this.

Lee *smiles and shakes his head.*

What?

Lee   Nothing.

Dave   What d'you reckon, eh? Go into business, all legit an' above board, work hard and build it up together.

A slight pause.

Our business'll be so successful we'll have our own fellas doin' the decoratin' for us, an'll have like a big office an' desks an' stuff. Fuckin' hell – we'll have briefcases, mate!

Lee *grins.*

Dave   You wait – we'll have so much money we'll have it comin' out of our ears!

A slight pause.

Lee   You still gonna go West Ham if you live out here?

Dave   Is the Pope Catholic?

Lee *grins.*

Lee   None a the supporters come from local any more, do they?

Dave   No. I reckon there's more on a train from Southend on a Saturday afternoon than there is having a walk along Green Street.

Lee *nods.*

Lee   So where've they gone then?

Dave   Who? The supporters?

Lee   No – The people who live here.

Dave   South a France.

Lee   Lovely.

Dave   Touch, eh? All cash in hand.

Lee   How d'you get this, then?

Dave   Sam's boss. Friend of his who I got chatting to in the pub.

Lee   Good, ain't it?

Dave   I tell you, mate – they are well posh.

Lee   Well why don't they get someone out the Yellow Pages?

Dave   Dunno. Tight, I s'pose.

Lee   What's he do?

Dave   Publishin'.

Lee   What about her?

Dave   Catering business.

A slight pause.

She's gotta great pair a boobs. You ever nobbed a rich bird? (**Lee** *shakes his head.*) Well, she can give me one. She can be right masterful an' smack my arse. (**Lee** *laughs.*) She could, mate. An' she can order me about in her posh little voice as much as she likes. If she's lucky, eh, Lee?

A slight pause.

Still, you're alright with Sherry, eh, Lee? She's a lovely girl. (**Lee** *nods.*) She's a bit straight but she's a good girl. I mean I love my Gina, but Gina's no good with her mum, an'

Sherry's been as good as gold, an' looked after her mum all through her divorce, an' stuck by her side.

Lee   What about the old man?

Dave   He's living in Woodford now with his new wife . . . Gina sees quite a lot of him, but him an' Sherry don't speak now.

A slight pause.

Shame, ain't it?

Lee *nods.*

Lee   Why did they get divorced?

Dave   He had an affair – with the lady he's hitched to now.

Pause. **Dave** *stands back from his work and admires it for a moment.*

Dave   Look at that, Lee. Work a fuckin' art, mate.

Lee *laughs.*

Lee   Does Gina know she's gettin' married to an artist?

Dave   Does she fuck!

Lee *and* **Dave** *laugh.*

Dave   You fancy doing some weights tonight?

Lee   Gettin' fit?

Dave   I might do.

Lee   Proper nineties man.

Dave   Yeah, bollocks.

A beat.

Come on. I fancy a bacon an' egg sanger.

Dave *puts down his trowel and exits.* **Lee** *shakes his head and follows.*

Act Two

One month later.

Scene One

Saturday morning, eleven o'clock. Barking Park. The weather's really sunny. **Sherry** *sits reading cross-legged and* **Gina** *sunbathes.* **Sherry** *has a tight top, 501s and swanky sunglasses.* **Gina** *is wearing denim shorts and a bikini top. Both girls have bags. A slight pause.*

Gina   So come on, darlin' – have ya shagged him?

Sherry *tuts.*

Gina   Are you tryin' to tell me you've been seeing him a month an' you haven't?

Sherry *tuts again.*

Gina   This isn't like you, Sherry. When you were seeing that lecturer I had all the gory details.

Sherry *shuts her book.*

Gina   Don't tell me – He's got a one-inch willy and you're going to therapy with him?

Sherry   Gina! – You're terrible!

Gina   I just like to keep an eye on me sister.

Sherry   An' her boyfriends by the sounds of it.

Gina   There's someone else apart from Lee?

Sherry   No!

Pause.

Gina   What do I detect?

Sherry   I've got no idea, Gina.

Gina   Is Sherry all luvvy-duvvy over Lee-baby, is she – is she?

Sherry   Piss off, Gina.

A slight pause.

I just want to get out.

Gina   Sorry. Sorry I opened my gob. Won't open it again today.

Gina *stands up and has a wander.* **Sherry** *re-opens her book.*

Gina   Is it good, Sherry?

Sherry   Shut up, Gina!

Gina   I'm bored.

Sherry   I thought you wanted a sunbathe?

Gina   I have. I'm bored.

Pause. **Gina** *looks at her nails.*

I'm glad I've got nails again, Sherry.

A slight pause.

I said, I'm glad I've got nails again, Sherry.

A slight pause.

What colour shall I do 'em Wednesday night?

Sherry   Any fucking colour – just shut up!

Gina *tuts.*

Gina   I don't know where Dave an' Lee have gone to. I don't know how long it takes to get an ice-cream.

A slight pause.

I knew we shouldn't've let 'em take the football with 'em, Sherry . . . They're gonna've forgot about the ice-creams . . . They'll be playing football . . .

Sherry *moves from her cross-legged upright position to lying on her front looking away from* **Gina**. **Gina** *tuts again and looks at her nails.*

Gina   Fuck!

Gina *scrambles over towards her towel and frantically rummages through her bag.*

Sherry   Gina!

Gina *fishes a ring out of her purse.*

Gina   There it is!

Gina *puts the engagement ring on her finger.*

Thank fuck for that!

Sherry   What're ya doing?

Gina   Putting me fucking ring on!

Sherry   What ring?

Gina   The engagement ring!

Sherry   What engagement ring?

Gina   The one Dave gave me, you silly cow!

Sherry   I didn't know you'd said yes?

Gina   I haven't!

Sherry   Well, why're ya wearin' it?

Gina   Because I said I would – provisionally – while I make up me mind.

Sherry   Gina!

Gina   I don't wear it all the time! I only wear it when I'm with Dave!

Sherry   But Gina . . .

Gina   What? It's what Dave wants – He said if I decide I don't want to, to give the ring back then – when I've thought about it properly.

Sherry   But Gina!

Gina   What?

Sherry   D'you think Dave thinks you'll ever take it off now it's on there?

Gina   He can think what he likes – an' I know it's not on there all the time.

Sherry   But he doesn't!

A slight pause.

Are you gonna marry him?

Pause.

Gina   I don't know.

Sherry   Geenie.

A slight pause.

But Dave thinks you're goin' a marry him.

A slight pause.

Have you spoke to Mum or Dad about this?

Gina   Dad, not Mum.

Sherry   What about Dave?

Gina   Well his're dead, ain't they, you silly cow!

Pause.

He's been trying so hard, Sherry.

Sherry   What d'you mean?

Gina   He's been on a diet. He's been goin' to the gym, an' he's cut down on the booze –

Sherry   But Gina . . .

Gina   What?

Sherry   Do ya love him?

Gina   Course I do – I mean, he makes me laugh, an' it's the best it's been at home for ages . . . He's really making an effort . . . He's really made an effort over the last few weeks . . . Come on – we've been together five years – course I love him.

A slight pause.

Sherry   Are you back sleeping together?

Gina   Sherry!

Sherry   What?

Gina   That's private!

Sherry *and* **Gina** *grin. A slight pause.*

Sherry   Are you?

Gina   Not really.

Sherry   What's that mean?

Gina   Not really!

Sherry   You haven't, have ya?

Gina   That doesn't matter – we've been together a long time.

Sherry   But you don't love him!

Gina   He's my best mate.

Sherry   You don't marry your best mate, Gina. You marry the man you love.

Gina   I know.

Sherry   If you're making a commitment.

Gina   I know.

A slight pause.

Sherry   I don't mean to go on at you, Gina.

Gina   It's alright.

A long pause.

Sherry   Here – I've got something for ya.

Sherry *rifles through her bag and pulls out a video tape.*

Gina   *Point Break?*

Sherry *nods and* **Gina** *takes it.*

Gina   You – are – a sweetheart!

Gina *smiles and kisses* **Sherry** *on the cheek.*

If only I had three-hundred-and-sixty-six Keanus. One for every day of the year an' two for me birthday!

Sherry *and* **Gina** *laugh.*

Sherry   There's only one Keanu.

Gina   There's only one Jamie Redknapp.

This now becomes semi-football-chant.

Sherry   There's only one Alan Shearer.

Sherry *and* **Gina**   Ffwwwwooooaaaa!

Sherry *and* **Gina** *fall about laughing.* **Lee** *and* **Dave** *enter. Both wear football shirts and shorts, and sunglasses.* **Lee** *carries a football.*

Sherry   Aye, aye – it's Robson an' Jerome.

Gina   I told ya – They've forgot the sodding ice-creams!

A slight pause. They take their sunglasses off and the girls detect the boys' sombre mood.

Sherry   Why've you been so long?

Lee   An' old girl's been mugged by the lake.

Sherry   You're joking!

Gina   No!

Lee   She's a right state. The ambulance had just arrived when we got there . . . She must've been eighty, Sherry.

Sherry   Oh, God.

Lee   Crying her poor bleeding heart out she was – An' the cruel fucking bastard killed her little dog. Obviously kicked it or somethin' when the bastard nicked her bag. Poor little thing's neck was broke.

Gina   No!

Sherry *covers her mouth.*

Lee   I've gotta go back over an' make a statement to the police – I saw some geezer running away when we were playing football – so it might've been him.

Dave   If I could get hold of that fucker!

Dave's *deeply felt, disturbing anger silences* **Lee** *and focuses their attention.*

If I could get hold of that cunt! What I'd do . . . That fucker wouldn't walk away from me.

A slight pause.

I'm so fuckin' angry – I'm so angry – If I saw that fucker now I don't know what I'd do to him!

Gina   I know.

Dave   You didn't see her, Gina! She was fucking black and blue!

Pause. **Dave** *is red-faced and his eyes have glazed over.*

What's wrong with this fucking world?! What's wrong with it, eh?! It's bank-holiday weekend, it's a fucking sunny Saturday morning and she was taking her dog for a walk in the park, for fuck's sake!

Dave *wipes away some tears and* **Gina** *wraps her arms around him. Pause.*

Lee   I think I'm gonna go back now.

Sherry   I'll come with ya.

Lee *nods and* **Sherry** *turns to* **Gina** *who nods.* **Lee** *and* **Sherry** *exit.* **Gina** *leads* **Dave** *back over to the towels.*

Gina   You alright?

Dave *nods and* **Gina** *digs out a tissue which she wipes his eyes with.*

Dave   I'm sorry – I've been a prat.

Gina   You haven't.

A slight pause.

Look at you.

A long pause. They sit silently side by side and **Dave** *makes a final wipe of his eyes.*

Dave   What've you been doin'?

Gina   Just sittin' here. Sherry's been readin'.

Dave   Bookworm, that girl.

Gina   Yeah.

Dave   Yeah.

A slight pause.

You got plenty a sun-block on? I don't want you gettin' burnt.

Gina *nods.*

Gina   I was pissed off cos I thought you'd go off playing football an' forget the ice-creams.

Dave   You're right.

Gina *smiles.*

Gina   It's horrible seein' something like that, eh?

Dave *nods.*

Dave   I've never seen anything like that before. I've seen punch-ups, an' I've had a few meself . . .

Gina   Yeah – I know.

Dave   But I've never seen nothin' like that.

Gina   It chokes ya, don't it? D'you remember when I seen that accident on Romford Road?

Dave   Yeah.

Gina   An' you couldn't understand why I was so upset?

Dave   Yeah.

A slight pause.

It's a terrible world sometimes.

Gina   It's a sad world, it is.

A slight pause.

Have you gotta go back an' make a statement?

Dave   I didn't see the bloke Lee saw runnin'.

A long pause.

I wonder if the old girl's got a family?

Gina   I should think so.

A slight pause.

Most've them've got someone. She's probably got some gran'children.

Dave   Yeah.

A long pause.

Gina   You know the last time I seen me mum an' dad together was me grandad's funeral.

Pause.

It was awful. I was with Dad an' Sherry was with Mum.

Pause.

Even with Grandad in a coffin it was still the same.

Dave   I wish I knew me gran'parents.

Pause. **Gina** *puts her arm round* **Dave***'s waist.*

Dave   I love you, Gina.

Gina   I know.

Dave   I'll make something better for ya than living round here if I have to work my fingers to the bone.

Pause.

I can't wait for ya to see the house on Monday, Gina . . . It's exactly the sort of thing that'll be great for bringin' up a family – an' the schools are terrific round there.

A slight pause.

It's good to have a big garden – the kids get used to bein' out in the fresh air an' you can put a climbing frame up so they get used to doin' things.

A slight pause.

I can't wait for you to see it cos it just shows what I'm aimin' for – What we're workin' for – all them hours I do mini-cabbin', an' decoratin', an' you on the tills . . . It half brings it home to ya.

A slight pause.

I'll make it happen for us, Gina. I will. An' Lee knows what I'm talking about now. He's as good as promised he'll put some money up to get the business going, Gina. He knows what it's all about. I'm gonna teach him a trade an' we're gonna work hard an' make a real go of things. You watch – we're gonna be the most successful decorators in Essex.

A slight pause. **Gina** *doesn't look at* **Dave**. *She just nods her head very slowly.*

Scene Two

Sunday afternoon, four o'clock. The living room of a terraced house in Barking, east London; **Beth**'s *house.* **Lee** *examines the family photo we saw him looking at earlier. He has jeans and a smart shirt on.* **Sherry** *enters, and smiles. Again she looks very natural, in a long summery dress.*

Sherry   She's fast asleep. (**Lee** *nods.*) She always has a kip after Sunday dinner. D'you wanna wash or dry?

Lee *doesn't seem to have heard what she said.*

You alright, babe?

Lee   Just thinking.

Sherry   'Bout what?

Lee   Dave.

Sherry   Yeah.

Lee   Yesterday. I've never seen him get that upset before.

Sherry   So?

Pause.

Lee   I dunno . . . I dunno what to say about this thing he's got about goin' into business.

Sherry   It's stupid.

Lee   But he's convinced about it, Sherry. It's all he's been talkin' about for the last month when we're workin' – an' he's been taking all this extra time to teach me stuff . . . When we finished Friday lunchtime he made this toast with these beers he brought to celebrate us finishin' the job – to our future partnership.

Sherry   Well, what've you said?

Lee   I haven't said anything! He's just on a mission, Sherry.

A slight pause.

An' I dunno where he's got it in his head from but he's got this idea I'm gonna put up the money for us to start – in return for me trainin' on the job.

Sherry   You haven't got any money!

Lee   I know – He thinks I can take out a loan on the flat – so we can get a van.

Sherry *shakes her head.*

Sherry   Why haven't you told me about this before?

Lee   Well, it's so bloody ridiculous! I dunno what planet he's on but he just keeps going on about getting married and us being partners. It's like a stuck record, Shell – I'm glad we've finished the job . . . I dunno what's going on up top, I really don't, Sherry! I mean, I like the geezer an' we have a laugh but I've only known him properly three months!

Pause. **Sherry** *sits down in the armchair.*

Sherry   You know Gina's not gonna marry him?

Lee *gives* **Sherry** *a look.*

Sherry   She just can't tell him.

Lee   The shit's gonna hit the fan, ain't it?

Sherry *nods.* **Lee** *looks again at the photo.*

Sherry   That was taken at Land's End.

Lee *nods.*

Lee   I'd like to meet your dad.

Sherry   Yeah?

Lee   Yeah.

A slight pause.

He sounds like a good bloke.

Sherry   Really?

A slight pause.

What's made you take an interest in me dad all of a sudden?

Lee   Well – I know your mum now – an' we come round here an' that – Might be nice to get to know your dad an' all.

Sherry   Well, I don't really see him, Lee.

Lee   Well, Woodford's not a million miles away.

A slight pause.

Sherry   What you gonna do now you've finished working with Dave?

Lee   I don't know . . . Look for another job, I s'pose.

Sherry *shakes her head.*

Sherry   What d'you wanna do?

Lee   I don't know.

A slight pause.

Why don't you wanna talk to me about your dad?

Sherry *tuts and stands up.*

Lee   Don't tut – you sound like Gina.

A slight pause.

Sherry   You say about my dad? – What about your family – your mum an' dad? You never talk about them – you never say anything about them.

Lee   They live in Saffron Walden – not Woodford.

Sherry   You not answerin' my question.

Lee   You're not answering mine.

A slight pause.

My mum and dad are cunts.

A slight pause.

D'you know what they are? D'you know, Sherry? They're washing machines an', and fitted kitchens, an' goin' to Weymouth every summer, an' slagging off their relatives, an' then smiling in their faces when they come over, an' decorating every six months.

Sherry   All right . . .

Lee   Me dad talks to the man at Texas about patios, an' the man at Anglian about double-glazing, an' the man at Dagenham Motors about new cars, an' about having his books on bookshelves an' he doesn't read 'em, an' me mum sees how many fucking shelves she can fill with bits of china, an' photos an' any fucking mediocrity they can fucking think of an' then call that living. Call that shite living! It's not living – it's not being alive – it's dead, it's being fucking dead, Sherry.

A slight pause.

D'you understand, Sherry? D'you understand?

Sherry   I understand. It's how a lot of people live. It's how we lived when me dad was here.

Lee   You know they've told all their neighbours they saved all their lives to retire where they are now?

A slight pause.

They've spent their whole fucking lives surrounding themselves with things pretending it means something, pretending they're more than they are. An' now they haven't even got the honesty to admit they've been lucky.

Sherry   Well they got you ya flat . . .

Lee   I know – an' sometimes I wish they hadn't.

Sherry   Lee, those things matter to people an' you shouldn't look down on 'em.

Lee   I just want something different.

Pause.

You know, Sherry – at the moment you're everything to me.

A slight pause.

Bein' with you – it's just brought it home to me how . . . much of a nobody . . .

Sherry   What d'you mean?

Lee   Not a nobody – that's the wrong word . . . Just – nothing. Nothing, Sherry. Me dad said when he was getting me me flat that it'd be great for me – I'd have me independence, I'd have some motivation, get meself up on me feet an' away . . . But it just made me . . . fucking lonely . . . An' I'd started gettin' round to thinking how I could do up the flat, an' how I'd get a job to do it up an' make it more like a home, an' I joined Juventus at the end a the season, an' I met Dave, an' he got me the work, an' I met you, an' you've made me happy – but what with Dave goin' on about this business, an' then you goin' a move in with me, I just keep seeing me dad, and me dad, an' can't get him out of me head.

A slight pause.

An' I see Dave an' Gina.

A slight pause.

An' it just worries me, Sherry.

Pause.

Sherry   Don't you want me to move in any more?

Lee   No, Sherry . . .

Sherry   I mean it's only been a month an' if you're not sure . . .

Lee   I want ya to live with me, Sherry. It's what I want. D'you still want . . . ?

Sherry   Yeah.

Lee   But d'you understand, Sherry?

Sherry *nods and gets up and embraces* **Lee**. **Lee** *speaks very quietly, intimately.*

Lee   I love you, Sherry.

Sherry   I love you too.

Sherry *and* **Lee** *kiss. The most loving, sexy, warm and gentle kiss.*

Sherry   A lot of people – most people – live like your mum an' dad, my mum an' dad, did – it's just normal, Lee.

A slight pause.

My dad is the nicest man you could ever meet. It's difficult for me to ever remember an unhappy day when I was a kid. He was the most funny, intelligent, most lovely an' brilliant dad you could ever have, Lee.

A slight pause.

An' then six years ago he met another woman an' he fell in love with her an' he left us. He said it broke his heart to leave his family, an' his daughters, but he said that he loved this – other – woman with all his heart and that he wanted to spend the rest of his life with her. An' I hate him for that, Lee. I hate him for taking all of that that we had away from us. I hate him.

A slight pause.

I'll never speak to him again as long as I live, but I admire what he did.

Lee *and* **Sherry** *hold each other tight. There is a knock on the sitting room door.*

Beth (*off*)   Sherry, love, Lee . . . Is it alright if I come in – I won't look . . .

Lee *and* **Sherry** *laugh.*

Lee   Come in – we're just talking.

Beth *enters and* **Sherry** *sits back down in the armchair.*

Sherry   Good sleep, Mum?

Beth   Yeah. I felt full up after that dinner – She cooks a lovely roast dinner, Sherry, don't she, Lee?

Lee   Yeah.

Beth   Did you like the apple pie?

Lee   Yeah.

Beth   You got that Marks an' Spencers, didn't you, Sherry? They do lovely food.

Sherry   D'you fancy a cuppa?

Beth   You wait, when she's running her own store we'll all be eating like kings an' queens.

Lee   Well, I'm looking forward to tastin' a lot a Sherry's cooking now.

Sherry   Lee.

Lee   Course – you won't be doin' it all yourself, will ya, darlin' – we'll take it in turns.

Sherry   Lee . . .

A slight pause.

Beth   What's he talkin' about, Sherry?

Sherry   I haven't said anything yet.

Lee   You said we'd talk about it after dinner.

Beth   What's he talkin' about?

Sherry   I haven't spoken at all about it yet.

Lee   But you said you had.

Sherry   Well, I haven't! I said we'd speak about it after dinner!

Lee   It is after dinner.

Sherry   I know.

Lee   I didn't bring it up over dinner, did I?

Sherry   No – but I haven't spoken to Mum at all yet.

Lee   But you said you had!

Sherry   I said I was going to.

Beth   Sherry – will you please tell me what's going on!

Pause. **Sherry** *gets up from the chair. A slight pause.*

Sherry   Well . . . Lee an' I . . . I – I've decided I'm goin' a move into Lee's flat with him.

Beth *laughs.*

Beth   You're not.

Sherry   I am . . . I want to, Mum – Lee wants me to.

Beth   But you've . . . you've only known him a few weeks.

Lee   Yeah – but – it's something we both want, Mrs Killick.

Beth   I don't think you really know what Sherry wants, Lee.

Sherry   Mum . . .

Beth   I'm her mother.

Lee   I know it's hard, Mrs Killick . . .

Beth   D'you think I've seen her all through university on my own so she can drop it all – drop her career like that – so she can just flounce off with the first bloke who comes along an' fills her head with silly ideas?

Sherry   Mum, I'm not dropping anything!

Beth   An' you've only known him a month, if that.

Sherry   Mum!

A slight pause.

Beth   I'm not sayin' I don't like ya, Lee, but Sherry can't just leave like this . . . she can't.

Pause.

Sherry   It's what I want to do, Mum. If I wasn't moving in with Lee – I'd be moving out on me own before long.

Beth   But I can't understand it – You do what you like.

Sherry   Mum . . .

Beth   You come an' go as you like – an' I don't mind Lee stayin' over here the night – I'm not old-fashioned like that, Sherry, you know I'm not.

Beth *goes to sit down in the armchair. Pause.* **Sherry** *glances at* **Lee**.

Beth   So you've made up your mind, have ya?

Sherry   Yeah.

Beth *nods her head slowly.*

Beth   So when are you thinkin' of movin' out?

Sherry   Week after next.

Beth *nods her head again.*

Lee   I'll go an' put the kettle on, eh?

Sherry *nods and* **Lee** *exits.* **Sherry** *goes and sits on the arm of the chair next to her mum who's quickly tearful.*

Beth   Don't leave me, Sherry – Don't leave me.

Sherry   I'm only gonna be round the corner.

Beth   You're leaving me just like your dad an' Gina's left me – She's been gone two years an' I don't see nothing of her.

Sherry   You do. You saw her last week an' you'll see her tomorrow . . . an' she's comin' over Wednesday.

Beth   An' what's Flash Harry there gonna be like in six months, eh? He's gonna be like the rest of them are, like your father was – he's gonna be fed up with ya. An' what ya gonna do then, eh?

Sherry   Mum . . .

Beth   I'm only thinkin' a you, Sherry.

A slight pause.

I'm gonna be here all on me own – Gonna be left on me own. I might as well be dead an' buried.

Sherry   For Christ's sake, Mum!

A slight pause.

You can't do this! You can't say this!

Beth   I can say what I like in my house.

Sherry   You can't just expect me to be here for ever.

Beth   All I want is some help from me kids.

Sherry   But we do help you.

Beth   What – by leaving me?

Sherry   Yeah.

A slight pause.

You've gotta start pulling yourself together, Mum . . . Christ, you're forty-two, forty-two, Mum.

Beth   I am – I'm workin' again now.

Sherry   An' what've you done for the last six years, eh, except feel fucking sorry for yourself?

Beth   I haven't!

Sherry   You have! You have! You go down the pub an' drink yourself silly, or ya sit there smoking your fags an' moan about me, an' Dad, an' Gina, an' you don't do nothin' for yerself! You don't do anything!

Beth   I didn't ask your father to leave me!

Sherry   But he has, an' he's gone, he's fucking gone, an' he's never coming back.

Beth   We're not a family any more.

Sherry   What d'you mean we're not a family any more? You've got us! You've fucking got us!

Beth   Don't swear, Sherry.

Pause.

Sherry   D'you know what Gina's been goin' through with Dave over the last six months, do ya?

A slight pause.

Course ya don't cos you're so wrapped up with yerself . . . D'you know how upset she's been with him treating her like shit? Course you don't. You don't even know he's asked her to marry him, do ya?

Beth   No one's told me.

Sherry   No one should need to tell ya.

Beth   I never see her, Sherry.

Sherry   When ya do see her you never ask her how she is, or talk to her.

Beth   If someone had told me . . .

Sherry   You should know when something's the matter with your daughter!

A slight pause.

You moan about Gina not comin' round here – when was the last time you went to see her in her flat? Eh? Eh? I'll tell you when! Christmas-before-bloody-last, that's when!

Pause.

Beth   Are Gina an' Dave gettin' married?

Sherry *shakes her head.*

Sherry   She doesn't love him any more, Mum – she wants to leave him.

Beth *nods. Pause.*

Beth   Must be hard for her?

Sherry   Yeah. It is.

Beth   I'll speak to her tomorrow. I promise I will.

Sherry *nods and gives her mum a hug.*

Scene Three

Monday afternoon, three o'clock. A bedroom in a house in Prittlewell, Essex. The wall **Dave** *was plastering earlier in the play has now been decorated. There is a dado rail dividing the top and bottom halves of the wall, which are crimson and a pink and white stripe respectively.* **Gina** *enters followed by* **Beth**. **Gina** *has a body and sarong on and* **Beth** *has dressed up in a long summery dress and is made-up.*

Gina   I think Dave said this one's goin' a be a nursery or something.

Beth   It's very posh.

Gina   They're loaded.

Beth   Where is Dave?

Gina   He said the tap ain't workin' properly in the kitchen so he's just havin' a look.

Beth *nods.*

Beth   You seem a bit quiet today, Gina?

Gina   I'm just tired.

Beth   You hardly said a word at Leigh . . . Is that all? You're tired?

Gina   Yeah. I had to work yesterday. I'm doin' a lot a hours.

Beth   You haven't seemed yerself lately.

Gina   Yeah?

Beth   Is everthing alright?

Gina   What?

Beth   At home. With Dave.

A slight pause.

Gina   Has Sherry been speakin' to you?

A slight pause. **Beth** *nods.* **Gina** *smiles.*

Gina   What's she said?

Beth   She said you wanna leave him. She said you don't love him any more, an' that's been even more difficult cos he's asked you to marry him. Is it true – what she said?

Gina *nods.*

Gina   She's a sly one, that one.

Beth   She's ya sister . . . Why haven't ya talked to me, Gina?

Gina   I don't see ya.

Beth   You can come round – it's what I'm there for.

Gina   I know.

A slight pause.

It's just cos a . . .

Beth   What?

A slight pause.

Gina   It's just cos of Dad.

A slight pause.

Beth   What d'ya mean?

Gina   I just felt . . . I couldn't.

Pause.

You know – I used to think I was the reason Dad left us.

Beth   Gina . . .

Gina   I did. I was terrible. I was in trouble all the time. I was a slag.

Beth   Now that's not true.

Gina   It is. (**Gina** *smiles.*) They used to call me BBF at school. Barking Bucket Fanny.

A slight pause.

I was a right fucking slag an' I was fucking evil, some a things I did to you an' Dad an' Sherry.

Beth   Now you don't have to use that language, Gina.

Gina *laughs. A slight pause.*

Beth   You was just a normal teenager – that's all.

Gina   Sherry wasn't like me.

Beth   Everyone's different.

Gina   Sometimes I think if I hadn't been so silly I might have a good job like Sherry.

Beth   You never know how things a gonna turn out.

Gina   I used to really hate me job on the tills. I'd look at all these miserable faces lookin' at me – starin' over piles a food, an' toilet rolls. An' I'd see 'em get out their purses stuffed full a money, an' their gold cards, an' I'd think if me an' Dave had your money we wouldn't be miserable. An' I'd resent them, an' me job, an' Dave, an' you an' Dad, an' Sherry for goin' university an' me bein' stuck in Tesco's.

A slight pause.

An' then I started thinkin' when I'd come home an' see the flat in such a state how it wasn't money, or nothin', or how I'd been such a dick-head when I was younger – it was . . . It's Dave. I woke up, Mum.

A slight pause.

I don't hate me job now, Mum. I know I'm working for meself now cos I know I'm leavin' Dave. I'm gonna work hard for meself now.

Pause.

It's makin' me feel drained though, Mum. I don't like how not bein' able to tell Dave's makin' me feel. I'm not laughin' any more.

Pause.

Beth   It's lovely bein' in the country, ain't it?

Gina   Yeah.

Beth   I used to love it when your dad used to take us out.

Gina   We went all over, didn't we?

Beth   Yeah.

Pause.

Gina   I've wanted to talk to ya.

A slight pause.

Beth   I know ya have, love. Did ya think I wouldn't notice that ring on ya finger?

Gina   I only wear it when I'm with Dave.

Beth   Gina . . .

Gina   I know. It's stupid. It's just so hard. His mind's so set.

A slight pause.

Beth   Sometimes I want your dad back so badly, Gina. It breaks my heart, it does.

A slight pause.

Sometimes I go to the pub an' ya get chattin' to these fellas an' they buy ya drinks but they're – I mean they're nice enough an' some of 'em make me laugh – but they're not ya dad, Gina.

Gina   But there'll never be anyone like Dad.

Beth   I know.

Pause.

Gina   It's hard with Dave – especially since he's been tryin' so hard lately.

Beth   What you gonna do?

Gina   It'd be easier if I had somewhere to go.

Beth   Course you've got somewhere to go.

Gina   Where? I've talked to the girls an' none of 'em have got any room.

Beth   Well – You can come home.

Gina *laughs.*

Beth   You can come home – you can have ya old room back.

Gina   I've left home, Mum.

Beth   I know, but if you need somewhere . . .

Gina   I can't come home.

Beth   That's what it's there for.

Gina   I can't – I don't feel right.

Beth   I could do with the company, Gina.

A slight pause.

Ya know Sherry's movin' in with Lee, don't ya? (**Gina** *nods.*) Well I could do with the company . . .

Gina   I want me independence, Mum – that's why I moved out first – that's why I wanna leave Dave.

Beth   You'll have ya independence – I won't bother ya.

Gina   I don't know . . .

Beth   You come an' go as ya like, Gina – I don't stop ya – I didn't stop ya when you was at home.

A slight pause.

You have a think about it, love. You have a good think an' ya can come over early before ya go out with Sherry an' the girls on Wednesday an' see what ya think a ya old room, eh, Gina? You do what ya like – but I'm just thinkin' a you, Gina.

Gina *nods. A slight pause.* **Beth** *looks out of the window.*

Gina   It's a big garden, ain't it?

Beth   It's lovely.

Gina   Dave's dead set on gettin' a place like this in years to come, d'you hear him?

Beth   Yeah. (**Beth** *turns back.*) He's a bit of a tearaway now but he'll make a good dad one day.

Gina *nods.*

Gina   Lee's nice, ain't he?

Beth   He seems alright.

Gina   I never thought him an' Sherry'd last.

Beth   She is a tough 'un.

Gina   Yeah. They get on, though.

Beth   What does he do?

Gina   Nothin' now they've finished the job.

Beth   How does he live?

Gina   He's got some savings – his mum an' dad won the lottery.

Beth   Lucky beggars.

Gina   Five numbers an' a bonus ball. They bought Lee his flat.

Pause.

I always thought I'd be the first to get married. I don't know now, Mum.

Beth   You'll find the right boy.

Gina   P'rhaps I'll always get the fellas like Dave . . .

Beth   Come on, Gina.

Gina   They say shit sticks – once a slag . . .

Beth   You should have more confidence, Gina.

Gina   P'rhaps I need to leave Barking an' go somewhere else.

A slight pause.

P'rhaps I should come out here an' set up a coffee shop, eh, Mum? – An' serve scones to the old country biddies.

Beth *laughs.*

What a laugh, eh? Gina Killick an' her country bumpkins . . .

Beth *laughs.*

I could marry a farmer – an' talk posh – No one'd turn their nose up at me then.

Beth   You don't wanna marry a farmer.

Gina   What?

Beth   They all smell a cow poo.

Gina *laughs.* **Dave** *enters. He has shorts on with a bright T-shirt and has a monkey-wrench and rag in his hand.*

Dave   Fixed it.

Gina *nods.*

Dave   Lovely house, ain't it?

Beth   Yeah.

Dave   We've done a good job, ain't we, babe?

Gina   Come on, Dave – let's go.

Dave   But you haven't seen downstairs yet.

Gina   Dave, I wanna go. I've got a stinkin' headache.

Dave   But ya mum hasn't had a chance to have a look, have ya, Beth?

Gina (*loses her temper*)   Dave!

A slight pause.

Beth   Well, if Gina's not well . . .

Dave   Come on, Gina – ten minutes, babe – ten minutes . . . I've put a lot a work into this place.

A slight pause.

Come on – I'll show ya the pool room first – Eh, we can have a game, Beth . . . I'll seven-ball ya!

Dave *turns to exit.* **Beth** *looks at* **Gina** *who nods and follows* **Dave** *out.*

Scene Four

*Wednesday evening, eight o'clock. The living room of a terraced house
in Barking, east London;* **Beth***'s house.* **Sherry** *sits in the armchair,
smoking and drinking from a glass of wine. She's dressed in some
clubby going-out gear and looks a little younger than usual.* **Gina**
*enters. She has a little portable stereo in one hand and a crumpled blue
dress in the other hand. She's a bit pissed and is dolled up in a short
dress, has her hair up and, if anything, looks a little older than usual.*

Sherry   You're pissed.

Gina   I'm not.

Sherry   You are.

Gina   Here look, Shell.

Gina *puts down the stereo and holds the crumpled blue dress in front
of her. It's electric blue and has tassels.*

Sherry   Bloody hell!

Gina   I found it at the bottom of me cupboard – D'you
reckon I could still get in it?

Sherry   Show us.

Gina *throws the dress to* **Sherry** *and it lands in her face.* **Sherry**
pulls it away.

Sherry   Errr – fish!

Gina   Piss off.

Gina *plugs in the stereo and puts some music on. It's Take That's*
Greatest Hits *– which plays until* **Sherry** *switches it off later in
the scene.*

Sherry   It's not as loud as I remember it.

Gina   I used to love that dress.

Sherry   I know.

Gina   Get a load of this, Shell.

Sherry   What?

Gina *shows* **Sherry** *her nails.*

Sherry   Fuckin' hell, Gina!

Gina   I like purple.

Sherry *shakes her head.*

Sherry   So where we goin', Geenie?

Gina   I dunno what pub the girls wanna go first but we're goin' Pulse tonight.

Sherry   Pulse?

Gina   Yeah.

Sherry *raises her eyebrows.*

Sherry   So who's comin'?

Gina   Vikki, Kelly, Debbie, Tina, Karen B, an' Karen C, and Louise . . .

Sherry   I only know Kelly.

Gina   You know Tina, don't ya?

Sherry   No.

Gina   She was my year at school, she works in HMV – You know – hair extensions an' a pierced belly-button . . . (**Sherry** *nods.*) We'll have a right laugh.

Beth *enters. She is carrying a big litre-and-a-half bottle of Lambrusco, and a glass tumbler.*

Beth   You left ya drink in ya bedroom, Gina.

Gina   Cheers, ma.

Beth *passes the drink.*

Beth   You alright, Sherry? – You're quiet.

Sherry   I'm just wonderin' where Lee is – He said he'd be here by now.

Beth   Ain't that lovely of him to come round an' keep me company tonight.

Gina   Ahhhh – he's such a nice boy, eh, Mum?

Sherry   You can shut up.

Gina *laughs.*

Beth   Have you seen the state of the nails?

Sherry   I know.

Gina   Eh – Guess what, Sherry? I've heard that Martin's goin' Pulse tonight.

Sherry   Martin?

Gina   Martin. Seventeen. Cold meats . . .

Sherry   That Martin!

Gina *nods.*

Beth   It was nice havin' a sort-out in ya room, weren't it, Gina?

Gina   Yeah.

Beth   I bet you didn't realise you left so much stuff here when ya moved out.

Gina   No.

The doorbell rings, off. **Sherry** *gets up.*

Sherry   That's gonna be Lee.

Sherry *exits.* **Beth** *takes* **Gina**'s *hand as she heads for the armchair.*

Beth   You're doing the right thing, love.

Gina *nods and kisses* **Beth** *on the cheek. Off we hear a door open and someone come in as* **Beth** *sits down.*

Sherry *(off)*   Oh – Hiya – I didn't expect to see you.

Dave *enters. He has a West Ham shirt and jeans on. He has a video tape in his hand.*

Dave   Yeah . . . Lee told me he was comin' round so I thought I'd keep him company.

Sherry *follows* **Dave** *in.*

Sherry   Lee's not here yet.

Gina   What ya doing here?

Dave   I thought I'd keep Lee company.

Gina *tuts.*

Dave   Alright, Beth?

Beth   Yeah. You, Dave?

Dave   Yeah. Lee not here yet, then?

Sherry   No . . . Is that video one a mine?

Dave   No – I brought it round for Lee an' me to watch.

Gina *tuts again and pours herself some wine which she downs and follows by pouring another.*

Dave   No Keanu Reeves I'm afraid, gels.

Beth   I don't know if I want to watch a video.

Dave   It's a good 'un . . . *Escape to Victory* – it's a classic, Beth.

Sherry   D'you want any wine, Dave?

Dave   No, thanks – You've not got a beer, have ya, Beth?

Beth   No – D'you want tea?

Dave   I'd love a cup a rosy.

Beth *nods and exits.*

Dave   You alright, babe?

Dave *bends down, kisses* **Gina** *on the cheek and then grins.*

Dave No wonder she wanted to get ready round here, eh, Shell? Didn't want me to see how short her skirt is, eh? Where ya goin'?

Sherry Pulse.

Dave Pulse? Me an' the boys have been down there.

Sherry You wanna fag, Dave?

Dave Didn't ya know? I've given up.

Sherry Yeah?

Dave Four days, Shell – four days.

The doorbell rings, off. **Sherry** *moves to answer the door.*

Beth (*off*)   I'll get it!

Dave That'll be Lee.

A door opens off and we hear someone come in.

Beth (*off*)   Hello, Lee.

Lee (*off*)   Hello.

Beth (*off*)   Oh, you shouldn't have.

Lee *enters, followed by* **Beth** *who has some flowers.* **Lee** *has jeans and a smart shirt on.*

Lee   It's alright.

Beth   Look – He always brings me flowers, this one.

Sherry   He's just a crawler, Mum.

Beth *goes back out.*

Sherry   Hello.

Lee   Alright.

Sherry *and* **Lee** *kiss.*

Lee   You're early, Dave?

Dave   Well I was just sitting at home twiddling me thumbs
. . . I mean I was tempted even to jostle the old apostle for
the minute – but I thought no – I've changed me ways . . .
I'll do it in bathroom, not in front of the telly . . .

Dave *laughs.* **Lee** *grins. The girls don't.*

Dave   I brought a video, Lee.

Lee   Yeah?

Dave   *Escape to Victory.*

Lee   Great.

Dave   Remember the bit where Ossie Ardiles does the old
flick of his back heel over his head, eh, Lee? They done it in
slow motion – pure poetry, mate.

Lee   Yeah.

Gina *has finished her wine and pours herself another one, which*
Sherry *spots.*

Sherry   Gina . . .

Dave   Yeah – I've been like a lost sheep since we finished
that job, Lee . . . I've rung you a couple a times as it goes
but you've been out – I just get the answerphone . . . I was
sayin' to Gina – we should think about investin' in one.

A slight pause.

Yeah – we had a lovely day on Monday, didn't we, Gina?

Gina   Yeah.

Dave   We took Beth to Leigh-on-Sea – had a lovely day.
We had a walk along the front an' got some ice-creams an'
that – an' then I took Gina an' Beth over to Prittlewell to see
the house, didn't I?

Gina   Yeah – he did.

Dave   They loved it, Lee – You thought we done a
smashin' job didn't ya, Gina?

Gina   Yeah.

Dave   It's a shame you haven't had a chance to get over an' see it, Shell. Still, the nobs ain't back till Sunday so if Lee wants to take you over, I've got the keys.

Beth *enters with* **Dave***'s tea.*

Beth   I just did a tea-bag, Dave, so I hope it's alright.

Dave *takes the tea.*

Dave   You heard any more from the old bill about the old girl?

Lee   No.

Dave *takes a sip and raises his mug.*

Dave   Well – Here's to you gels having a good night out.

Lee   What's that dress?

Sherry   What?

Beth   That's Gina's old dress.

Sherry   This?

Sherry *lifts the old blue dress, which* **Lee** *has a look at, and turns off the music which is starting to irritate her.*

Dave   You weren't thinkin' a wearin' that?!

Lee   I'm sure I recognise this from somewhere.

Sherry   I'll tell ya later.

Dave   You're quiet, Gina – Cat got your tongue?

Beth   Match your nails, that dress, Gina.

Gina   Yeah.

Sherry   Have a look, Lee.

Lee *and* **Sherry** *look at* **Gina***'s nails.*

Gina   Nice, ain't they?

Lee   Bit loud, ain't they?

Beth   You can say that again.

Gina *looks proudly at her fingers stretched out in front of her.*

Dave   Show us.

Suddenly **Gina** *notices she hasn't got the engagement ring on and she clasps her hands together and turns away from* **Dave** *who peers over her shoulder.*

Show us.

Sherry   Gina?

Gina   I need the toilet, Dave.

Dave   Go on – show us, Geen.

Gina   I just wanna pop to the toilet.

Gina *moves to exit but* **Dave** *stands in her way.*

Gina   Dave . . .

Sherry   Gina?

Dave   Come on – They can't look that tarty! Come on – Be nice to see what's gonna do all that damage to me back later on – If I'm lucky, eh, Lee?

Pause.

Come on – what's all the fuss?

Gina   Dave – I really need the toilet.

Dave   Well, just show us your nails.

Pause. Slowly **Gina** *opens her hands and shows* **Dave** *her nails. A slight pause.*

Dave   Well, I have to say, Gina – I'm shocked. They're purple.

Dave *laughs and gives* **Gina** *a hug, and slaps her bum, as he releases her and makes way for her to exit.* **Sherry** *follows* **Gina** *out.*

Dave   She's in a funny mood. Pissed, eh, an' she has a go at me.

Beth   She likes a drink that one.

Beth *sits down in the armchair again.* **Dave** *wanders over to the sideboard, puts his mug down and picks up the photo we've seen* **Lee** *looking at earlier in the play. He has a look at it and smiles.*

Dave   Yeah – I've been tryin' a get hold a you, Lee – so we can talk about how we're gonna go about setting up the business.

Lee   Well, Dave, I have been givin' it some thought.

Dave   You know it makes sense, don't ya, Beth? Thought the job we did on that house was fantastic, didn't ya, Beth?

Beth   Yeah, it was good.

Dave   You watch, Lee, she's gonna have us round here before long, doin' this place up – buck-she an' all.

Dave *laughs.*

Now I was thinkin' we should go and see the bank together – Cos they have these business plans, ya know.

Lee   I think you should leave it to me, Dave.

Gina *comes back in, followed by* **Sherry**. **Gina**'s *a bit red-eyed.*

Dave   Alright, love? I was just saying about me an' Lee goin' a see the bank.

Sherry   Lee?

Lee   Well nothing's final.

Gina   Oh for fuck's suck, Dave!

A slight pause.

Dave   Eh? Eh? What's all this?

A slight pause.

What's all this? Gina . . .

Dave *tries to touch* **Gina** *and she turns away. A slight pause.*

Dave   Gina . . . Babe . . . Sherry? Lee?

A slight pause.

Lee   Well, Dave . . . Ya see . . . I've been thinking about what you've been sayin' about the business an' that . . . an' . . . well . . .

Sherry   Just tell him, Lee.

Dave   Tell me what? What, Lee?

Lee   Well – I don't . . . I don't think I'm ready to go into business yet.

Dave   What? Come on – We've been talkin' about it for weeks – haven't we?

Lee   You have, Dave.

Dave   But I mean – We did a good job on the house – We work well together – We're mates.

Lee   Yeah – I know . . . But I just don't – I'm not ready to make that sort a commitment . . . I can't handle it, Dave.

Dave   I mean, you know I'll give you good trade – I'll teach ya good if that's what you're worried about . . . You should see him unblock a sink, Shell – he can turn it round in five minutes now, can't ya, Lee?

Lee *nods.*

Dave   Eh, Lee – I've thought've a name for the business . . . Mahtsew. What do ya reckon, eh? West Ham backwards. It'll be great. Mahtsew – Renovation, Decoration, an' Refurbishment . . .

Lee *nods again.* **Sherry** *has her head in her hands. A slight pause.* **Dave** *smiles.*

Dave   Course, I know we've only known each other three months – an' I know Gina won't . . . won't mind me saying now – but like, when we get hitched, I'd like you to be best man.

Gina   Dave!

Sherry   God.

Dave   Now I know this is a bit of a surprise, Beth – but see me an' Gina've been together five years now . . .

Gina *starts to cry.*

Sherry   Dave . . .

Dave   And I've asked Gina to marry me. Now my mum an' dad have passed away, God rest 'em, but I'd like your permission – an' Gina's dad a course when I get over to see him.

Pause. **Gina** *wipes her eyes.*

Beth   Gina isn't gonna marry you, Dave.

Dave   Now I know I'm bein' old-fashioned but we don't need you to –

Beth   Gina isn't gonna marry you, Dave.

Dave   Yes, she is. We love each other an' she's gonna marry me.

Beth   No, she's not. And next week she's movin' her stuff out of the flat and she's movin' back into her old room here.

Dave   No, she's not!

Beth   She is, Dave – Aren't ya, love?

Gina *nods.*

Dave   You're not – You're fuckin' not, Gina!

Lee Dave . . .

Dave You keep your nose out a this!

Beth She doesn't love you any more, Dave, an' she's gonna stay with her mum for a while – while she gets herself together, ain't ya, darlin'?

Gina *nods. Pause.* **Dave** *fights back the tears now.*

Dave Well, well, well . . . I'm the last to know all this, am I? Am I?

Pause.

Listen, Gina – if this about – about Lee not comin' in with me in the business . . .

Sherry It's not, Dave.

Dave I can tell ya, darlin' – I'll do it on me own – I'll do it . . . So what? I can do it – I can. I've grown up fuckin' orphan – I've struggled, an' worked me way – an' I'll do it again. I've done markets, I've sold newspapers to get a few quid an' I've gone out an' thieved cars before now to put a few quid in me pocket an' some dinner on the table an' I'll do it again to put a roof over your head, an' look after you, Gina!

Gina No, Dave.

Dave What can I do?! What more can I do, Gina? I work, I work, I work, work, work, work! What can I do?

Gina I don't love you any more, Dave.

Dave *lets out a pained cry and clenches the framed picture tightly between his two hands.*

Gina Dave!

Dave *snaps the picture frame in half, the glass shatters, and he tears the two halves apart.*

Gina Dave!

Beth   My picture!

Lee   Dave!

Dave   Fuck you all! D'you hear me? Fuck you all!

Dave *exits, we hear the front door opened and slammed behind him.* **Gina** *cries and so do* **Beth** *and* **Sherry** *as they kneel down and examine the broken picture.* **Lee** *looks at the three women, looks at the open sitting room door and he exits through it after* **Dave**. *We hear the door open but* **Lee** *doesn't close it behind him.*

Sherry   Lee!

Gina *lets out a cry of pain as she cuts her knee on some glass.*

Gina   Fuck, I've cut me knee!

Sherry   There's glass stuck in it – I can see it.

Gina *gets up and exits.*

Sherry   Gina!

Beth   Oh, Sherry . . . Sherry, look . . .

Beth *holds the two broken halves of the picture together in front of her.*

Look . . .

Sherry   Oh, Mum . . .

Beth   That's it, Sherry – that's it. I haven't even got the negative any more . . . Look, Sherry, it's broken . . .

Sherry   I know, Mum.

Sherry *puts her arm round her mum's shoulder.* **Gina** *enters in floods of tears, a toilet roll in her hand, and blood running from the cut in her left knee.*

Gina   I've broken the fuckin' toilet-roll holder.

Sherry   Oh.

Beth   Oh, Gina.

Beth *laughs, then so does* **Sherry**, *and finally even* **Gina** *a little bit.*

Beth   The screw's probably just come out of the wall – it's loose, Gina.

Gina   Come an' fix it, Mum.

Beth *places the two halves of the picture on the floor in front of* **Sherry**. **Gina** *goes back out and* **Beth** *follows. Pause.* **Sherry** *picks up the two halves of the picture and looks at them as* **Beth** *did.* **Lee** *enters, breathless.*

Lee   I chased him, Sherry, but his car was parked round the corner an' he drove off.

A slight pause.

Lee   You alright, Sherry?

Sherry *nods.*

Lee   Is Gina alright?

Sherry   She cut her knee on the glass.

Lee   That was bad, weren't it?

Sherry *nods.*

Sherry   This was one a the last things of me dad's we had – me mum burnt nearly everything when he left. She got pissed an' built a great big bonfire in the garden. This escaped cos Gina had it.

Pause. **Lee** *comes closer and takes one half which he looks at.*

Sherry   That was hard tellin' Dave, yeah?

Lee   Yeah.

Sherry   Dave'll be alright.

A slight pause.

Lee   Is Gina gonna be alright here?

Sherry   Yeah. She'll pick up the pieces – she'll start again.

Pause.

I don't know how Mum'll get on with Gina here – She's got more of a temper than me.

Lee   Your mum'll be alright.

Sherry   Yeah.

A slight pause.

Lee   You sound as if ya sure mostly everything'll turn out alright.

Sherry   You can never tell, Lee.

Lee   An' what about us?

Sherry *laughs.*

Lee   What?

Sherry   What a time to talk about us.

A slight pause.

We're gonna have a great summer . . .

Lee   Yeah.

Sherry   An' make the most a the nice weather cos it'll soon be September.

Lee *laughs.* **Sherry** *leaves her half of the picture on the floor and stands.*

Sherry   What?

Lee   You sound like my mum.

Sherry *and* **Lee** *both smile.* **Sherry** *exits.* **Lee** *looks at his half of the picture and throws it on the floor. He exits too.*

Under the Blue Sky

For Ruth and Stevo – my favourite teachers

Richard   . . . It's important. History. Our Lives.
Robert Holman, *Today*

Irina   Tell me, why am I so happy today? As if I were
sailing, with the wide blue sky above me, and great white
birds soaring in the wind. Why is it? Why?
Anton Chekhov, *The Three Sisters*

Under the Blue Sky was first presented at the Royal Court
Jerwood Theatre Upstairs, London, on 14 September 2000,
with the following cast:

Helen	Samantha Edmonds
Nick	Justin Salinger
Michelle	Lisa Palfrey
Graham	Jonathan Cullen
Anne	Sheila Hancock
Robert	Stanley Townsend

Directed by Rufus Norris
Designed by Katrina Lindsay
Lighting by Johanna Town
Sound by Rich Walsh

Characters

Helen, *aged twenty-seven*
Nick, *aged twenty-eight*
Michelle, *aged thirty-eight*
Graham, *aged thirty-six*
Anne, *aged fifty-eight*
Robert, *aged forty-two*

Setting
Leyton, east London; Hornchurch, Essex; and Tiverton,
Devon.

Locations
A kitchen and living area, a bedroom and a patio in
a cottage garden.

Time
February 1996, May 1997 and August 1998.

Note
This play should be performed without an interval.

Act One

As the house lights dim, the long thunderous sound of a huge bomb exploding and police sirens wailing are audible.

February 1996. The kitchen and living area. A flat in Leyton, east London. Seven p.m.

Nick *crushes a clove of garlic in his crusher and empties the contents into a pan. He then peels and chops a large onion with a knife larger than he needs for the job.*

Nick *is twenty-eight.*

A slight pause.

Helen *enters. She is drinking a glass of red wine.*

Helen *is twenty-seven and looks good in her outfit.*

Helen The ceasefire's over.

Nick It was a bomb then?

Helen Yeah. It's on the television.

Nick Where?

Helen They've bombed the Docklands. Canary Wharf, I think.

Nick Was anyone killed?

Helen I don't think so.

Nick And you thought it was thunder?

Helen D'you want any help?

Nick *tips the onion into the pan.*

Nick You can chop up that green pepper.

Helen *puts down her wine and takes the knife* **Nick** *was using. She makes a start gutting the pepper.*

Nick Cheers, Helen.

Nick *adds olive oil to his garlic and onion and switches on the hob. He gives it a stir with a wooden spoon.*

Helen   Your hair looks great short like that.

Nick   Thanks.

He watches **Helen** *as she chops the pepper. He pours himself a glass of red wine.*

Is that new?

Helen   Yeah. D'you like it? It's from Principles.

Nick   Yeah. It's very flattering.

Helen *smiles at* **Nick**.

Helen   Shall I put this in?

Nick   Not yet.

He drinks. The onion and garlic begin to sizzle.

I knew it was a bomb. The flat shook. It shook, didn't it?

Helen   It unnerves me to think we were close enough for that to happen.

Nick *stirs the onion and garlic and then hunts around in the fridge for the mincemeat. A slight pause.*

Nick   Stop looking at my arse, Helen.

Helen   Why would I be looking at your arse?

Nick   You know you're obsessed with my arse.

Helen   I'm not obsessed with anyone's arse. Let alone yours, my dear.

Nick *takes out the mincemeat and shuts the fridge door.*

Nick   Apparently Amanda Harrison's going to send me a valentine's card with 'sexy bum' on it.

Helen   Amanda Harrison?

Nick   In year eleven.

Helen   Lovely.

Nick   So the other girls tell me.

Helen   I've never had a card from a pupil.

Nick   You've never had a card full stop.

Helen   Yes I have.

Nick   What? You sent to yourself when you were thirteen?

Helen   You're such a git.

Nick   Didn't you ever fancy a teacher?

Helen   No.

Nick   Really? I thought everyone had an adolescent crush on one.

Helen   No. Not that I remember.

Nick   I think the reason people fall for teachers the way they do's because of that. I don't think it's any of that stuff about it being a noble profession. The person who puts his own ambitions and dreams to one side. That's all crap. That's the sort of thing people who don't know us say. No. I think it's because you remember that person who made school worth coming to. Like a first love. And then later on in life when you meet a teacher you fancy and you go out and you sleep together, you can't help it. You're a devoted fourteen-year-old all over again.

Helen   You do talk complete rubbish, don't you?

Nick *laughs and takes the knife from* **Helen** *and slices open the packaging around the mincemeat.* **Helen** *takes her wine and drinks it.*

Nick   Are you going to Sarah's party?

Helen   I don't know. When is it?

Nick   Wednesday night.

Helen   Who's going?

Nick   The usual lot. Sort of sad single-people get-together. Drink tequila, get very pissed and reveal secrets and then stagger home at four in the morning, with some dim light in your brain saying 'Shit. Year seven first lesson.'

Helen *smiles.* **Nick** *empties the mincemeat into the pan and stirs it together with the onion and garlic.*

Helen   Well, this is about time.

Nick   What?

Helen   You've been in here a year and this is the first time you've invited me over.

Nick   It's not.

Helen   It is.

Nick   You've been over here?

Helen   You know I've not.

Nick   No?

Helen   And how many times have I cooked for you? Had you over for dinner parties and drinks?

Nick   Sorry.

A long pause.

Helen   So what's this thing you want to talk to me about?

Nick *looks at* **Helen** *and thinks.*

Nick   Let's wait until after dinner. Yeah? OK, darling?

Nick *smiles.* **Helen** *drinks.*

Helen   You're such a flirt.

Nick   And you're so bloody serious. So boring. Why are you my friend?

Helen *smiles and pours herself some more wine.* **Nick** *stirs the meat and onions.*

Helen   Watch it, haircut one hundred.

Nick   Shit.

Helen   What?

Nick   I forgot to pick up fresh chillies.

Helen   Use powder.

Nick   Powder? Powder . . .

Helen   D'you want this wine all over your clean shirt?

Nick *laughs and raises his glass.*

Nick   To a good one.

Pause.

Helen   I put my bag in your room.

Nick   OK.

Helen   Is that OK?

Nick   You can sleep in my room, if you like.

Helen *smiles and drinks.*

Helen   Can I?

Nick   If you want to, you can.

Helen   Really?

Nick   Yeah. Course you can.

Helen   I might like that.

Nick   I haven't tried out the sofa bed yet. Perhaps tonight's the night I get my head down on there. Three hundred quid it cost me. I think it should be down to the PE department because they're the only ones who've had the benefit of it.

Helen   It's all right. I'll sleep on the sofa bed.

Nick   Whatever you fancy.

Helen *laughs.*

Helen   Yeah.

Nick   What?

He opens a cupboard and takes out the dried chillies.

I remember I overdid it once with the dried chillies and when I burped and farted it stang.

Helen   Nicholas . . .

Nick   Don't Nicholas me.

Helen   So what is it you want to talk about, Nicholas?

She drains her wine and pours herself another.

Because to be honest I think I'll be half cut by the time we've eaten that chilli.

Nick   Well, the future.

Helen *laughs and laughs.*

Nick   What?

Helen *downs the whole glass of red wine.*

Nick   Ding bloody dong.

Helen *puts down her glass, wipes her mouth and folds her arms.* **Nick** *looks at her and then shakes his head and begins to sprinkle the dried chillies over the meat and onions.*

Helen   I've got a pretty good idea what you want to talk about.

Nick   Have you?

Helen   Yeah.

Nick   What?

Helen   I think it's obvious.

Nick   Is it?

Helen   It's about us, isn't it?

Nick   What?

Helen   All the time we've been spending together. And going out. And all that. All that stuff.

Nick *stirs the meat and thinks.*

Nick   Look, Helen, I think you've got this . . .

Helen   I've noticed things have been changing. Things have been developing in a way they haven't before, haven't they?

Nick   No, Helen . . .

Helen   Admit it. They have, haven't they?

Nick   Helen, I wanted to talk to you because I'm thinking of leaving.

A pause.

I'm applying for another job.

He stirs the meat. A long pause.

Helen *is embarrassed and wounded.* **Nick** *goes over to hug her but* **Helen** *shies away.*

Nick   I wanted to talk to you first, Helen.

Helen   Yeah.

Nick   It's not far. Half-hour tops on the train from Stratford.

Helen   Yeah. Not far.

Nick   You can take those driving lessons you've been saying you're going to take. Pass your test. You're the only teacher I know who doesn't drive.

Helen   How stupid of me.

A pause.

Nick Helen.

Helen What school is it?

Nick It's in Essex. To start in September. I drove up
there at the weekend to have a proper nose around. It's
a lovely school.

Helen Is it?

Nick The football team were playing at home and
I watched the first half. Then I had a look at the dining halls
and then I got talking to the chaplain. He showed me round
the chapel. You should have seen it. There were these long
rolls of honour. Of old boys who passed away in the two
world wars.

Helen It's an independent school, is it?

Nick Yeah. So?

Helen A public school?

Nick It doesn't feel much like one but I suppose so.

Helen Why do you want to go?

Nick You know I've been feeling tired.

Helen Of what?

Nick Of the kids. I'm good at crowd control but I do
want to actually teach at some point as well, Helen.

A slight pause.

*He goes to the cupboard and takes out a tin of chopped tomatoes and
a small tin of kidney beans.*

You know teaching? I've had enough of being a bloody
social worker, Helen.

He takes a tin-opener from the drawer.

And I want to teach A level again.

Helen Well, there are plenty of colleges in the borough.

Nick   And I've been thinking I want a change from the East End. I want to move.

Helen   Well, I don't know about that.

A pause.

Nick *looks at* **Helen** *and takes the tin of chopped tomatoes which he starts to open. He tips the opened tin of chopped tomatoes into the pan, which he stirs.*

Nick   I'm tired of spending all day telling kids off. I want to be challenged. Intellectually. Every time I read a novel there I am fantasising an epic sixth-form discussion about it.

He smiles.

Now that is not normal. That is sad. That is very boring. Remember, you're boring. I'm not boring.

Helen   Don't make fun of me.

Nick   Come on. I'm meant to be teaching them English and about half the bloody kids haven't even got it as their first language.

Helen   You're exaggerating.

A slight pause.

I think you'll be making a mistake.

Nick   Why?

Helen   I think you should stay.

Nick   Why? I want a career.

Helen   Things are going to get better.

Nick   I want a department of my own. I want a career. Not a slog.

Helen   Things are getting better. We were only saying last week how things have improved since the inspection.

196 Under the Blue Sky

Nick Things have improved a little bit. No one's pulled a knife on you in six months. Big deal.

Helen Don't make fun of that.

Nick I'm sorry.

A slight pause.

Helen Things are getting better at school. I wouldn't have been in favour of it before, but the kids wearing blazers and a proper uniform has made a difference.

Nick It's great. But it's not enough.

Helen Well, I would rather be where I am than silver-spooning a bunch of toffee-nosed brats from Essex.

Nick *studies* **Helen**. *A pause.*

Nick Fine. OK. Fine.

A slight pause.

Helen *picks up the knife and points it at* **Nick**.

Helen 'Fuck off, Miss, I'll fucking kill you. I'll fucking stab your heart, Miss. You bitch. You bitch-whore.'

Nick I know what happened. I was there.

Helen And have you seen me running away?

Nick *takes the tin of kidney beans which he opens with the tin-opener.* **Helen** *puts the knife down. A pause.*

Nick It isn't my duty to be unhappy. I owe it to myself to be happy in my work and I'm not. Why are you trying to put me on this huge guilt trip?

Helen I'm not making you feel guilty. You feel guilty. If you're feeling guilty don't blame your guilt on me.

Nick Helen, you're being so hard on me.

Helen Am I?

Nick I thought I could talk to you about this?

Helen   Things will get better. I promise you, Nick.

Nick   I want a change . . .

Helen   And things will change.

Nick   Don't you see I need a change? This is like talking to a brick wall. I need to move on.

A slight pause.

I need to move on now. I've had enough. I know I've had enough. It's been hard but I've enjoyed cutting my teeth here and that is it.

Helen   So having cut your teeth you can piss off and leave the kids that need good teachers like you?

Nick   Helen, I need to move on. And I think it's a terrific department.

Helen   Well, the kids can't move on anywhere. You know the department?

Nick   Not really.

Helen   You've already been for an interview, haven't you? You have, haven't you? Last week. Last Tuesday. I thought it was strange.

Nick   Yeah.

Helen   You told me you had an inset. Why didn't you tell me? Why did you lie to me?

Nick   Stop it. Just stop it. Please. Stop this. It isn't fair. I wanted to talk to you. All I wanted to do was talk to you. Please. You're my friend. You're my friend, aren't you?

Helen   Yeah, I am.

Nick   Then let me go. Let me try and do this. Help me to do this. Be here for me. Understand, please. Please try and understand. I'm so fond of you.

Helen   I know, but . . .

Nick   You must have been able to tell I've been unhappy? Why I've been needy. Spending time with you. Talking over and over things. And then I saw this job. And everything was clear.

Helen   But you've not been honest with me. You've not told me anything. I can't believe you didn't tell me about it. I can't believe you lied to me.

Nick *takes the kidney beans and tips them into the chilli which he stirs. Pause.*

Nick   You know I'm going to miss you, Helen.

Helen   Are you?

Nick   Yeah. I am really. I don't know if it's going to work out or not in this school.

Helen   I'm sure it will.

Nick   It's totally new to me. The only time I've ever been in a public school was when I was a lad. Our comp played them in a friendly. They gave us sausage, chips and beans beforehand and a cream cake and tea afterwards. It was like a dream.

A slight pause.

He smiles.

Can you imagine me getting up on a Saturday morning to teach year-seven boys?

Helen *shakes her head.*

Helen   First form. You'll have to get used to calling them first form.

Nick   See. You know more about it than I do. There's me getting all misty-eyed over the chapel on a guided tour. But can you see me in a front pew down on my knees with my hair parted?

Helen *laughs and shakes her head.*

Nick   I don't know whether I'll like it, but I want to give it a go. If I get it.

A pause.

Helen   I'm going to miss you so much.

Nick   And so will I.

Nick *tips the pieces of chopped green pepper into the pan. He stirs the chilli. A slight pause.*

Helen   We're still going to see each other, aren't we?

Nick   Yeah. Course we are. You can come up and stay.

He studies **Helen***. A pause.*

If I'm honest I guess I have been thinking about us as well.

Helen   Have you?

A pause.

Nick   Yeah. Well, we are close.

Helen   Yeah.

A pause.

Nick   Maybe it won't be a bad thing for us to see not quite so much of each other.

Helen   Why?

Nick   I don't know what us has been all about. I know I love us being friends.

Helen   So do I.

A pause.

Nick   Why can't you say what you feel?

Helen   Say what?

A pause.

Nick   I'm confused. You're clearly not. But you only ever meet me halfway emotionally. And I don't know if that's good. I don't know how I feel about it. Us. I feel really confused.

Helen   So am I.

Nick   I don't think you are. I am.

Helen   So what do you want me to do?

Nick   Just talk to me. Honestly. I wanted to talk to you about moving on. Going to another school. I admit it. Of course I wanted you to talk about your personal feelings.

Helen   Personal feelings?

She can't believe it. A slight pause.

So I can put my heart and guts on the floor in front of you? Sob and wail like a widow and hope it might change your mind? And in the process confirm your gut feeling it might be good for us to see less of each other. Good for you to see less of me. While you create a new life for yourself in Essex. Is that what you want? Well, you can get stuffed.

Helen *tries to leave.* **Nick** *stands in her way.*

Nick   Talk to me.

Helen   Piss off.

Nick   Come on.

Helen   Get lost. I mean it.

Nick   I'm sorry.

Helen   I can't tell you how I feel about you.

A long pause.

I could never.

Nick   Do you love me? Are you in love with me?

A long pause.

Helen   Why are you doing this? You've just been telling me you want to leave. You want to move away. This isn't fair and it isn't right.

Nick   You're the most important person to me in the world.

A slight pause.

But I don't know if I love you. I don't know if I can love you. If I'm capable of loving you.

Helen   You arsehole. You fucking arsehole.

A long pause.

Why are you torturing me like this?

A pause.

I can't talk any more. I feel so exposed.

A pause.

Nick   Sometimes I think it was a mistake I slept with you. I'm sorry.

Helen *looks at* **Nick**. *A slight pause.*

Helen   A mistake?

Nick   I don't know. Yeah. I think it was.

Helen   What, just that night or our whole friendship?

Nick   No . . .

Helen   I mean, you wanted it. You wanted to sleep with me.

Nick   And you didn't?

Helen   I knew I thought a lot of you. That I was feeling like I liked you more than just fancying you.

Nick   We were both drunk.

Helen   No, you were drunk and you wanted it.

Nick   So are you saying I forced myself upon you?

Helen   No.

A pause.

This is so ugly. I don't want this. Why are you talking about this?

A pause.

To be honest, I think it wasn't a fantastic thing that it happened when it happened but I know it did something.

A pause.

Like you cracked something. And it all leaked out.

A pause.

I felt different then.

A pause.

With every word I say I feel I'm betraying myself. I'm shrinking in front of you.

A pause.

The things you said to me.

Nick   When?

Helen   That time. Then.

Nick   I was drunk.

A slight pause.

I didn't know what I was saying.

Helen   You were heavy and pissed and you moved me around the bed like I was a prone body. But your words? The things you said. Your promises.

Nick   I don't know what to . . .

Helen   No.

Nick *stirs the chilli and turns the hob down. A slight pause.*

Helen   Your memory of it is that we were both drunk but I was sober. I remember every clumsy movement and every word you said like it's shot through my memory.

A slight pause.

I thought tonight would be my turn. You know that? To fall on you. Half cut.

A slight pause.

I feel so awful I wish the earth would swallow me up.

A long pause.

Nick   I reckon the chilli will be about another fifteen minutes. Perhaps I should boil the kettle and get the rice on? I got some lovely fresh bread from Sainsbury's.

Helen   Lovely. Really splendid. Lovely. I love chilli. And you make the best chilli, Nicholas.

She thinks. A pause.

A lot of damage out there, I expect. I suppose if you're a terrorist. If you're proud of your culture. But you don't have any structure to fulfil or contain that sense of identity. Then that bomb isn't an unnatural response. Is it?

Nick   I don't know.

Helen   It's not enough believing in something. Having a passion. You have to have a voice to voice it.

Nick   That's why we do what we do, isn't it?

Helen   I was in the bar at university with some people and this Irish guy was talking about the 1916 uprising. The rebels were shot and martyred. The ringleader was a schoolteacher. Another bloody romantic, I suppose. Anyway, this girl joined in and said how she objected to these mythic pasts. It was like our Poppy Day. The myth of sacrifice. I didn't really understand what her objection was but I thought it's not your bloody history. Then this other bloke said Remembrance Sunday made him feel proud. He said he'd been on a school trip to the war cemeteries and heard the last post being played. And we were all quiet. Then the girl left and someone else said she was uptight and she needed a good nobbing and they all laughed. I hadn't said anything.

Nick   What are you talking about this for?

A slight pause.

Helen   I don't know.

A slight pause.

So really I should be booking up my driving lessons, shouldn't I?

Nick *studies* **Helen**.

Nick   Well, you need a car.

Helen   So hopefully even allowing for failing my test three times, or something hideous like that, I should have a car by the time you start work in Essex.

Nick   You'll pass first time, I'm sure. I haven't even got the job yet.

Helen   You'll get it.

A slight pause.

I could get a Clio or a Fiesta or something like that, couldn't I?

Nick   Yeah.

Helen   Can we talk about your school?

Nick   I don't know if I want to any more just now.

Helen   I'd like to talk about your school.

Nick   Can't we talk about something else?

Helen   What else have we got to talk about? Our friendship? Our relationship? Whether making love three years ago was a mistake?

Nick   Helen.

A slight pause.

You're making me feel edgy.

He takes a saucepan which he fills with water. He turns on the hob. When it boils neither of them takes any notice.

Helen   You know, I just can't work it out? All the things we've done together. All the times we've got drunk and talked about what's important to us. All the times. Yet in three years. This is the first time. The fact that we spent a night together is mentioned.

She fights back the tears. A long pause.

How many kids are there? There. At your new school.

Nick   Over a thousand not including the prep.

Helen   What's the uniform like?

Nick   Blazer. Grey trousers. Not that much different from ours.

Helen   Have they got a swimming pool?

Nick   An open-air one.

Helen   An open-air one?

Nick   But they're thinking of rebuilding.

Helen   Is it a rugby or a football school?

Nick   Football.

Helen   That's right. You said earlier.

Nick   Stop this.

Helen   I want to know.

Nick   Please stop this.

Helen   I'm your friend. You're going. I'd like to know.

Nick   Then be my friend and try and understand. I'm sorry. I've messed things up. I've said things badly. Things have come out wrong. Don't you think I wish I didn't feel so confused?

Helen *starts to weep. A slight pause.*

Nick   I'm sorry. I'm sorry. I think the world of you.

Helen   Do you?

Nick   I've never gone out with anyone, have I?

Helen   What?

Nick   In the time we've known one another. There's been no other relationship. I've not wanted anyone.

Helen   You've gone out with people.

Nick   I've had dates. But who's there been?

Helen   No one that I know about.

Nick   No one.

Helen   I saw that guy for a month. We've never been going out. You don't have any right . . .

Nick   I know I don't.

A slight pause.

Perhaps I felt something about that?

Helen *really cries.*

Helen   I only saw him because I wanted you to . . .

Nick   What?

Helen   I don't know . . .

Nick   Fight over you?

Helen   No. I wanted you, not him.

Nick   But I didn't know how I felt. I still don't. But the longer it's gone on the more certain I've become that if I really wanted us. Us. In that way. Surely I would know? What am I holding back? What's holding me back?

Helen   Nothing.

Nick   There's something.

Helen   There's nothing stopping you. Just let it be . . .

Nick   All I know is I love you as a friend and this is ugly, Helen. It's hurt us both but all I wanted to try and do was talk to you. I want to leave and that is it.

Helen   I don't want you to go.

Nick   It's what I want.

Helen   Stay with me.

Nick   I can't . . .

Helen   Let me see you every day . . .

Nick   This is no good.

Helen   I know you're not sure how you feel but don't just . . .

Nick   Helen.

Helen   Leave me and go from me. Don't do that. Please.

A pause.

Nick   It's no good. I want this job. I don't know if our friendship can be any more than it is.

Helen *is heartbroken.*

Nick   Please don't cry any more.

Nick *goes to* **Helen** *but she picks up the knife. It is unclear whether she intends to hurt* **Nick** *or herself.*

Helen   You're not going.

Nick   Please . . .

Helen   You're not leaving me . . .

Nick   Give me that knife.

Helen   I'm not going to let you leave.

Nick   Helen. Just pass me the knife.

Helen   Tell me that you'll stay.

Nick   I can't say that.

Helen   Then I will do something . . .

Nick   No. Calm down and give it to me.

Helen   I think about you all the time . . .

Nick   I know . . .

Helen   I can't help it . . .

Nick   I know.

Helen   I think about the things we do . . .

Nick   Yeah?

Helen   And I think about all the things we're going to do . . .

Nick   We've had a right laugh, haven't we?

Helen   Like when we went to Warwick.

Nick   That's right.

Helen   To see your friends.

Nick   Billy and Susan. They thought you were great.

Helen   And I was embarrassed because they thought. They presumed I was your girlfriend.

She calms a little. A pause.

It was a lovely meal. And I was drinking Billy's Jim Beam by the end. You must have been ashamed of me.

Nick   No.

A pause.

Please. Give me the knife.

Helen   No.

Nick   You can't force me to stay. It's no good.

Helen *clearly threatens* **Nick** *with the knife.*

Helen   You're not leaving me. I'll kill you. I'll kill you right here and now.

Nick   No, you won't.

Helen   I will. I'll put this right through your heart.

Nick   If you really loved me you wouldn't hurt me like this.

A slight pause.

Remember when that boy threatened you?

Helen *wipes away a tear and nods.*

Nick   How you felt?

Helen *nods and cries.*

Nick   You told me how scared you were.

Helen *nods and sobs.*

Nick   You're scaring me, Helen.

A slight pause.

You'd never hurt me. You'd never threaten me with that if you truly love me.

Helen   I do. I thought if I just waited.

Nick   I know. But this isn't helping anything, is it?

Helen   No.

She shakes her head and completely breaks down. **Nick** *embraces her as she cries and cries.*

I'm sorry, I'm sorry, I'm sorry, I'm sorry.

Nick   I'm sorry too.

Helen   I'd never hurt you.

Nick   I know you wouldn't.

Helen   I'd never ever hurt you.

Nick   You're just upset.

Helen   I can't stand the thought of not seeing you every day.

Nick *kisses her forehead as he comforts her.*

Helen   I can't stand it. I don't know what I'm going to do without you.

Nick   You're not losing me.

Helen   I want you, I want you, I want you.

Nick   Let's just be friends now, eh?

Helen   I am your friend.

Nick   Let's not analyse us. Let's just be. Let's just be us.

Helen *nods.*

Nick   I don't know. Maybe I'm just not ready yet.

Helen *nods.*

Nick   No more tears now. Eh?

Helen *nods.* **Nick** *roots around in the cupboard and takes out some rice and the bread.*

Nick   It's easy-cook rice. By the time it's done the chilli should be ready.

A pause.

He tips some rice into the pot on the hob.

Helen   It's awful, isn't it?

Nick   What?

Helen   The bomb.

Nick   Yeah. It is.

Helen *studies* **Nick**. *He takes the knife from her, wipes it with a cloth and uses it to slice the bread.*

Helen   When you go I'll come and visit.

Nick   If I go.

Helen   Of course you'll go.

A slight pause.

I'll learn to drive. I'll pass my test. I will.

Nick   You can do it. No problem.

Helen   I'll come and see you.

Nick   Whenever you want to.

Helen   We can go out for meals. And go to the cinema. Have days out like we always do?

Nick   Yeah. We can.

Helen   And Essex'll be nice, won't it? It'll make a nice change. I'll pass my test and I can drive us off out into the countryside and we'll find quiet pubs that do good food.

Nick   Yeah.

Helen   And we can make plans to do things together like we always do.

Nick *nods. A slight pause.*

Helen   Maybe we can book a holiday. It's something we've talked about loads of times but we've never got round to it.

A slight pause.

Somewhere hot. Away from this country.

Nick   Why don't we talk about it when I've got dinner dished up? We can talk about what I'm going to do and where we can go away. If we want to. Then, can't we?

Helen   What about the south of France? July. A farmhouse. Or a cottage or something. Maybe an apartment with a pool.

Nick   I'd like that.

A pause.

Helen   Just me and you. Somewhere we can be.

Nick *nods.*

Nick   I'd like that, Helen. The two of us on our own. We can spend proper time together and catch up on everything we've been doing.

Helen   Can we?

Nick   Come on, let's just have a good evening.

Helen   Yeah.

Nick   Let's have a good evening and put the last half-hour behind us.

Helen   Yeah.

A pause.

Nick   Water under the bridge. Yeah?

Helen   Water under the bridge.

A slight pause.

Nick   Promise?

Helen   Promise.

Helen *smiles. She walks towards* **Nick** *and they embrace.
A slight pause.*

Slow fade.

Act Two

May 1997. The bedroom. A house in Hornchurch, Essex. One a.m.

Michelle *and* **Graham** *enter, snogging furiously. They are all over each other and through the next scene undress each other – not always successfully as they are both pissed.*

Michelle *is thirty-eight.* **Graham** *is thirty-six.*

Michelle   I want it.

Graham   Do you?

Michelle   I want it. Give it to me.

Graham   How do you want it?

Michelle   I want it inside me.

Graham   You can have it inside you.

Michelle   Can I? Tell me I can.

Graham   You can.

Michelle   I feel horny.

Graham   You can have it all.

Michelle   Give it all to me.

Graham   It's hard for you.

Michelle   It is. Isn't it?

Graham   Yes it is.

Michelle   I want to touch it.

Graham   No, don't touch it.

Michelle   I want to.

Graham   In a while.

Michelle   Show me it.

Graham   Let me see your breasts first.

Michelle   Do you want to see them?

Graham   I want to see them.

Michelle   I want you to see them.

Graham   I've thought about seeing them so many times.

Michelle   Tell me.

Graham   So many times it's hard to pick.

Michelle   Tell me you've thought about my breasts.

Graham   Last week. On the athletics track. You were supervising second-form girls and you had a tight white polo shirt on.

Michelle   Did you want to rip it off?

Graham   I wanted to rip it off and clasp them.

Michelle   Clasp them.

Graham   Yes. Clasp them. Two huge balls of love fun.

Michelle   Go on. Clasp them now.

Graham   Yes, I am.

Michelle   Do you love it?

Graham   Yes, I love it.

Michelle   You're wearing your army uniform.

Graham   My CCF uniform.

Michelle   Tell me you're back from the war.

Graham   I'm back from the war.

Michelle   Tell me you've only got three hours.

Graham   I'm back from the war.

Michelle   A hero.

Graham   Battle-scarred.

Michelle   Battle-scarred. Yes.

Graham   I've only got an hour. God, your nipples are hard.

Michelle   An hour?

Graham   Yes, an hour. Sister.

Michelle   Sister. Sister?

Graham   You must remember last time I returned from the front? You nursed me and pleasured me.

Michelle   How did I pleasure you?

Graham   We only had an hour then but you did everything.

Michelle   I did everything, didn't I?

Graham   You were so naughty I wanted to put you over my knee and spank your bottom.

Michelle   But you couldn't, could you?

She pushes **Graham** *over on to the bed and sits astride him, pinning his arms down.*

Because you were weak from your wounds and I tended to you.

Graham   Yes, you did.

Michelle *kisses* **Graham** *softly.*

Graham   Is this all right, Michelle? I mean, this is pretty wild.

Michelle   Shut up, Graham, you're spoiling it.

Michelle *slaps him.*

Graham   That's nice.

Michelle   This naughty little nurse wants to see your rifle.

Graham   No, don't.

Michelle   Your naughty little nurse wants to see your rifle.

Graham   No, please don't . . .

Michelle   Let me see your bang-bang.

Michelle *puts her hand inside* **Graham***'s trousers.*

Graham   Michelle.

Michelle   Oh dear.

Graham   What?

Michelle *laughs.*

Graham   What are you laughing at?

Michelle   What? Look what you've done already. It's all sticky.

Graham   No it's not.

Michelle   Yes it is.

Graham *tries to kiss* **Michelle** *but she laughs and moves away to avoid the kiss.*

Graham   Why are you stopping?

Michelle   Why do you think, dimbo?

Graham   What?

Michelle   We can't carry on now, can we?

Graham   Yes we can. I want to. I want to feel your body.

Michelle   Of course we can't carry on.

Graham   Well, why don't we wait for a while?

Michelle   You've had a bottle and a half of wine. I don't think so, Graham.

Graham   It'll be all right.

Michelle　For God's sake, man, don't be so ridiculous.

Graham　Are you upset with me?

Michelle　No, Graham. I'm not.

Graham　Then why are you being like this?

Michelle　Do you want me to spell it out for you?

A pause.

Graham　I'm sorry. I'm drunk and I've made a complete fool of myself.

Michelle　I wouldn't worry. You're not the first one, Graham.

She gets up off **Graham** *and starts to rearrange her clothing.* **Graham** *starts to cry.*

For God's sake, don't be such a baby, Graham. All you did was come in your pants. You haven't got a terminal illness or anything.

Graham *cries some more.*

Michelle　Stop blubbing, Graham, and go and get me a drink if you want to do something useful.

Graham *wipes his eyes and starts to rearrange his clothing.*

Michelle　I knew this was a mistake.

Graham *watches* **Michelle**.

Graham　Can't we just lie together?

Michelle　Why?

Graham　On the bed.

Michelle　Now?

Graham　We've had a great laugh. Think of the years we've known each other. Tonight's the first time we've been out for a meal and it's been excellent. Until now.

Michelle   Yeah. Until now.

Graham   You're humiliating me, you know?

Michelle   Well, that never did anyone any harm every now and again.

Graham   Thank you.

A slight pause.

Michelle   I knew this was a mistake.

Graham   Was it that bad?

Michelle   What? That's my question. What? The only thing that happened was that you couldn't control yourself.

Graham *starts to cry again.*

Michelle   Stop crying.

She shakes **Graham**.

If you don't stop crying and behave like a man I'm going home. And I'll never speak to you again. Do you hear me, Mr Tibbotson?

Graham *nods.*

Michelle   Please can you go and get me a drink before I yell.

Graham   I'm sorry.

Michelle   Don't be sorry. Just get me a Bacardi.

Graham   I've made a complete fool of myself.

Michelle   Let's just be friends. Let's just forget this silly part of the evening ever happened, shall we?

Graham   Yeah. That's right.

A slight pause.

Michelle. I have valued your friendship and good advice over the years we've been colleagues.

A slight pause.

Michelle   So have I, Graham. You've always listened to my problems.

Graham   When I first met you I did, didn't I? I listened.

Graham *turns and exits.* **Michelle** *tuts and looks around the room for her handbag. A slight pause.*

Michelle *spots it and takes it. She roots around inside and pulls out a packet of condoms. She shakes her head and puts them back in. Then she finds her cigarettes and lighter. She lights up a fag and puts her head in her hands. A slight pause.*

She looks around for something to flick her ash into. She checks in the drawer of the bedside cabinet. She takes out a copy of Modern History Review *and underneath it a copy of* Razzle *which she looks at. She hears* **Graham** *coming and quickly puts the magazines back in their drawer, spilling ash on the duvet as she goes.*

Graham *enters. He has a bottle of Bacardi and a bottle of Diet Coke and a tumbler. He spots* **Michelle** *smoking.*

Graham   Is it all right if you don't in my bedroom? It's my asthma.

Michelle   Sorry, Graham.

She stubs her cigarette out on her packet and puts the half-cigarette in the packet.

Can we just forget about what happened?

Graham *nods.*

Michelle   It was a lovely Chinese meal and you didn't embarrass me at all. When you started leaping around the dance floor.

Graham   You said I looked like a demented baboon.

Michelle   Thank you for dinner.

A slight pause.

And you must show me the photographs you took down in Dorset. I didn't realise you were such a keen ornithologist.

Graham   I don't show them to anyone. Birding is a private thing.

Graham *passes* **Michelle** *the tumbler and pours her a large Bacardi and then adds some Coke.*

Michelle   Cheers.

Graham   Do you mind if I change? Put my dressing gown on.

Michelle   No.

Graham *takes his shirt off and puts on his dressing gown before taking off his trousers and socks.* **Michelle** *finishes her drink and pours another, which she has straight.*

Michelle   I'm going to drink myself silly. And then I'm going to pass out on your bed. Is that all right?

Graham   If you want to.

Michelle   And do you know why? Because I have been dumped and had non-sexual intercourse with the least sought-after member of the common room in one day. And I feel like a drink. That's why.

Graham   What do you mean, you've been dumped?

Graham *perks up.*

Michelle   Nick finished with me this morning.

Graham   Did he?

Michelle   You don't really think I would have cheated on Nick with you, do you?

A pause.

Nick said he can't be with anyone right now.

A pause.

And do you know what? That is bollocks. That is bollocks.
What's really gone on is that jumped-up little hamster he
taught with in Leytonstone has got in the way. I would like
to get hold of her prissy little head of hair and rip it all out.
Very slowly. Jumped-up bitch. She's obsessed.

A pause.

Every weekend she's been up visiting in her silly little green
car. Making herself at home. Cooking omelettes for him.
I said to Nick, don't you see what she's doing? She's
obsessed with you. She wants to break us up. But he won't
hear a word said against her. It's like she's his conscience or
something. And then this morning he drops the bombshell
that his conscience is coming to our school. I said, I thought
she wouldn't teach in an independent school? But he said
she feels much more comfortable working in the private
sector now. I said what a load of crap. She wants you for
herself. And then he said they were just good friends and in
the same breath he confessed he'd slept with her twice.
Twice? I said you fucked her twice and you expect me not
to feel threatened? He said the last time was fifteen months
ago and the time before that three years. And both times
they were drunk. I said it's either me or her and that's when
he gives me the speech about commitment and not being
ready for a relationship. Wanker.

Pause.

Well, he was fantastic in bed, but that's all I'll miss. That
bitch can have him as far as I'm concerned.

She looks at **Graham**. *A pause.*

You know that is a complete lie? That is a complete fucking
lie.

Graham   Is it?

Michelle   I think I'm in love with him, Graham.

She downs her drink. A pause.

Fucking hell.

Graham   Lucky you, eh?

Michelle   What?

Graham   Who have I ever had?

Michelle   Probably no one.

Graham   No. No one. As you put it. The least sought-after member of the common room.

A pause.

Michelle   And you know the ridiculous thing, Graham? You were meant to make Nick jealous.

She is beside herself with laughter. **Graham** *is gutted and quiet.*

My oh my. I'm an embarrassment.

A slight pause.

You're a great pal, Graham. Where would sixth-form theatre trips be without you and me? Bottoms up.

Michelle *drinks.* **Graham** *sits on the bed beside her.*

Graham   Yeah. That's right. So you can pour your heart out to me. Your problems and your adventures.

Michelle Don the schlong. He was the first one, wasn't he, Graham? And I fell for him like a silly teenage girl. Now when was that? When did I confide him in you? My first.

Graham   Riverside Studios. All the way round the North Circular to Chingford on the minibus. And I was driving.

Michelle   Well, let me tell you something about Donald.

Graham   You told me all about him. You tell me about all your sordid little affairs when we go to the theatre. Yes. Forty-two visits in all.

Michelle   Come on, Graham.

A slight pause.

I remember him clear as day sidling up to me in the
common room. I'd been at school precisely two days and
what did Don go and do? Brought me a coffee and a Jammy
Dodger, brushed my hand and asked me if I was a pianist.
He said I had delicate elegant fingers.

A slight pause.

And I fell for it. I fell for it, didn't I, Graham? You know,
when he got me into bed forty-eight hours later. And went
down on me. Which was heavenly. He even fed me some
crap about his expert technique and playing a wind
instrument.

A slight pause.

He even persuaded me to go to a soul weekender at Caister,
didn't he? Don was in full *Miami Vice* mode. New sparkling
white trainers, arms on his jacket rolled up eighties style. He
even brought his saxophone. And I met my nemesis.
Lorraine. In the chalet next door. She invited us in for a
Malibu and pineapple and Lorraine and Don hit it off. Told
him all about crawling out of her window when she was
fifteen to go down the Lacy Lady in Ilford. To hear one of
the funk mafia play. Don had been to the Lacy Lady and he
layed it on thick.

A slight pause.

I was in a foul mood, of course. Which confirmed Don's
feeling he'd be having a better time with Lorraine. Who was
a dog clipper. And my mood got worse when I spilt a glass
of Bacardi and Coke down the cozzie I'd hired for the toga
party. Don wasn't sympathetic. Said to get a sheet off of the
bed and get it round me as we had to meet Lorraine and
Karen. Her mousy friend. One minute I was Aphrodite.
The next a crap ghost at a Hallowe'en party.

A slight pause.

Karen, who worked for Barclays, turned out to be a marked
improvement upon Lorraine and we got on like a house on

fire. Had a laugh with two firemen and didn't even notice
Lorraine and Don had slipped away.

A slight pause.

I opened the door of the chalet an hour later, jazz is blaring
out and what do I see? Don having sex with Lorraine from
behind. And she'd been sick all over my Bacardi-stained
toga. What a slut.

Michelle *pours herself another Bacardi.*

Graham   I went to a soul weekender once.

Michelle *ignores him.*

Graham   Don't you want to hear about it?

Michelle   No.

A long pause.

Graham *takes the Bacardi and has a swig and nearly gags.*
A slight pause.

Graham   I don't know why you have to be so awful
to me.

A slight pause.

Michelle   When we took the sixth form in that pub at
Liverpool Street. That was another one, wasn't it, Graham?

Graham   Stephen.

Michelle   Your friend in the history department.

A slight pause.

We'd just started going out. He was lovely. I adored him.
I don't know why I . . . He treated me so well. You know,
we didn't sleep together for six weeks? And for me that was
a world record. He stroked my hair. Kissed the small of my
back.

A pause.

He could cook too. And he was so funny. A great mimic.
Do you remember the impressions he used to do of all those
characters in the *Carry On* films? And the old sitcoms. Rigsby
in *Rising Damp*. The headmaster. That silly bitch who does
the catering. He had them all down to a T. I used to get
annoyed with him when he mimicked me. I was silly. So
silly. I don't know why I betrayed him. It was too easy
somehow. With him. I know you're going to hate me saying
this but he was too nice.

A slight pause.

I hate myself.

A slight pause.

I do. I hate myself when I think about him. It. All of it.
I hate it. He's up in Bishop's Stortford now, isn't he? Head
of department.

Graham *nods.*

Michelle   Good for him. I was so very jealous when
I heard he'd married.

Graham   They've got a baby now. A little girl.

Michelle   I didn't know that?

A pause.

Graham   Chloe.

Michelle   I always wanted to call my little baby Chloe.
If I do. When I do. Perhaps I will. Still.

A slight pause.

Graham   Stephen was a good bloke. He still sends me
a Christmas card.

A slight pause.

Michelle   I was bored with Stephen. He bored me. But
Colin . . .

Graham Colin was a cunt.

Michelle I didn't know that word was in your vocabulary?

A slight pause.

Colin. Christ.

A slight pause.

He was a thrilling lover. And an utter, utter brute.

Graham *swigs from the bottle. A slight pause.*

Michelle *actions for* **Graham** *to pass the bottle to her. He does and she takes a swig too.*

Michelle Do you know what he forced me to do?

Graham I don't want to know that.

Michelle A thousand humiliations behind closed doors and yet so, so pleasant on parents' evening.

A slight pause.

And yet he sometimes found a tenderness I can only describe as. Childlike.

Graham *covers his ears.*

Michelle Listen to me. Listen. You wimp. You stupid wimpy man. Listen.

Graham *uncovers his ears.*

Michelle I was pregnant by Colin. I was pregnant.

Graham Were you?

He thinks. A pause.

Did he make you get rid of it?

Michelle No. I miscarried. I had a miscarriage. There. You didn't know that, did you, Graham?

A slight pause.

About a month later we were queuing for hamburgers in Romford. And he asked me how I was. And he said he thought maybe what had happened was for the best. And I knew it was over.

A slight pause.

I made my excuses and I locked myself in the disabled toilet. And I slid on to the floor and cried so hard it hurt. This spotty teenage lad broke the door in for me.

A slight pause.

I laughed and lied. Said my mother had just passed away. I got caught. Wanted to be alone. And the little lad gave me a handful of napkins and a free Diet Coke. I asked him if he was dropping a hint. He said he wasn't. Said I looked great. And there I was in Burger King's disabled toilet. Mascara all over the shop. Flirting with a boy who could have been one of my fifth form. That was when I started playing again. And there have been so many, haven't there, Graham? Until Nick. Until my darling, darling Nick.

A slight pause.

And you've been my confidant. Thrilling you with my stories. Another expedition for our theatre club. Another snatched half-hour or so feeding your fantasies. Your adolescent little fantasies.

Graham   Don't do this to me.

Michelle   So many. Disasters. Torrid affairs.

Graham   No . . .

Michelle   That sixth former I had in my car.

Graham   No more now . . .

Michelle   In the back of my car. All over his exciting lean body.

Graham   Please.

Michelle   The groundsman I had all weekend. Snogging him outside the tobacconist's for all to see.

Graham *shakes his head.*

Michelle   The biology teacher I met at the gym. He had a wife. I didn't care.

Graham   Please.

Michelle   The adultery thrilled me.

Graham   You're a slut.

Michelle   My next-door neighbour with bad breath and nasal hair.

Graham   You're just a slut . . .

Michelle   And the parent. The parent with the blue BMW and his set of golf clubs.

Graham *covers his ears again.*

Michelle   His endless unfunny quips. About his son getting a good school report after the extra I was getting.

Graham   You foul . . .

Michelle   And then my beautiful Nicholas. Oh, my Nicholas.

Graham *shakes his head.*

Michelle   The joy being weak-kneed and girly.

Graham   Stupid cow . . .

Michelle   That I might sacrifice my Nicholas? Nicholas that has been taken away from me for you?

Graham   I can't stand you any more.

Michelle   You. Pathetic. Limp-wristed. Silly. Bore.

Graham   Do you really hate me?

Michelle   When I see you shouting and screaming at the kids doing CCF, I abhor you.

Graham   What?

Michelle   When I see you playing soldiers with the cadets. The public-school cadet force. Pretending you're a real man screaming and shouting at quivering fourteen-year-old boys. I despise you. Captain Tibbotson. Commando section. No longer the weak-willed ineffectual history teacher. Now leader of men. Soldier. I saw you no more than a month ago. I was with Nicholas. And you had some boy out of his line. You were humiliating him. Your snide little attempts at humour and your horrible vile temper. Why was it? Something pathetic? Like not having shining boots? Not snapping his foot down quick enough on parade?

A slight pause.

I wish that boy were here now. I wish I could tell him. And watch him laugh. Mr Tibbotson. Captain Graham Tibbotson CCF Commando section a come-in-his-pants sissy.

A slight pause.

I wanted to sleep with you to get revenge on Nick, but to see you entertaining? Flirting with the idea? Really thinking I wanted you. Was going to cheat on Nicholas with you. Seeing the smug flicker of a shabby weak man. A man feeling empowered in the way humiliating teenage boys usually only fulfils. It makes me want to watch you tumble down flights of stairs. I've learned to despise you on our cosy little theatre trips, Graham, but not so much as this evening. I go home and snigger into my bathroom mirror when I remember you agonising. Trying to hide your erection. In some tatty theatre foyer or other. Your tortured attempts to flirt with me.

A slight pause.

Over the seven years I've known you, yes, I have grown to hate you. You're clearly the only the man who wants me and that's not something I admire.

She laughs and laughs to herself.

And to watch you try and dance this evening. A demented baboon complements the spectacle with humour. But it wasn't even funny watching you fling yourself around. All I could do was hide my face and think why build a Chinese restaurant with a dance floor?

Graham   I used to be a good dancer.

Michelle   I don't care what you used to be.

Graham   I went to discotheques when they were still discotheques.

Michelle   I really don't give a damn.

Graham   And I did go to a soul weekender once. I went with my cousin.

Michelle   Well, you would have got on well with Lorraine.

Graham   I used to do the stomp.

Michelle   Really?

Graham   And I can waltz.

A slight pause.

I can waltz. You couldn't manage anything half so graceful. Your slovenly frame couldn't move with the precision and charm of a waltz.

Michelle   I want my Nicholas. He belongs with me. I've waited too long for someone like him.

A slight pause.

I want his kisses to shower the nape of my neck. I want his fine hands to steady my spinning, spinning nature. That's what I want. That cow Helen's not having him. He's mine.

A slight pause.

Graham   You. You . . .

Graham *can't get what he wants to say out.*

Michelle   What, you coward?

Graham   You . . . maths teacher! You fucking maths teacher!

Graham *storms out of the bedroom. A pause.*

Michelle *purposefully takes out her cigarettes and lights one up. A slight pause.*

Graham *enters. He has a huge bouquet of flowers. They are embarrassing they are so huge and he tears open the cellophane and grasps a handful of stalks which he throws at* **Michelle***.*

Graham   I got them for you! Have them, you bitch!

Michelle *is slightly taken aback even after everything else.*
Graham *throws more flowers at her.*

Graham   I got them for you!

A slight pause.

I went to the high street at lunchtime and I got them for you. After dinner. A Chinese meal. Back here. I'd give them to you. And you would like them. And be delighted and happy. That there were such beautiful flowers. For you.

He throws more flowers at her and throws the bouquet on the floor. He stamps on the bouquet and kicks it.

You go on and on and on about me but who are you? You're just a selfish cow. You've been at the school seven years and you still haven't even got your own form. You never get involved with anything or anyone. You're just

interested in drawing your salary and your sordid succession
of men.

Michelle   Which you wank yourself silly over . . .

Graham   And the theatre club? You only do that so you
can pour out your disgusting mind to me and to try and
appear cultured at school. You don't care about anything.
You don't know anything. You have a mind that connects
with numbers and that is about it because you certainly
have no soul!

A slight pause.

I'm a man, a man. Although I don't feel much like one
sometimes!

A slight pause.

Yes. Sometimes I don't feel like a man. I haven't even
managed to find myself a wife.

A slight pause.

I had one hope.

A slight pause.

From being a gawky shy twenty-eight-year-old who'd never
kissed a girl. But you? You don't believe in a bloody thing,
do you? I've been hiding away all these years but now I've
had enough. I've followed you in my car and watched you
go drinking with Don. Argue with him in Indian restaurants
in Upminister. I watched Stephen leave in the morning and
blow kisses at you. And that afternoon I heard Colin fucking
you. I heard you whining he was hurting you. Your
incessant whine. I saw you giving Adams a blow job in the
back of your car. I saw that.

A slight pause.

I came into your room when you were asleep in Edinburgh.
I saw your breasts exposed. How I wanted you. How I
wanted to just take you. Have you.

Michelle *looks for her coat.*

Michelle   You're sick.

Graham   No . . .

Michelle   You stalker.

Graham   No. You are.

Michelle   It's you, isn't it?

Graham   What?

Michelle   You've been opening my mail? In my
pigeon hole.

Graham   No, I haven't . . .

Michelle   I knew someone was tampering with my mail.

Graham   I haven't been doing that.

Michelle   I'm going to report you to the second master
for this.

Graham   No, you won't.

Michelle   I certainly will. Do you really think I want to
see your horrible face in the common room again?

Graham *walks around the bed and opens the drawer of the bedside
cabinet. He takes out a brown manila envelope.*

Michelle   What are you doing?

Graham *opens the manila envelope and passes* **Michelle**
photographs. At least twenty prints. **Michelle** *looks at them
and gasps.*

Graham   You and that sixth-form boy. The parent with
the golf clubs. On top of him in the park. That lab
technician you've been quietly bonking.

A slight pause.

That's right. I know about that.

A slight pause.

Your body. Beautiful. In the moonlight. In your room.
I thought it was my last chance. At the festival. My
last chance.

A slight pause.

Michelle   What do you want from me?

Graham   Teach me.

Michelle   What?

Graham   Do your duty to me. I've waited seven years.

Michelle   I don't understand?

Graham   Make me a man. Teach me. Show me. Show
me. Make me a man. Show me. Give yourself to me. Show
me how. Show me. Have me. Now. Have me.

A long pause.

Michelle   Don't make me do that.

Graham   I've waited so long.

Michelle   Please.

Graham   You were going to before. Weren't you? You
were. You wanted to take my cock in your hands. You
wanted me. You wanted to use me.

He moves towards **Michelle**. *She flinches.*

I'm not going to force . . .

A slight pause.

Please.

Michelle   I can't.

Graham   You can. I want you to.

Michelle   What about the pictures?

Graham   What about them?

Michelle   You know what.

Graham   I like them. I feel close to you.

Michelle   Can I have them?

Graham   Let's see, shall we?

Michelle   You won't show them?

A long pause.

Let's just forget any of this happened.

A slight pause.

Let's just pretend we've only been back ten minutes. We've had a drink. And you've put your dressing gown on.

A slight pause.

Graham   Touch my face. Tenderly.

Michelle *touches* **Graham**'s *face.*

Graham   Am I your soldier?

Michelle   You're my soldier.

Graham   And you're my nurse?

Michelle   Yes.

Graham *slips off his dressing gown.*

Graham   My shoulder's been bruised.

Michelle   Has it?

She looks.

Oh yes. I can see it. And there are bruises all over your back.

Graham   Will you kiss them better? Like the girl does on the ship. In *Raiders of the Lost Ark*.

Michelle   There, there.

Graham   That's nice.

Michelle   Does that make you feel nice?

Graham   Yes.

Michelle   What happened to you?

Graham   I escaped from the Gestapo. I was being tortured.

Michelle   You poor thing. You're brave.

A slight pause.

Graham   I've never kissed a girl before.

Michelle   Haven't you?

Graham   No.

Michelle   Why's that?

Graham   I'm shy. I'm very shy.

Michelle *sits next to* **Graham** *on the bed. She smiles at* **Graham**. *He is like a little boy.* **Michelle** *finds it very difficult through the next.*

Graham   Will you kiss me again, nurse?

Michelle   Yes.

Michelle *kisses all over* **Graham**'s *back.*

Graham   That's nice.

Michelle   It is, isn't it?

Graham   Will you kiss my lips?

Michelle   Yes.

Michelle *kisses* **Graham**'s *lips.*

Graham   That's lovely.

Michelle *kisses* **Graham**'s *neck and then his chest and his nipples.*

Graham   That's lovely. Really lovely.

He kisses **Michelle** *and her neck and then starts to unbutton her top.*

Graham   When the war's over I'm going to marry my nurse and have a nice house.

Michelle   That's right . . .

Graham   We're going to have children and live in a nice street.

Michelle   Yes . . .

Graham   And after the war's over everything will be better, won't it?

Michelle   Of course it will . . .

Michelle *goes down on her knees and pulls at* **Graham**'s *underpants.*

Graham   The streets will be clean and we'll look after the sick people and the elderly people. And we'll educate the young properly. Show them how to behave. That's what we're fighting for, isn't it?

Michelle *looks at* **Graham** *and laughs.* **Graham** *grabs* **Michelle**'s *hair.*

Graham   Is this what Colin did? Did he pull your hair? Did he grab it? When you laughed at him? I'm tired of you laughing at me. Of these games. These silly, silly games. I'm so tired.

Michelle *shakes her head. She is frightened.*

Graham   After the war we won't have to worry about anything, will we? We can stay in bed all day. When the war is over.

Michelle   Yes.

Graham   But now time is precious, my love. I've only got an hour and I have to be on a train to Portsmouth.

Michelle *nods.*

Graham   Mission behind lines. Top secret. I may be risking my life. Maybe I'll come back a hero.

Michelle *looks away.*

Slow fade.

Act Three

*August 1998. The patio. A cottage garden in Tiverton, Devon.
Ten a.m.*

Anne *sits at the garden table with her feet up on another chair. The
table is littered with the remnants of a barbecue and party from the
previous evening.*

Anne *is fifty-eight.*

Robert *stands opposite* **Anne** *across the patio.* **Robert** *has
a portable CD player in his hands with a long extension lead running
from it back into the cottage.*

Robert *is forty-two.*

Anne   No.

Robert   You promised.

Anne   No, no, no.

Robert   You promised me.

Anne   Robert, if you think I'm dancing with you now
you've got another think coming.

Robert   Now, you made a deal.

Anne   I don't care what I said last night.

Robert   I know you didn't want to dance to Spandau
Ballet but this is Neil Sedaka.

Anne   No.

Robert *puts down the CD player and folds his arms. A slight pause.*

Anne   Are you sulking?

Robert   No.

Anne   What are you doing standing like that, then?

Robert   I'm waiting.

Anne   Well, you better get some sunblock on your nose because you're going to have a long wait standing there.

Robert   You know, sometimes you're no fun at all.

Anne *laughs.*

Anne   That's not what my sixth form think.

Robert   Well, compared to my lot they're a pretty shabby bunch. On results day mine got me an inflatable sheep and a bottle of Dom Perignon. Now, correct me if I'm wrong, but your lot bought you a packet of Celebrations and half a litre of Sainsbury's gin. Pathetic.

Anne   That's not what you said last night. When you were busy bonding with them. Anyway, they're normal kids. They haven't got Mummy or Daddy to buy champagne for teacher.

Robert   I thought one or two of them needed taking under my wing. A bit of pre-university guidance.

Anne *laughs.*

Robert   What?

Anne   From you? Robert, you started out on dramatic societies and ended up telling them to shag anything and watch out for modern languages students called Helen.

Robert   Which in retrospect does seem unwise.

Anne   Given that there are two Helens in my sixth-form set. One of whom's doing Spanish and law and the other who's doing German.

Robert   Proves my point.

Anne   What?

Robert   Find a university modern languages department and you will find the biggest concentration of Helens in the country.

Anne *laughs.*

Robert See. You know it's true.

Anne I don't think it was the association of their name and modern languages that offended them. More to the point that they should be steered clear of.

A slight pause.

Kids from Devon are more sensitive than they are in Essex.

Robert I took them under my wing. They loved me.

Anne *laughs. A slight pause.*

Anne The teacher who died. The geography teacher. She was called Helen, wasn't she?

Robert Yeah. Very sad that.

Anne Helen. I like that name.

A pause.

Robert Will you dance with me? You'll make my day.

Anne Will I?

Robert *picks up the CD player and grins.*

Anne Don't make me. Please.

Robert OK.

A slight pause.

As long as you promise me next time you have a party you'll dance with me. Even if it's 'True' by Spandau Ballet.

Anne Even if it's not 'True' by Spandau Ballet.

Robert *feels funny and rubs his head.*

Anne Are you all right, Robert?

Robert Nave of wausea.

Anne Wave of nausea?

Robert Nave of wausea. Not good.

Anne   Have you had a Resolve?

Robert   No. Not yet.

Anne   There's a sachet in the bathroom cabinet. Or I've got some co-codamol?

Robert   Yeah. Resolve. I think I need Resolve.

Anne   I thought you seemed uncharacteristically energetic. What time did you get to bed?

Robert   Four.

Anne   Four?

Robert   Ish. We were listening to Nina Simone.

Robert *holds his head.*

Anne   What is it?

Robert   I'm sweating. I feel like shit.

Anne   It's hot already.

Robert   No. That's better. My stomach just did something gymnastic.

Anne   What were you drinking?

Robert   Stella. Red wine. Most of that Sainsbury's gin. Oh, and the brandy we brought back from France last year.

Anne   Robert . . .

Robert   But your sixth formers did love me, didn't they?

Anne   You were the entertainment down from Essex. There's no one like you in Tiverton. That's for sure.

Robert   You watch. When they go to university you'll be going through me to keep in touch.

Robert *studies* **Anne**. *A slight pause.*

Robert   All your sixth form were asking what was going on between us.

Anne   Were they?

Robert   They said you're always going on about me in class.

Anne   Did they? What did you say?

Robert   We're mates.

A slight pause.

When you showed them the pictures. From Mexico. One of the Helens asked me about the sleeping arrangements.

Anne   Cheeky little cow. What did you say?

Robert   I told her the truth. We had a twin.

Anne   What did she say?

Robert   Nothing. I said we get on well and we always share a room when we go on holiday. To save money.

Anne   What did she say to that?

Robert   She said she thought it was a shame. She said she thought it was romantic. Holidaying together. She couldn't believe we've been going away together for six years. I said we were good friends for two or three years before that. When we first taught together. In Essex.

A pause.

She asked me if I'd been married. And I said no but I told her you had been. Was that all right?

Anne   Yeah. My sixth form know that anyway.

A pause.

Robert   I said we once shared a kiss but never a bed.

Anne   You didn't say that, did you?

Robert   No. And what if I had?

Anne   Then you would have been bloody silly.

Robert   Why?

Anne   You know perfectly well why.

A pause.

Do you want some toast? Do you want something to eat?

Robert   I don't know.

Anne   I can make you scrambled eggs on toast?

Robert   I'm actually not that hungry. I finished off the tuna pasta before I went to bed.

Anne   Did you see I had the spare room painted?

Robert   Yeah. By the way. One of your students was sick in your stockpot. I covered it over with tinfoil.

Anne   Thanks.

A slight pause.

Robert   What time are we going to lunch?

Anne   I didn't know if you had to go?

Robert   No. We always have lunch before I go.

Anne   OK. Well, we can have a pub lunch.

Robert   I'll drop you off here and then I'll get on my way. Is that all right?

Anne   Yeah.

Robert   When I'm over we always have lunch and . . .

Anne   Then we'll have lunch.

Robert   Though I don't know if I can stomach a roast. Will you take the piss out of me if I have a salad? Tossed.

Anne   No, Robert. I won't.

Robert   And we need to talk about half-term.

A slight pause.

I don't know about you but I fancy Italy.

Anne OK.

Robert Tuscany might be nice. Late October.

Anne Lovely.

Robert Now, do you know the dates, because I've got two weeks off?

Anne Yeah . . .

Robert I loved Mexico.

Anne I loved Mexico. I didn't expect to like it as much as I did. I don't know why. I felt uneasy about it.

A slight pause.

I felt uneasy about going away.

Robert Did you?

A slight pause.

Anne I did feel uneasy about us going away this summer.

Robert Why?

Anne I don't know.

A long pause.

Robert We've had some wonderful holidays.

Anne I know.

Robert Remember our Scandinavian cruise?

Anne *smiles.*

Robert We read *The Wild Duck* by the fjord in those plastic Viking helmets I got. And those Americans took pictures. It was so funny. And Mexico was splendid, wasn't it?

Anne Yes it was.

A slight pause.

Robert *smiles.*

Robert   I wouldn't mind a sachet of that Resolve now, Anne.

Anne   Robert, I'm not sure about half-term.

Robert   Why?

Anne   I've been thinking about it since we got back. I think I'd like to go to Belgium.

Robert   Belgium?

Anne   To Flanders.

Robert   Why?

Anne   I'd like to go to visit the war cemeteries at half-term. With my Auntie May. She asked me to take her. And I want to go. I've never seen them. She can't go on her own.

A slight pause.

Can she?

Robert   No.

Anne   Since I've been down here we've become close.

Robert   I know that. So I'll see you at Christmas.

Anne   She wants to go there before she dies. I can't refuse her that, can I?

A slight pause.

She's so bloody difficult though. You know what the weather's been like. First sun in weeks and she wouldn't even let me run her into Taunton.

A slight pause.

I want to go. I'd like to see those cemeteries for myself. Apparently the silence is humbling.

Robert   What does she want to go now for?

Anne   She has a ghost she wants to lay.

A slight pause.

When we came back from Mexico I went over to see her. And she told me a story I'd never heard before.

A slight pause.

My Auntie May was fourteen when the First World War broke out. Sometimes her father allowed her to attend tennis parties. To field the balls for the adults. And it was on one afternoon like that just after the war broke out my great-aunt met this young man. Arthur.

A slight pause.

He was eighteen and Auntie May said he was hopeless at tennis. Everyone kept falling about laughing at him but he was so good-humoured he just laughed along with everyone else. But in the end he gave up and instead he amused himself fetching the tennis balls with May.

A slight pause.

Apparently, they hadn't been fielding long when the ball went into the ornamental part of the garden at the end and Arthur and May went chasing after it. She was light on her feet and located it quite quickly but Arthur, seeing she'd got hold of it, yells out to everyone: 'Lost ball. Carry on with another till we can find it.' And then he came over to her sitting in a little hideaway. With the lost ball. May said he was very handsome and although he was afflicted with some acne he had golden curls of hair. And bright blue eyes like the sea, she said. Arthur told her he expected to go overseas and he began to stammer. She said he was trying to pluck up the courage to ask her permission to write to her. She said she got goose pimples all the way up her arms and legs. And Arthur went to the front line and saw action at Ypres.

A slight pause.

She showed me the letters. There were six in all. And they were the most beautiful letters I have ever read in my life.

A slight pause.

When Auntie May showed me them I held them so
delicately. They were almost brown and they felt like
they might crumble. This treasure might crumble in
my fingertips.

A slight pause.

I feel I spoil his writing trying to paraphrase his words.
Précis those delicate love letters. But I had this powerful
feeling reading them. The feeling of being young and in
love, I suppose. My aunt never received another letter
from him.

Robert   Didn't she?

Anne   No. No news at all. Then in 1916 May went to
France with her mother and the Yeovil Red Cross
Ambulance. She said she never stopped loving Arthur.
Then in August 1917, when May had been at the front
eighteen months, she saw him.

A slight pause.

Those thought likely to die were assembled in a great
marquee tent. The surgeons had to concentrate their efforts
on the ones they might be able to save. And consequently
May didn't come across Arthur for some time after he
arrived.

A slight pause.

There was one surgeon serving there who prided himself on
choosing one of the men from the marquee. Bringing one of
the men everyone else had given up on back from the dead.
And he settled upon a chap whose legs had been shattered
and turned septic already. But May heard a voice from the
stretcher beside him call her name.

A slight pause.

He was covered in mud and across his stomach was a rough
dressing soaked in blood. Although it was all matted and

muddy May recognised his blond curls and his blue eyes. And he said, 'My angel.'

A slight pause.

The surgeon asked May what was going on. May asked him if he'd consider attending to Arthur but he said he'd chosen for that day. He allowed her five minutes to wash Arthur and change his dressings. May said she noticed he'd matured and she could see his acne had disappeared. He said that he loved her.

A slight pause.

Then Matron marched through the tent. Like a dreadnought. When she saw May crouched at the side of a tommy in the marquee she was furious and sent her to the surgeon's side straight away. They hacked off this poor man's legs and May said he vomited blood and screamed. He died on the table as May held his arms. But she said she was happy his suffering was over and she could return to Arthur. But he was gone. May went out towards the lines of bodies covered with blankets and greatcoats. She said she hesitated pulling them back but eventually she found him. The face she'd washed was smeared with mud again, she said, but his sightless blue eyes still shone in the sun.

A slight pause.

She clenched her fist around the thermometer still in her hand and splintered glass deep into her palm. May showed me her scarred hand.

A slight pause.

That's it. The story she told me.

A slight pause.

Robert   Did she stay at the front?

Anne   She served out the rest of the war. Then she returned to Yeovil and led a fairly solitary life. She only married for a very brief spell in her twenties.

Robert *nods. A pause.*

Anne   She says Arthur was her one and only true love.
Innocent and unconsummated as she accepts it was. She
wants to visit his grave. She says it's haunted her her whole
life she wasn't able to tell him she loved him.

Robert *nods. A very long pause.*

Robert   What time are we going to lunch?

A slight pause.

Anne   Is that all you've got to say? In response to
her story?

Robert   I'm sorry.

A pause.

I don't know what to say. I don't know why you've told
me it.

Anne   I don't think my auntie and Arthur were in love.
Really. She met Arthur and in a moment he was gone and
there was a gap. With nothing but the imagination to fill it.
She created this love of her life. From a sunny afternoon
and half a dozen beautiful letters.

A slight pause.

They needed each other. She created this romantic love and
it got them through the horrors they faced.

A slight pause.

I think what really haunts my auntie is guilt. That she never
provided him with any more comfort in those conditions.
That she didn't plead, beg the surgeon. She has this
enormous guilt that she couldn't do more.

A slight pause.

No. I don't believe they were in love. They were only kids.
Think of a sixth former of mine or yours going out with a
third-form girl. It happens occasionally, doesn't it? They

might seem smitten. They might even be good friends, but would you say they were in love?

Robert   I don't know. Probably not.

Anne   May's story has preoccupied me.

Robert   You know, in the time we've known each other, this is the most I've heard you discuss any relationship.

A slight pause.

Anne   It touched something very deep inside me. I wanted to tell you about it. I've woken at night thinking . . .

Robert   About your own life.

Anne   When I was a sixth former I was so madly in love with my English teacher. I adored him. He was relaxed and compassionate. Daring. And he seemed fond of me as well. I expect he was gay. How I loved him and how I missed him when I went to university. My husband never came near him. And then when I least expected it. After years of disastrous marriage and divorce, another English teacher appeared in my life. And I discovered feelings I'd long since given up on unlocking.

A slight pause.

It's been much easier since I've been down here, us still being friends, but I've not been entirely happy. And then May's story triggered something. This idea I've had of us. Of a sort of. Compromise. On both our parts. Being friends. It's a sham.

Robert   I agree.

Anne *studies* **Robert**. *A pause.*

Anne   In the time we've been friends I've loved us holidaying together.

Robert   So have I.

Anne   But I don't know if we should continue.

Robert   What? But why?

Anne   Robert, surely you should be doing other things in the holidays?

Robert   Like what?

Anne   You're nearly twenty years younger than me.

Robert   What difference does that make?

Anne   When you meet people. Don't they think it's strange we go off holidaying together?

Robert   No. Why should they?

Anne   It's not even like we're teaching at the same school any more.

Robert   So we can't be pals because we're no longer strictly speaking colleagues?

Anne   No. But you're often saying to me you don't have enough friends of your own age. People in a similar position.

Robert   What do you mean?

Anne   We can both feel lonely. I certainly can feel lonely down here. I know you can. You need to make other friends you see regularly. Who aren't married. Or haven't got kids.

Robert   What's that got to do with us?

Anne   And what about girlfriends?

A pause.

Robert   What about girlfriends?

Anne   Well, it's no wonder you have trouble dating when you're booked up to go on holiday with me all the time.

Robert   I don't understand this . . .

Anne   If I was dating you and you were booked up three months in advance to go on holiday with a female friend I probably wouldn't like it . . .

Robert   Who cares? I don't want to date anyone else . . .

Anne   But Robert?

Robert   What? Tell me. Tell me please.

A long pause.

Anne   I know you want a family. I know you want to get married.

Robert   What?

Anne   I'm holding you back. I know I am. Why do you think I moved down to Devon in the first place?

Robert   You said you were tired of a six-day week.

Anne   I've been thinking about it since we got back from Mexico. I don't think we should go on holiday together any more.

Robert *thinks. A pause.*

Robert   You don't know what I want.

A slight pause.

When we started teaching together you gave me confidence. I was shattered teaching in state schools. You built me back up.

A slight pause.

All of this talk about your aunt? About us? About phantom relationships crushed under the sheer weight of their circumstances? It's bollocks. It's such an evasion. Such a cop-out. You're not taking proper responsibility for your feelings and your actions. For us. You talk about history? Sell me a bloody story instead of talking honestly about me and you? You know, you want to talk about history, Anne. I've grown up being taught most of what's happened the last eighty years has been because of that dreadful war your aunt lived through. The Easter Rising. The Balkans. And Adolf. That aberration in the middle. At the heart of it.

Now I keep hearing this conclusion, that the reason he did what he did was because the man was sexually frustrated. But whatever it is. What he got up to with his niece. Versailles. It all seems to offer him an explanation. An excuse for what he did. But he was responsible. People look back and try and make sense of who we are. How we got where we are. It's natural. It's a moment. We're educated and we're used to explaining the world around us. We teach. We should know better than anyone else.

A slight pause.

But it's about what I've done and what I haven't done. What I do and what I don't do and then how I choose to remember it. Do you understand me? What I'm saying? Anything else is the biggest abrogation of responsibility. It's shit. And I believe that.

Silence.

You don't know what I want.

A slight pause.

Anne   Well?

Robert *loses his confidence.* **Anne** *gives up. A slight pause.*

Anne   The teacher who died. It was an accident, wasn't it? Helen. How did she die?

A slight pause.

Please tell me.

Robert   I never really knew her but a bloke in the English department was good friends with her. In fact, they taught together at a comprehensive in Leytonstone. In the East End. Well, they were good mates and she followed him out into Essex. Started last September. He was really popular with the kids but I never liked him very much. Bit of a lad out boozing with the PE department. Anyway, Helen joining caused some trouble because he'd been going out with Michelle Didsbury.

Anne   Slapper.

Robert   Yeah.

Anne   Is Graham Tibbotson still in love with her?

Robert   I don't think so. They fell out May before last.

Anne   Why?

Robert   No one knows. Anyway, the English department has been lumbered with running sixth-form theatre trips now. Anne, why won't you –

Anne   But what about this girl?

Robert   Michelle was jealous of Helen's friendship with Nick and they broke up over it a few times. But then it comes out Michelle had been having an affair with one of the lab assistants and Nick was in pieces about it. Anyway, Michelle left Nick's place and he rang Helen. It was raining hard but Helen said she was getting straight in her car.

A slight pause.

She lost control of her car. I think there's going to be a memorial service for her in the chapel at the start of term. For some reason the Rev's asked me to read a poem.

A slight pause.

Of course, Michelle's dumped her lab technician and she's been trying to get back with Nick. But I don't know if he's even going to make it back to school.

Anne   Why?

Robert   I saw him in the pub last week. He was on his own. A bit of a mess. As I said, I've always thought he was an arsehole but I felt sorry for him and I talked to him. He said it was his fault but I said it wasn't. He said he asked her to come over. He said he knew she'd always do what he wanted.

A slight pause.

He said he's thinking of going back to Leytonstone to teach in the comp again. It has no meaning. Teaching in a private school. Helen would have wanted him to go back but I said that was bollocks. Wherever you teach you're doing the most important job there is. He said he thought teaching should be a calling. It was for Helen. He only ever wanted to be a professional footballer. I said very few of us are doing it as a first choice and it's not a mission. It's a job. And as it happens I think it's one of the best jobs you can do. And you know what? He cried. Wept like a child. So I gave him a hug. And then my mate turned up and took the piss.

Anne *smiles.*

Anne   I think you're wonderful.

A slight pause.

Was she in love with him? Helen?

Robert   Yeah. Obviously. You know, this Nick guy was your replacement.

Anne   Was he?

Robert *nods.*

Robert   Nick knew Helen loved him and he didn't want her but he wouldn't let her have anyone else. Selfish, eh?

A slight pause.

He accosted me when I was leaving the pub. He was saying what a brilliant bloke I was. And then he said, 'I loved her, you know. I really did.' And I don't know if it was because I'd had a few beers or what, but I said to him, 'No you didn't, Nick. You didn't love her. It was all about your fucking ego, mate.' And it was like I'd got hold of his neck and squeezed every ounce of blood up into his face. But I was that clear what I thought of him.

A pause.

What did you want to be, Anne?

Anne   What?

Robert   What did you want to be? Before you were married and took up teaching? Come on. What did you want to be?

Anne *thinks and smiles.*

Anne   I wanted to chef. You know I wanted to be a chef.

Robert *nods. A pause.*

Robert   I wanted to be a musician. A pianist.

A pause.

Anne   The thought of you sitting at a piano fills me with the most happy feeling.

A slight pause.

Robert   I want you to do something for me.

Anne   What?

Robert   If this is it. If as far as you're concerned we're not going to see each other in the holidays any more then I want you to dance with me now.

Anne   We'll still see each other in the holidays . . .

Robert   We won't end up seeing each other. You know what it's like. If you don't make plans . . .

A slight pause.

You know what it's like. Dance with me.

Anne   It's half past ten in the morning.

Robert   Dance with me.

Anne   What about the music?

Robert   What about it?

Anne   It's Sunday.

Robert   Dance with me. Like you promised you would last night.

Anne   I was embarrassed last night. In front of my sixth form.

Robert   Please.

Anne *nods.* **Robert** *fiddles around with the CD player.*

Anne   Robert . . .

Robert   I want you to dance with me. If it's a slow one it's a slow one. If it's 'Oh Carol' I'll go mental.

'Breaking Up Is Hard To Do' by Neil Sedaka plays from the CD player.

Fuck it.

Anne *can't believe what's playing either.* **Robert** *shakes his head and laughs. He turns it up. He dances and is funny. He sings all the words.* **Anne** *is reluctant.*

Anne   Robert, the neighbours . . .

Robert   Fuck the neighbours . . .

He unbuttons his shirt and flashes his belly. He wobbles it.

Neighbours! You dour Devon bastards. I am from Essex and I am dancing!

Anne *laughs and shakes her head and* **Robert** *pulls her up to dance. They dance, singing all the words very loudly. They twist and twirl each other round. They do funny little movements and make each other laugh. After bopping,* **Robert** *encourages* **Anne** *into an ill-fitting waltz.*

Anne   I love this song . . .

Robert   It's a brilliant song . . .

They continue until the song finishes. **Robert** *turns the CD player off. They are breathless and laugh to themselves until they are silent. They look at each other. Very suddenly* **Anne** *turns away as if she*

might cry but **Robert** *approaches and kisses her on the lips.*
A slight pause.

They kiss for a very long time. It is teenage and a joy to see. They stop
and look at each other. A slight pause.

They kiss again and can't let go. A slight pause.

They look at each other.

Robert   I'm sorry that I covered it over.

Anne   What?

Robert   The sick in your stockpot. But I didn't know what
to do with it. And the tinfoil was handy.

Anne *smiles but is then serious.*

Anne   I don't know what this means. I came down here to
Devon . . . I'm holding you back.

Robert   No.

Anne   I don't know where . . .

Robert   No. Listen to me.

Anne   But my age . . .

Robert   No.

Anne   I can't . . .

Robert   You can.

Anne   But what about what you want?

Robert   What?

Anne   We're at different stages in our lives.

Robert   I don't care . . .

Anne   We want different things . . .

Robert   I don't think we do.

A pause.

I want you.

A slight pause.

I don't know what love is but I do know that your face is the face I think about every morning.

A slight pause.

Your twinkling eyes and your hair. Your appalling bad manners in restaurants. Reading me favourite bits out of books you're reading. I think about your lined hands and kissing them. I think about the way you used to stand proudly in assembly. Then turn to me and catch my eye conspiratorially.

A slight pause.

All the places we've been in the world and the hung-over mornings we've had. The laughter, the endless laughter. Going out with our sixth formers because they're far more interesting than some of our fuck-shit boring colleagues. I don't know what. I can't say it. You know it all. Everything we've done. Everything we do. It's not just in my head. For God's sake, I'm completely in love with you. I've loved you for years and I love you now with a passion I never knew I had. I love you.

Anne I know. I love you.

Robert *smiles and* **Anne** *laughs.*

Anne What are we going to do?

Robert You're going to pack in teaching.

Anne And do what?

Robert And sell this place.

Anne I can't . . .

Robert You can . . .

Anne And do what?

Robert   We're going to buy a little place. To eat and drink.

Anne   Robert, we can't do that. Where?

Robert   Somewhere in the middle. I don't know. Oxford. Anywhere. We'll serve food we like. Fish. Halibut and risotto. Monkfish on noodles. And fishcakes. Our place. I'll cork wine bottles and put a piano in the corner and I'll play.

Anne   Will you?

Robert   Every night of the week. We'll do it.

A slight pause.

And we will do it and it doesn't matter that we're starting out later in life because I've found you and it's not nine years too late because it's now and it's us and I love you and I know I'm just a fat English teacher who drinks too much and insults your students but I think you love me in fact you said a minute ago that you did so let's please do it and be happy because I know we can because you make me happy in a way no one else can and if it doesn't work out it doesn't work out and I'll bugger off back to Essex and play snooker but I think it will I know it will because I believe I make you happier than anyone else ever has or can. Am I right?

He is out of breath.

Anne   I think you need to start going to the gym.

Robert   Well, what do you think?

Anne   I think I'd like to. I'd love to.

Robert *grins. A slight pause.*

Robert   Now, what is my mother going to say about this?

Anne   What's my son going to make of this?

They both think and look at each other. **Anne** *seems worried.*

We can't just give up teaching. We've kids expecting us to see them right through their upper sixth.

A pause.

Robert   Anne, we've been teaching nearly all our adult lives. And I've loved most of it. But sometimes I feel like I'm watching from the sidelines. The times I've discussed kids and I've used the phrase 'This concerns the rest of their life'. Well, fine. But this is my life. Our chance. We've done our bit. We've taught in state schools, grammar schools, private schools, the lot. We've got nothing to feel bad about. All right. Maybe we're not going to pack in teaching, but Anne . . .

Anne *thinks.*

Robert   Please come to Italy with me at half-term.

Anne *laughs and shakes her head.*

Anne   What about May? My Auntie May. I'd love us to go too but I feel duty-bound. I made a promise I'd take her to see the cemeteries.

Robert *groans, thinks and then has an idea.*

Anne   What is it?

Robert   Anne, this November's the eightieth anniversary of the armistice. Why don't you go then? It'll be a better time to visit. More poignant. There are probably going to be organisations for the old nurses represented. We could find out, couldn't we?

Anne   Yeah. We could.

Robert   The head'll let you have two or three days off. Your head's all right, isn't he?

Anne   Yeah. Great.

A slight pause.

Anne *nods. They don't know what to do. A pause.*

Robert *looks at his watch.*

Robert   Are we still going to lunch?

Anne   Yeah.

Robert   What are we going to do for a couple of hours?

Anne   I don't know, Robert.

Robert *looks at* **Anne** *hopefully, then hesitates.*

Robert   Will you come to bed with me?

Anne *looks at* **Robert** *and then away. A pause.*

Anne   I've got a video of my second-year production of *The Hobbit.* You haven't seen it yet, have you?

Robert   No.

Anne *hides underneath her sun hat.* **Robert** *laughs. Pause.*

Anne   I'm feeling quite hungry.

Robert   How do you fancy knocking up some scrambled eggs on toast?

Anne   OK. You can load the dishwasher.

Robert   Have you got any bacon?

Anne   I'll defrost some.

Robert   Excellent.

He looks up. So does **Anne**.

Look at that sky, will you. Not a bloody cloud.

Anne   It's perfect.

Robert   I love it.

Anne   It is extraordinary. Not a cloud.

Robert   I wish every day could be like this.

They continue looking up.

Anne   Look, there's a plane!

Robert   Where?

Anne   There! It's trailing a sign.

She points.

What does it say?

They try to read the banner.

Robert   'B & Q Summer Sale. Ends Today.'

They both laugh.

Anne   I thought for a moment someone sent one up for us.

Robert   Sort of like – 'Rozza and Azza together for ever.'

Anne *looks at* **Robert**. *He nods.* **Anne** *looks back up at the sky.*

Anne   For a minute I thought the whole world knew.

Robert   Yeah. They will.

They look at each other.

They will.

Anne   Will they?

Robert   I promise you.

Anne   I don't know if I can . . .

Robert   You can. Don't spoil it. Not now.

They both look back up at the sky.

Anne   Just look at it, Robert.

Robert   Perfect.

Anne   Completely blue.

A slight pause.

The last post plays quietly as **Robert** *and* **Anne** *continue to look at the sky.*

When the last post ends, **Robert** *and* **Anne** *look at each other.*

Slow fade.

I am deeply indebted to all the teachers who talked to me about what they do and to Lyn MacDonald's brilliant books, *1915 The Death of Innocence, The Roses of No Man's Land* and *To the Last Man: Spring 1918*, which inspired aspects of the third act. As she says, 'In the end it is the people who matter.'

And special thanks to the Royal National Theatre Studio for time and space to work.

DE, August 2000

M.A.D.

M.A.D. was first performed at the Bush Theatre, London, on 23 April 2004. The cast was as follows:

John	Lewis Chase
Alice	Jo McInnes
Kelly	Lee Ross
Luigi	Gerald Lepkowski
John	Daniel Mays

Directed by Hettie Macdonald
Designed by Jonathan Fensom
Lighting by Jason Taylor
Sound by David Benke

For Peter Thomson and James MacDonald

Acknowledgements

I would like to voice my admiration for Roy Williams, Gary Owen, John Sullivan and Robert Holman and the debt I owe them for their inspiration.

I would like to express my gratitude to Sarah Whitehead at the BBC for providing archive documentary material.

And finally I would like to offer heartfelt thanks to Michael McCoy, Ruth Little, Dawn Walton, Peter Thomson, Caroline Finch, Simon Stephens, Mike Wadding, Rufus Norris and Hettie Macdonald for their wise advice, and to Mike Bradwell and Nicola Wilson for their patience.

DE, March 2004

One

*Monday 24 September 1984. A semi-detached house in Collier Row,
Romford, Essex. A living room. There's a battered sofa and a matching
armchair propped up by a baking tin. There's a seventies-style coffee
table, a TV and a record player with at least a hundred LPs and
seven-inch singles. There's a boy's West Ham United football shirt
drying over a radiator, along with a pair of underpants and a
handkerchief. There's a bookcase but there are only a few books on it –
well-thumbed Mills and Boon novels and the odd* Beano *annual.
There is one picture of* **Kelly** *and* **Alice**, *much younger, on their
wedding day on the side and one of* **John**, *aged five. There's a small
dining table and on it is a piece of plywood covered with a Subbuteo
pitch, which has been glued to it. Model fencing rings the pitch, which
has a huge tea stain across the middle. There is a serving hatch through
which you can see into the kitchen, which is very small. The room looks
as if someone started to decorate, but then gave up after an hour or so.
Some of the wallpaper has been scraped off and there is no skirting
board. You can see from one patch of wallpaper where a picture or
mirror has been removed, and there is no lampshade covering the bulb,
which hangs from the ceiling.*

*Stacked where there is space against the walls are six dozen pairs of
shoes, tied in bundles of a dozen each. There's also a large cardboard
carton.*

John *packs away his Subbuteo players. He has his school uniform on.*

Alice *enters. She has two plates of ham, egg and chips. She watches*
John. *She puts the plates down on the middle of the pitch.* **John**
scowls at her. She exits.

John   Mum.

A slight pause.

Mum?

He picks up the plates. **Alice** *enters with knives and forks and tomato
ketchup.*

John   I said I'd do it.

Alice   It'll get cold.

They sit down and eat.

John   Is Dad still getting tickets for the Arsenal?

Alice   I don't know. I think so, babe.

John *dips chips in his egg yoke.*

Alice   I told you no fingers, mister man.

John   I'm looking forward to it.

Pause.

Do you still like Ray Stewart?

Alice   I don't like Ray Stewart.

John   You do. You said he's your favourite.

Alice   No I didn't. Eat your dinner.

John   You did.

A slight pause.

Alice   I quite like Geoff Pike.

John   Geoff Pike? Err. Yuk. Yukky-yuk-yuk. Geoff Pike.

Alice   Geoff Pike seems polite. He was on the radio.

John   You fancy Geoff Pike.

Alice   Shut up, John.

John   Geoff Pike's ugly.

Alice   Shut it, John.

John   You're bound to be ugly with a name like Pike.

Pause.

Do you think we've got a chance of winning the Milk Cup?

Pause.

Alice *nods.*

John   Am I ugly?

Alice   As sin.

John   No, I'm not, I'm handsome.

Alice *looks at his plate.* **John** *continues to eat his meal.* **Alice** *can't finish hers. Pause.*

Alice   Geoff Pike could give me a cuddle.

John *laughs and throws a chip at his mum.*

John   Can I put the radio on?

Alice   No.

John *does some hand-dancing and nods his head.*

John   Go on.

Alice   You wally.

John   I is an handsome wally.

Alice *laughs and* **John** *waggles his fingers on the way out.*

Alice   You can get your soldiers out after you've done your reading.

John   It's not a book, it's a – fat thing. What's wrong with *Danny the Champion of the World?*

A slight pause.

What about my other books?

Pause.

Can I go to the market on Saturday?

Alice   No.

John   Why?

Alice   I told you why.

Pause.

John   I don't want to bring my stuff down now.

A slight pause.

Alice   I thought you wanted to play down here?

John   I'm not playing.

Alice *studies him. Pause.*

John   What?

Alice   What are you doing, then?

John *exits.* **Alice** *feels in her pocket. She pulls out a little model tank.*

Alice   John? John. I found something.

Pause.

I said, I found something, John.

Silence.

John *enters with a custard cream.*

John   We give City such a thrashing.

Alice   I know.

John   Tony Cottee's goal was blinding. Where did you get that?

Alice   Guess?

A slight pause.

In the washing machine.

John *takes the tank and dips the biscuit in his egg.*

Alice   John?

John   What, Mum? Merm? Mum? What, Merm?

Alice   That's disgusting. Give it here, please.

John *eats it.*

Alice   What's the marking on the side there?

A slight pause.

John   Ray Stewart got one.

Alice   That red marking. There. Does that mean it's on a team?

John   No.

Alice   I can see where you painted it. There was some paint on your duvet.

A slight pause.

John   Cottee got the second one.

A slight pause.

It's not on a team. Dodo.

A slight pause.

It's the Second Guards Tank Army.

Alice *smiles.*

Alice   What?

John   They're the Russians.

John *hides under the table.*

Alice   What's the matter with you, silly?

John *pops his head up.*

John   Nothing.

Alice   I think it's good that you read the paper and take an interest.

Pause.

They look at each other. **Alice** *turns as she hears a noise.*

John   Team, you spas? You Joey. Joey Deacon. You spas.

Alice   Stop it.

A slight pause.

John   When they drop the bomb I hope it burns your boobs off.

Alice   That's nice. I hope it burns your willy off.

John   You said willy! You said willy!

Alice *and* **John** *roar with laughter. She moves to collect his plate.* **Kelly** *and* **Luigi** *enter.* **Kelly** *has his market pocket on top of a box.* **Luigi** *throws* **John** *a Walnut Whip. He has some fish and chips wrapped in newspaper under his arm.*

Kelly   This all right?

Alice   Yeah, we've had ours.

Alice *clears the plates and exits.* **John** *clocks this and unwraps his Walnut Whip.* **Luigi** *offers the takeaway.*

Kelly   Go on, Lulu, do the honours.

Luigi *follows* **Alice** *out into the kitchen.*

John   Luigi, can I have some fishy chips?

He is beside himself with laughter. **Kelly** *puts the box and the pocket on the floor.* **Kelly** *clocks the carton.* **John** *clocks the carton as well.*

Shall I?

Kelly   Go on.

John *leaps up and along with his dad quickly throws shoes and boots from the carton.* **Kelly** *helps him in and then covers his son with the shoes and boots.*

Kelly   Stop moaning, you wally.

Kelly *leaves him be and then goes to his pocket. He counts out the money – about two hundred pounds.* **Luigi** *comes back in with the fish and chips for him and* **Kelly**. **Luigi** *has a Scotch egg in his mouth and looks for* **John**. *He gives* **Kelly** *his food and then sits down.* **Kelly** *gives* **Luigi** *fifteen quid.*

Kelly   Give us a bite.

Luigi *passes the half-eaten Scotch egg.* **Alice** *enters with Dickens'* David Copperfield.

Alice   Where's John?

Kelly   In his room I think, love.

Alice   John!

Kelly   Have a look in there.

Alice *opens the box* **Kelly** *brought home. It contains a Betamax video recorder.*

Alice   Where did you get that?

Kelly   Lulu got it, didn't you, mate?

Alice   Where did you get it?

Luigi *shrugs.*

Kelly   Don't ask.

Alice   What do we need that for?

Kelly   There's some tapes in there. There's one of *Fools and Horses*. And *Stars Wars* an' all.

Alice   I thought we agreed.

Kelly   The fella came up the stall today, didn't he, Lu?

Alice   I thought we agreed?

Kelly   It was cheap, babe.

Alice   I bet it was.

Kelly   Don't fucking start.

A slight pause.

Alice   Who did you get it off?

Kelly   I don't know.

Alice   What do you mean, you don't know?

Kelly   Luigi saw him, didn't you, Lu?

Alice   Got it from the same place you got the telly, was it?

Kelly   Stroll on.

Alice   We agreed, Kelly.

John *pokes his head up out of the carton.* **Alice** *jumps, screams and* **Luigi** *spills his fish and chips all over the carpet.*

John   Have we got a video?

Kelly *laughs.* **Luigi** *tries to clear up the mess.*

Alice   Get out of there, John.

John *climbs out.* **Alice** *helps* **Luigi**.

John   Is it a Betamax? Put it on, Dad. Michael Eddy's got one. Go on, put it on. Put *Star Wars* on.

Alice   I told you.

Kelly   Give over.

Alice   You're a prat, you know that?

Kelly *goes to get the Betamax.* **Luigi** *starts eating the chips that are mostly back on his plate.*

Alice   I mean it.

John   Put *Star Wars* on. Merm.

Alice   If you think you're putting that thing on now you can shit in your hat and punch it, mate.

Kelly   Don't talk to him like that.

Alice   I'm not talking to him.

John   Who's he?

Kelly   What do you reckon, Lu?

Alice, **Kelly** *and* **John** *all look at* **Luigi**. *They wait for some time for a reply, but after a while he just shrugs and continues eating his chips.* **Kelly** *looks at* **Alice** *and smiles.* **John** *looks at the Betamax.*

Alice   What?

Kelly   I built my life around you, did what I –

Alice   You can bore off.

Alice *exits.* **John** *fiddles with the cables.* **Kelly** *goes to the LPs, looks for one and puts it on.*

Kelly   Come on Lulu.

'Ain't No Pleasing You' by Chas 'n' Dave plays. **Kelly** *sings.*

Go on, the Lulu.

Luigi *puts his plate of chips down on the sofa and gets up.* **Kelly** *and* **Luigi** *link arms and high-kick their legs in time.* **Luigi** *sings the words in Italian.* **John** *laughs and does some hand-dancing.* **Alice** *darts back in. She watches them fart around for most of the song, then lifts the arm of the record player before the end.* **Alice** *gives* **John** *the book.*

John   Mum?

Alice   Come on, you.

John *takes the book.*

Kelly   Leave him alone. He wants to play with his tanks.

A slight pause.

Alice   You've got to do your reading. I mean it.

A slight pause.

Kelly *thinks.* **Luigi** *eats his chips.*

John   If you hit me on the head with this I think I'd die stone dead.

Kelly   Do as your mother says.

Alice   Go on, John.

Kelly *shakes his head.* **Alice** *goes out into the kitchen.*

Kelly   Go on, son.

John   I used to like reading. I'm going to ring Nana.

Kelly *laughs.* **John** *exits.* **Kelly** *and* **Luigi** *look at each other and laugh.* **Luigi** *leaves his chips and helps* **Kelly** *set up the video.* **Kelly** *looks through the videos that came in the box.*

Kelly   Which one's the porno?

Luigi *passes* **Kelly** *a tape.*

Kelly   *The Jazz Singer?* Fucking hell, what's that, the lesbian version? Neil Diamond with his cock out in a cowboy hat?

Pause.

It's horny seeing a girl playing pool, ain't it?

A slight pause.

High heels. Denim skirt. Touch of red lipstick. Boner.

John *enters.* **Kelly** *hides the tape.*

Kelly   Go on. Out, Johnny.

John   She's in a mood.

Kelly   In the kitchen, plonker. Go on.

John   *David Copper-bollocks poo.*

Kelly   Don't swear.

John   You call it *David Copper-bollocks.*

Alice *enters.*

Alice   I'm giving you two minutes.

A slight pause.

John   I don't want to do it now.

Kelly   Do as your mother says.

A slight pause.

John   I'm not reading it.

Kelly   If you don't do your reading you'll end up flogging high heels like me.

John   I don't care. I'm not doing it.

Alice   You are.

Kelly   Shut it, will you, Al?

Alice   You shut it yourself.

A slight pause.

John   I don't want to do it. I want to go to Marshalls Park. I don't want to do it any more.

A slight pause

I mean it. I'm not going.

Luigi *stops what he's doing.* **Kelly** *goes to* **John** *but he runs out.* **Alice** *starts to follow.*

Kelly   Leave him alone.

Alice   That's right. Just like you.

Kelly   He's had enough. Leave him alone.

Alice *sits at the table instead. She looks at the little tank. She glares at* **Kelly***, who kneels by* **Luigi***. He switches on the television and inserts a tape in the video recorder.*

Alice   Turn that thing off.

Kelly   Leave off.

The sound of the Star Wars *theme begins but it soon segues into an episode of* Coronation Street.

Here, she's had her hands on this while I wasn't looking, eh, Lu?

Luigi *shrugs and sits back.*

Kelly   It's got *Stars Wars* on there.

Luigi   It's got *The Jazz Singer* on the other tape.

Alice   Have you got *The Jazz Singer?*

Kelly   No.

Pause.

Alice   I wanted to see *The Jazz Singer*.

A slight pause.

He wouldn't take me.

Pause.

He said we're saving up to go on holiday. Some chance.

Pause.

He never takes me to the pictures.

Kelly   Babe, I'd rather pass a cheese grater.

Pause.

See that little tank she's got there?

Alice   Who's she?

Kelly   John-boy's got loads of them in his room. All marked up. Few model planes as well.

Alice   You're always knocking him.

Kelly   I'm not.

Alice   You are.

A slight pause.

Kelly   Do you think he's in the shed again?

Alice *shrugs. They watch the television for a minute or two, then* **Kelly** *switches it off, stands and exits.* **Alice** *throws* **Luigi** *the tank. He looks at it and throws it back to her.*

Alice   Kiss me.

Luigi *shakes his head.*

Alice   It's true what he says. John's got loads of them and he's mad on maps.

Luigi *moves towards her. He takes her hand, turns it over and kisses the palm.*

Luigi   *Voglio averlo adesso. Lo voglio. Lo voglio. Desidero che eravamo soli.*

Alice   I love it when you speak like that.

Luigi *kisses her wrist.*

Alice   Will you come round?

Luigi *kisses her arm.*

Alice   Will you kiss my neck?

Luigi *nods. He moves to kiss her neck.* **Alice** *smiles.*

Alice   Not now, you pillock.

Luigi *puts his hand on her hip. He stares at her intently.*

Alice   Will you kiss my tits? Just here. And here.

Luigi *nods.*

Alice   I want to watch you run your tongue all over my tits and my nipples. Right down my body. In my belly button, it's all right, I'll bath. No fluff. Right down, down, down. If I shut my eyes I can feel you doing it to me now, Luigi, on my fanny.

Luigi   You know you're a beautiful lady, Alice, but you're no poet.

Alice   You can write me a poem any day. Write me one. Oh, write me one. I'm not interested in bluebells and champagne. Write me something sexy. Write words that make me melt. All melted like I am now. Hot, sticky and hot. I bet you can put down words. There's so much going on inside you, isn't there? I can see it. If they was upstairs I'd go down on you now. I'd suck you dry. When I'm finished with you you'll have bollocks like a pair of shrivelled raisins. I'm good at it. Shall I send them out for a loaf? Milk, we need milk, I'm sure.

Luigi *moves away from* **Alice**, *who follows.* **Kelly** *enters. He clocks them both.*

Alice   How's John?

A slight pause.

Kelly   He's all right.

A slight pause.

Alice   That's good, then.

A slight pause.

Kelly   He doesn't want to do his exam.

Luigi *sits down and picks at his fish and chips.* **Kelly** *watches him.*

Kelly   He's a stubborn little basket.

A slight pause.

Like his mother.

Alice *sticks two fingers up at* **Kelly**.

Kelly   Why did you tell him he can't come down the stall?

Pause.

John *saunters in with two shoeboxes, one under each arm.*

Kelly   What have you got there, boy?

John   Nothing.

Kelly   Come on, I'll give you a game of Subbuteo. Bagsy Ajax.

John   I don't want to play Subbuteo.

Kelly   Come on.

John   Mum?

Alice *ignores them and sits next to* **Luigi** *on the sofa.*

Kelly   Come on, wally.

John   I don't want to.

Pause.

Can we put *Star Wars* on?

Kelly   It's not *Star Wars*.

John   You said it was *Star Wars*, Dodo.

Kelly   I know, but it's not on the tape, son.

John   You don't let me do anything I want. You never let me do anything I want.

Kelly   You get your own way all the time!

Alice   Leave him alone!

John *wants to cry but bites his lip.*

Kelly   Come on, give us a game.

John *thinks.*

John   Will you give us a game, Luigi?

A slight pause.

I'll be West Ham. You can be Ajax.

Kelly   He'll want to be Juventus, won't you, Luigi?

Alice   He wants you to be Ajax, Luigi.

They both look at **Luigi**. *A slight pause.*

Luigi   Have you got Tottenham Hotspur?

John   Dad trod on the box and Mum hoovered up one of the players. She always does things like that. I was going to glue it as well.

Alice   Who's she?

John   You always do things like that.

Alice   No, I don't.

John   We're not even allowed to wipe our hands on the towel in the bathroom.

Alice   Don't be silly.

John   It's for show.

Luigi *gets up and heads over.*

Luigi   What team would you like me to be?

John   Ajax.

John *and* **Luigi** *put the players out on the pitch.* **Kelly** *sits on the sofa next to* **Alice**, *but as soon as he gets comfy she gets up and sits in the armchair.* **Luigi** *throws* **Kelly** *the money pocket.* **Alice** *pointedly sits facing in the other direction.* **Kelly** *takes his asthma inhaler from the pocket and has a puff.* **John** *is about to kick off when* **Luigi** *turns to* **Kelly** *and* **Alice**.

Luigi   I think I should be making a move.

Kelly   I think that might be an idea, mate.

Alice   No, you stay.

A slight pause.

John   Take no notice, Lulu. You know what they're like. If you want we can swap ends so you don't have to look at them while you're playing. It would put me off.

Kelly   Watch your cheek.

Alice   Like you watch yours.

Luigi   OK. We kick off then.

Luigi *and* **John** *begin their match. They play for at least three minutes before anyone speaks.*

John   Go on, Pike. He's Mum's favourite, ain't he, Mum? Merm.

Alice *watches the game.* **Kelly** *watches her.*

Kelly   I never thought Subbuteo was a spectator sport.

Luigi *turns and* **John** *scores a goal.*

Luigi   Eh!

John   Goal! Goal! Cottee! Goal!

John *runs around the room singing 'I'm Forever Blowing Bubbles'.*

Kelly   Go on, John-boy!

Alice   That's not fair, John, that's cheating!

Kelly   He's done you right up, mate!

Luigi   The spirit of Paolo Rossi always wins in the end.

Kelly *stands.*

Kelly   Come on, John, Luigi's had his turn.

Alice   He's playing Luigi.

A slight pause.

Kelly *advances.* **Luigi** *moves out of the way for him.*

Kelly   Come on, give your dad a go.

John *walks away from the table and takes one of the boxes of soldiers.*

Kelly   Come on, son, don't sulk. Give your dad a game.

John *takes one of the boxes and sits in the armchair. He lifts a soldier from the box. It is painted blue.*

John   The blue ones are NATO and the red ones are the Warsaw Pact. Do you know what the Warsaw Pact is, Luigi?

Kelly   John?

John   They're the commies.

Kelly   Why won't you give me a game? That's not fair, is it?

John   Making me do things all the time's not fair.

Kelly   Sod you, then. Sod the pissing lot of you! I've pissing had it up to my eyeballs with both of you, you self-centred bastards! I've pissing had enough of it here – you can get on with it, the lot of you!

Alice   Go on, you ignorant bastard! You push it! It'll take me two minutes to get my cases out of the loft!

Kelly   Then do it. Don't keep threatening me – do it!

Kelly *storms into the kitchen.*

Alice   Go on, you bloody kid! Like you always do, you pig!

Kelly *darts back in.*

Kelly   And you! In your bedroom and do your reading now!

John *darts to* **Alice**.

Kelly   In your room now!

Alice   Leave him alone!

Kelly *takes his belt off.* **John** *hides in* **Alice***'s armpit.*

Kelly   Get in your bedroom with that book now or I swear your arse is going to be red raw.

Alice   You so much as dare and I'll fucking brain you.

Pause.

Kelly   And if you think I'm going take you to Upton Park again you've got another think coming!

He exits. **Alice** *nips out after him.* **John** *hides in the corner of the sofa.* **Luigi** *isn't sure what to do. He picks up his fish and chips and continues eating. He sits down on the sofa.* **John** *turns and looks at* **Luigi**.

Kelly (*off*)   Just fuck off and leave me be!

Pause.

John   Did you see that *Threads* last night?

Luigi *nods. A slight pause.*

John   Do you think there's going to be a war, Luigi?

Luigi *shakes his head.*

John   I do.

A slight pause.

That's going to happen to us. It is.

A slight pause.

They're going to drop nuclear bombs on London.

A slight pause.

Did you see it, Luigi? Dad didn't want me to watch it but Mum said I could because I need general knowledge for me entrance exam. Did you see it, Luigi?

Luigi   Everyone saw it, I think.

He stands with his plate.

Do you want me to stay for a while?

John   They'll be all right. It always blows over.

He nods towards the sofa. **Luigi** *smiles. A slight pause.*

Mum and Dad'll die because Dad won't have bothered to lean the doors to for a shelter.

He sits down. A slight pause.

I hope I die. Like the boy with the game. Probably won't.

A slight pause.

I'll have to drag their bodies out. But there won't be any bin bags because they'll all be melted. The fallout looked nice, didn't it? Like snow. It never snows, does it?

Luigi *sits down. A slight pause.*

John   Do you remember when I was sick on the stall? Imagine being sick all the time. I've only ever been sick for half an hour and that was nasty.

A slight pause.

They'll be legs sticking out of the rubble at the end of our road. I hope it's Mrs Saunderson. She never throws me back my football. I'll have to wrap up Dad in the carpet. Might use their duvet if it's not too singed. It'll be horrible because me dad's slippers will be poking out of the end. Don't know what I'll do with Mum.

A slight pause.

Me mum says she wants to be cremated. P'rhaps I can drag some bits of furniture and do it in the garden, eh, Luigi? Like a Viking Queen or something. I don't know if I could do it, Luigi. Do you think that's silly? Could you do that? She gets right on my nerves, but she's not that bad, is she?

Pause.

They'll probably be all right. They're always all right, ain't they, Luigi? Just my luck that'll be, I never get any peace and quiet.

A slight pause.

Dad'll be in the market selling radiated shoes for tins of rusty baked beans. Mum'll be moaning about the cold, looking for water.

A slight pause.

Did you see the woman cuddling the dead baby? All them black bodies? Reminded me of dead seagulls after an oil slick.

A slight pause.

Dad says he hates seeing a stray dog. Says they're like old soldiers who need a kip. That's what he says, eh, Luigi?

A slight pause.

I'll have to go out looting. I think it'll be scary. And exciting. Creeping round the smashed-up houses. I can kill rats to sell and find things that have survived. Like a video game.

There was one in *Threads*, wasn't there, Luigi? I'd like a video game. I better not get caught. I'll end up prisoner in the tennis courts up Lawns Park. Traffic wardens'll have guns to guard us. I might get shot.

A slight pause.

Mind you, they'll probably run right out of bullets. Knowing my luck I'll get hung. From the market frames in the market place. Everyone'll be watching. Me legs'll be dangling down and I'll be dead as a dodo.

A slight pause.

There won't be anything left, will there, Lulu?

A slight pause.

Nothing.

A slight pause.

Upton Park'll be ruined.

A slight pause.

Romford Market'll be gone. All the frames will be twisted.

A slight pause.

At least I won't have to go to the posh school.

A slight pause.

I think you're right, Luigi. It won't happen, will it?

Luigi   I'm sure.

John   What do you reckon, then?

Luigi   It's the nuclear bombs which make the peace, John-boy. By threatening each other all the time, Russia and America – they keep the peace. I promise you.

John *leans on* **Luigi**, *who puts his arm around* **John**.

Luigi   You OK?

John   Are you going to get married, Luigi?

Luigi   I don't know. Maybe one day.

John   If you get married and you get your own house, can I come and stay sometimes?

Luigi   If you want to.

John   Can I?

John *smiles and leans his head in* **Luigi***'s lap.*

Luigi   What?

John   Luigi, you're the bee's knees.

Luigi *laughs.* **John** *spots his tank.*

John   You can have it, if you like. Go on.

Luigi   It's OK.

John   Go on, I've got loads of them. I'd really like you to have it, Lulu.

Luigi   Why?

John   Because.

Pause.

Luigi   Would you like a fishy chip?

John *gives* **Luigi** *the tank, which he puts in his pocket.* **John** *takes the plate and picks up a chip, which he examines.*

Luigi   They're nice cold.

John *puts down the plate but holds up the chip.*

Luigi   Don't you like them cold?

John   No.

A slight pause.

There. Look. It's one of Dad's toenails.

Blackout.

Two

It's late, the room is dark, lit only by some spill from the kitchen.

John *enters. He wears some pyjama bottoms and is barefoot. He shivers and looks for his West Ham shirt, which he takes from the radiator. He looks around and goes to the TV and video. He examines the tapes. He switches on the TV and puts one of the tapes in. He turns down the volume a touch and fiddles with the channels until the* Star Wars *music comes on.*

John   Yes.

The Star Wars *theme segues into* Coronation Street.

Poo.

He switches the tape off and puts another one in. A porn film comes on. The sound of a couple fucking and moaning is audible. **John** *watches open-mouthed – for some time.* **John** *looks down his pyjamas to see if anything is happening – there isn't. Suddenly* **John** *hears a noise. He panics, switches the TV off, and tries to eject the tape, but it's stuck.* **John** *looks around the room until he spots the large cardboard carton. He darts to it and clambers in.*

Kelly *enters. His hair is sticking up and he is wearing only his battered slippers, a vest and underpants. He scratches his arse and feels something. He looks around. He takes his pants off and puts them on the sofa. He fetches the pants from the radiator and puts on the clean pair, and then goes into the kitchen and puts some milk on the stove. He enters and switches the TV on. The programme is* Newsnight, *hosted by John Tusa. An American commentator is speaking. It's 10.42 p.m. The panel is discussing the docu-drama* Threads *and the documentary* On the Eighth Day, *screened immediately before* Newsnight. **Kelly** *watches until, in reply to Robin Cook's remark, 'You cannot fight a nuclear war, there can be no victory,' he says:*

Kelly   Go on, you ginger prat.

He goes back into the kitchen. He comes back in with a mug of hot milk, sits down in the armchair and watches the programme until, in reply to George Walden's remark, 'Any film which is really worth its salt is not simply going to arouse people's fears,' he says:

Yeah, you'll be all right, you toffee-nosed prick, you'll be in a comfy little shelter.

He drinks his milk. After a couple of minutes **Alice** *enters. She is in her nightdress and dressing gown.*

Alice   John's not in his room.

Kelly   He's probably having a shit. I think he's a nocturnal dumper.

Alice   He's not in the toilet.

Kelly   I don't know.

Alice   Do you think he's gone anywhere?

Kelly   He's probably sulking in the shed.

Alice   Well, go and have a look.

Kelly   You go and have a look. You've got your dressing gown on.

Alice *moves.*

Kelly   Leave him. It'll do him good.

Alice   What, catching his death?

She spots the underpants on the sofa and looks at them.

If you leave another shitty pair of pants in here I'm going to shove them so far down your throat they'll come out the other end.

A slight pause.

Kelly   Come and give us a cuddle.

Alice *switches the TV off.*

Kelly   Stroll on.

Alice   Go down the shed and I might think about it.

Alice *switches the light on. It hurts* **Kelly**'s *eyes.*

Kelly   It's like pulling teeth.

A slight pause.

I bet old Maggie don't treat Dennis like this. I bet she's there in Number Ten now in a cheeky lacy number with a gin and tonic for the old boy in her fluffy blue mules.

Alice   Go out the shed. Go on.

Kelly   I bet she's down on that expensive carpet sucking him like a nancy boy in a spaghetti-eating race.

Alice   You, you're like a dog on heat.

Kelly   I wish.

A slight pause.

I wish. I'm jealous of that Alsatian they've got next door. He's shagging left, right and centre. I saw him having a go at old misery guts' Labrador behind my van. When he'd finished the cheeky bastard had a piss over my new panelling as well. I find I identify more with that mongrel. The one who wanders round the market with the moccasin I give him last Christmas.

A slight pause.

I swear he winked at me when I flicked him a chip on Saturday.

Alice   You don't want John to do this exam, do you?

A slight pause.

Be honest.

Kelly   If he doesn't want to do it, he doesn't want to do it.

A slight pause.

Alice   You didn't answer my question.

Kelly   I did.

Alice   John's not going to volunteer to take an exam that will take him away from all his mates, is he?

Kelly   I know it's a good school, babe, but what's the point if he's not going to be happy there?

Alice   How do you know he's not going to be happy there?

Pause.

Kelly   The boys there, the people that send their kids there, they're not like us.

A slight pause.

I hope he gets in. I hope he gets the education, babe. I hope he makes some good mates.

Alice   You don't help. You don't encourage him. You always leave it to me.

Kelly   Listen, you're not the one freezing your bollocks off queuing up for tickets at West Ham at nine o'clock in the morning. I bet Luigi has a field day.

Pause.

Alice   What do you mean by that?

Kelly   What do you think I mean?

Kelly *whistles and makes a gesture with his hand.*

Alice   Luigi wouldn't?

Kelly   Don't be stupid.

A slight pause.

Alice   Don't talk to me like that.

Kelly   He has a bite. Where do you think he got that video? I tell you what, babe, it wasn't from Rumbelows.

Alice   I knew it was knocked off!

Kelly   So's the telly.

Alice   I said to you –

Kelly   And the cooker.

Alice   I said to you, no video.

Kelly   Fucking stroll on.

Alice *thinks and then sits on the arm of the armchair.*

Alice   I want him to do well.

A slight pause.

Kelly   I don't think it will take the strain, Al.

Alice   Bog off.

Alice *kisses* **Kelly** *on the cheek.*

Kelly   Next time aim a bit lower.

Alice *gives* **Kelly** *a whack.*

Kelly   That hurt.

A slight pause.

It's doing my brains in.

Alice   What is?

Kelly   He's in a world of his own.

Alice   He's not.

Kelly   He is. He's in his room, full of these ideas. All these soldiers and tanks. What's all that about? I'd have thought he'd have grown out of Subbuteo by now, babe.

Alice   That's rich.

Kelly *laughs.*

Kelly   You know what he said to me on the stall on Saturday? I had three birds on the go, Luigi's disappeared and I've got wally at my elbow – 'Dad, Dad.' So I said, 'What d'you want, son?' And he said, 'Do you think that if the Russians shoot down another plane America will launch its nuclear missiles as a reprisal?'

Alice *laughs.*

Kelly   I said, 'I've got no idea, boy, but if you don't get me a pair of lilac slingbacks in a size five quick sharp there'll be a few reprisals going on round your earhole.'

Alice *kisses him on the cheek.*

Kelly   You encourage him. Reprisal? Babe, I had to ask the Toby what it meant, he didn't know either and he had to get the dictionary out of the office.

A slight pause.

What's he going to be like at public school?

A slight pause.

Alice   He's growing up and getting a mind of his own, that's all. He's bright.

Kelly   He's changing.

A slight pause.

I don't like it.

Alice *cuddles* **Kelly** *and gives him a kiss on the cheek.*

Kelly   Why won't you kiss me on the lips?

Alice *looks at him. She gets up. Pause.*

Kelly   If I make us another cup of milk, will you come to bed with me?

Alice   I'll just go down the shed.

She nods.

I'm tired now.

Kelly   I don't mean to go to bed and go to sleep.

Pause.

I don't know what I've done wrong.

Pause.

What if he doesn't get a scholarship?

Pause.

Market's dead.

Pause.

Alice   I can go back to work.

Kelly   You're all right.

Pause.

What was going on earlier?

Alice   What do you mean?

Kelly   You and Luigi.

Alice   Nothing.

Pause.

You're being silly.

Kelly   Am I?

Alice   You are.

Pause.

I'll go and get John and I'll put my cap in.

Kelly   Don't do it just because I've said something.

Alice   Well, what do you pissing want then?

Pause.

What do you want me to do? Shut my eyes and pretend you're not there!

Kelly   You could try!

A slight pause.

Alice   I didn't mean it like that.

Pause.

I have tried.

Kelly   You haven't. You've not even given me a wank.

Alice   Fuck off, Kelly.

Pause.

Kelly   I don't know what I'm doing wrong.

Alice   You haven't done anything wrong.

Kelly   Then why do you turn away from me?

Pause.

Alice   If you want the truth, I don't love you like that any more.

Kelly *turns away, anguished. Long pause.*

Alice   What, do you want me to lie?

Kelly *looks at her. He is very upset. Pause.*

Kelly   What are you still doing here with me, then?

Pause.

Alice   Why do you think?

Kelly   I don't know, you tell me!

Alice   Because of John! Because of John, why do you think?

She starts to weep.

I do love you.

Kelly   That's not what you said, is it, babe?

Alice   I do love you.

Kelly   Don't try and turn it round!

Alice   I can't help it.

Alice *really cries. Pause.*

Kelly *gets up and goes over to the TV. He switches the video on and presses the eject button. It is still stuck. He explodes.*

Kelly   He's been fucking about with this video! It's not been in here five minutes and he's been fucking around with it and it's broken! That's it. John! John!

Kelly *storms out.*

Alice   I'm sorry! I'm sorry, I'm sorry, I'm sorry! I'm so sorry!

Kelly *hovers in the kitchen. He comes back in.*

Kelly   You've cut me in half. You –

Alice *wipes her eyes.*

Kelly   I could have gone. Don't you think I could have pissed off?

A slight pause.

What sort of life do you think I've got?

A slight pause.

I'm up at five o'clock every pissing morning of the week!

A slight pause.

If I'm not back in here by half past seven I get the third degree! There's not a pissing soul I can call a mate. All I've got is a life of misery with you!

Alice   What sort of a life do you think I've got?

Kelly   Go on. Go on!

Alice   Since we had John I've never had a life!

Kelly   You could get a job!

Alice   I wanted to work on the stall!

Kelly   You've never wanted to work!

Alice   I wanted to be on the stall with you!

Kelly   What, so you're on my back twenty-four hours a day, driving me round the twist?

Alice   As soon as John started school I said to you I didn't want to be at home!

Kelly   And what happened?

Alice   You've never given it a go!

Kelly   You turn up at ten o'clock, you're offhand with the customers –

Alice   Because you were flirting with them!

Kelly   Because I was trying to sell them a pair of shoes, darling, because, I know you might not be the sharpest knife in the drawer, but that is the aim of the operation!

Alice   You were flirting with them! I know how you are!

Kelly   All fucking day – nag, nag, nag, moan, moan, moan. It's wet. It's cold. What do you expect, it's fucking December! What, do you think I enjoy putting the stall out at six o'clock in the morning when it's pissing down with rain? It's all right for you to swan down there at half past ten –

Alice   Half past ten now!

Kelly   And you slope off at three o'clock!

Alice   I was picking John up from school! Being a good mother! Though you wouldn't know what that means. Trying to bring up a child!

Kelly   That's what you call it, is it? Making him into a fucking mummy's boy?

Alice   All you want him to do is run wild!

Kelly   I don't want him to run wild!

Alice   All you want him to do is sit on the stall, just like you!

Kelly   I don't, I don't!

Alice   You do, Kelly.

Kelly   I do want him to toughen up a bit. What's wrong with being a bit streetwise?

Alice   You're just frightened and jealous, jealous that he's got something that you haven't and you want to keep him down, bring him down to your level!

Kelly   No I don't, no I fucking don't!

A slight pause.

Don't you think I wish I had an education? Don't you think I wish I went to a good school? That my mum and dad dreamed for me to go to university instead of sending me down the market! I was ten! Ten! Ten, hobnail boots, plimsolls and horrible bastards in Roman Road! Don't you think I wish that, you fucking hard-nosed cunt?

Pause.

You've hurt me. You've really hurt me.

Long pause.

Alice   I do love you.

Kelly   Don't mug me.

Alice   I wanted to work on the stall with you.

Kelly   Don't you make a monkey out of me.

Alice   I do love you.

Kelly   Don't you mug me.

Alice   You're always moaning about money but you'll have Luigi on there. You'll have a tea leaf but you won't have your wife.

Kelly   Wife?

Alice   Yeah, that's right.

Kelly   Yeah, great pissing wife, why don't you just piss off out of it!

Pause.

Alice   I don't want to split up. You know I don't want that. I love –

Kelly   If you loved me you'd want to be with me!

Alice   I do want to be with you!

Kelly   Then be my wife!

A slight pause.

Alice   If the fucking's so important to you, then fuck me. You can fuck me all you want and I'll keep my mouth shut, just like I always do.

Kelly   I've got more chance of winning the pools than you keeping your trap shut.

Alice *pulls off her dressing gown.*

Alice   Go on. Fuck me.

Kelly   Put your clothes on.

Alice   Go on, fuck me now.

Kelly   You're out of your mind, you're loopy, you are.

Alice   Go on. Fuck me.

Kelly   Just piss off and leave me alone.

Alice   Suck your cum out of my arsehole. That's what you want. That's what you like, you horrible bastard.

Kelly *slaps* **Alice**. *She attacks him. The fight is vicious. They roll into the armchair.* **Alice** *hits* **Kelly** *with the baking tin.* **Kelly** *gets up holding his head.* **Alice** *attacks him again and he falls into the bundles of shoeboxes. He hits her with one. They use them to attack* *each other. Stiletto shoes fall out.* **Alice** *grabs a stiletto.* **Kelly** *pushes her back and they crash into the table. The Subbuteo pitch and players fly everywhere.* **Alice** *attacks him with the heel of a stiletto. It takes* **Kelly** *by surprise and she gets the upper hand quickly as she hits him around the face with the shoe.*

Kelly   Stop it, stop it, you'll fucking kill me! You'll kill me!

Alice *drops the stiletto and moves away.* **Kelly** *sits up. His face is bloody.*

Alice   Oh Christ, Kelly. I didn't mean to –

She quickly takes the handkerchief from the radiator. She goes to **Kelly**, *kisses him, wipes his face, kisses him again.* **Kelly** *pushes her away. Pause.*

Are you all right?

Kelly *nods.*

Alice   Are you sure? Let me –

Kelly   You get away from me.

A very long pause, much longer than you think you can get away with.

I've never wanted anyone else.

Long pause.

Women come down the stall every day of the week and I know I can have my pick.

A slight pause.

I could have my pick like Luigi does.

A slight pause.

But I don't want that. I've never wanted that.

A slight pause.

Why do you think I have him on the stall? He's only got to bat his eyelids and speak a bit of Italian and a one-legged,

blind, geezer-bird would still walk away with some ankle
boots and a pair of pop socks.

A slight pause.

He puts more money in my pocket than he ever takes.
Hundred times over. Don't you knock Luigi. He's all right.
He doesn't take a liberty.

A slight pause.

He's the one who chats up the birds. Not me.

Pause.

I've got my faults but I'm not a bad man.

A slight pause.

Alice   I know you're not.

Kelly   Do you? I don't think you do, babe.

Alice   I know you're not a bad man. Why do you think
I've stayed with you? Why do you think I love you?

Kelly   Don't keep saying that word.

A slight pause.

I'm not a bad father. Don't you think I wish I was here with
him?

A slight pause.

No, I'm the mug who'll be putting the cricket flannels round
his arse.

Alice   I know.

Kelly   Why do you think I want him to come to the stall?
Why do you think I like John-boy on the stall with me? But
you won't let him.

Alice   I do.

Kelly   You suffer it. I'd never see nothing of him. You'd
like that.

Alice   I don't want that.

Kelly   I've never ever so much as looked at anyone else.

A slight pause.

We went in the boozer after we'd packed up tonight. And there was some bird in there playing pool. I thought she was giving Luigi the eye but she wasn't – she was looking at me. She was bending right over in front of me, showing her arse to me, making excuses to brush past me to get the chalk.

A slight pause.

All I could think about was when we first went out. I used to watch you fiddling with your hair, thinking about us getting home and being together.

Alice   I'm bored, Kelly, I'm bored out of my mind, I'm going mad with it, I'm so bored!

Long pause.

Jean came round.

Pause.

She's got three girls working for her now. She's just taken on a fella to clean the carpets and pick up and drop off the ironing. Both her kids are at prep schools. She said she's been nominated for the Essex Award. Best new business.

Pause.

My sister was always the slow one.

Pause.

Why can't we talk like this all the time? What's wrong with us, Kelly? What's wrong?

Pause.

Do you think one of us should go and get John?

Kelly *turns away. Pause.*

Alice   Please, Kelly.

Kelly *nods.*

Kelly   What's my face like?

Alice   Pig ugly.

Kelly   That's not funny.

Alice   Why have we got to have a row like this to be honest?

Pause.

Kelly   We haven't got to any more, have we, babe? Not now it's out in the open.

Alice   Until the next time.

A slight pause.

I wish I'd never met you. I wish I'd never had John. You're making me into a bully.

Kelly   You're not.

A slight pause.

Don't be silly.

A slight pause.

I think you're lovely.

Alice   Still?

Kelly *nods.*

Alice   Even though I tried to smash your face in?

Kelly   Don't be silly.

A slight pause.

I can try harder. I will, babe. I promise you.

He looks around the room.

We'll get this room finished, eh?

A slight pause.

We can do it together, eh, babe? I'll get up the yard and get the skirting cut up. I've still got the bit of paper with the lengths.

A slight pause.

Bit each night after work.

A slight pause.

P'rhaps you can have your own pitch on the market, eh? Down the other end. You can do Men's and I'll do Ladies'. We'll be like Mr and Mrs.

A slight pause.

Fresh start, eh?

A slight pause.

You're a bloody nightmare, you are, but I love you and I've loved you since the minute I see you dancing round your handbag in the Lamb.

Alice   I know.

Pause.

Kelly   I won't go near you if you don't want me to.

Alice   I do.

Kelly   I don't want you to leave me.

A slight pause.

Alice   I don't want to.

A slight pause.

I think it's too late, Kelly.

Kelly   It's not.

Alice   It is.

Kelly   You said you still love me.

A slight pause.

Alice   I've done something terrible.

A slight pause.

Kelly   It's just a few nicks and bruises.

A slight pause.

Alice   I think we should call it a day.

Kelly *explodes.*

Kelly   Then call it a day then! It's always hanging over me! You either want me or you don't want me, just don't keep making my life a misery!

Alice   What, like my life?

Pause.

Kelly   What?

Alice   Nothing.

Kelly   What?

Alice   I said, nothing.

Kelly   What is it?

A slight pause.

Alice   I slept with Luigi.

Kelly   You what?

Pause.

Alice   I said, I went to bed with Luigi.

Pause.

Kelly   I knew. I knew something –

Kelly *is dazed. He knocks into the sofa.*

Alice   I've ruined everything. I know.

Kelly *howls, something from deep inside the gut, but he doesn't cry. Long pause.*

Alice   I don't want to leave. I don't want you to leave me. I know what I've done.

Kelly *gets to his feet.* **Alice** *wipes her eyes.*

Kelly   Why did you do it?

Alice   I don't know.

Kelly   Am I that much of a useless bastard?

Alice   No.

Kelly   Why have you done it, then?

Alice   I don't know.

Kelly   When did it happen?

Alice   It doesn't matter.

Kelly   It matters to me.

A slight pause.

Alice   When he come to get the boots. Last week.

Pause.

Say something. Please. Say something, Kelly. Please, babe. Say something. I'm going mad.

Kelly   I thought you couldn't say anything more than you've said already tonight. To hurt me so much. But now you have.

A slight pause.

Alice   Forgive me. I'm begging you, babe. I'm sorry.

Kelly   I – can't – breathe.

He takes his inhaler from the bookcase and exits. Pause.

Alice *wipes her face. She weeps and then she wipes her face again when the tears stop. She tries to tidy the room a bit and then thinks.*

She switches on the TV. Newsnight *is still on. She watches it for a minute or so. Robin Cook speaks. After Cook says, 'Possibly even the extinction of the human race,' she turns.*

Alice   John?

She exits. Long pause.

John*'s fist punches through the side of the carton.*

Fade.

Three

The next morning.

All of the stock is cleared from the room except the large carton, the contents of which are now in a bin bag. **Kelly** *is sorting and putting his LPs and singles into the carton.* **Alice** *sits at the dining table, smoking.* **John** *has the Subbuteo pitch spread out on the carpet in the middle of the room. He has drawn a rough map of Europe on the pitch. He has his soldiers and tanks nearby.* **John** *studies his parents.* **John** *is still wearing his West Ham shirt and pyjama bottoms.*

John   Are you going to put out the stall?

Kelly   Not today.

John   Why's she smoking?

Pause.

Kelly   If your mother wants to kill herself that's her look-out. Why aren't you ready for school?

Pause.

Alice   Why don't you ask me?

John *turns away from her.*

Alice   Who's she?

John   I'm going to make breakfast.

He ignores her and arranges the soldiers and tanks on the map: red on one side and blue on the other.

Dad?

Kelly   What?

John   Come and look.

Kelly *stops what he's doing and crouches by* **John**. **Alice** *stubs out her cigarette and exits.*

John   It's not poofy.

Kelly   What's not poofy?

John   This.

Kelly   I know it's not, boy.

John   The red ones are the Warsaw Pact and the blue ones are NATO.

Kelly   Can you show me this later, son?

John   No.

A slight pause.

This is the Second Guards Tank Army. That's going to go up there to capture Denmark.

A slight pause.

This is the Twentieth Guards Army. This one's going to cross the river and capture Hanover. The British Army will fight this one.

A slight pause.

This is the Third Shock Army. This one's going to go towards the capital of West Germany.

A slight pause.

This is the Eighth Guards Army. This one is going towards Frankfurt.

A slight pause.

This is the First Guards Tank Army. This one is going to try and capture Stuttgart.

A slight pause.

It's not a game. It's a history of the future. It's what's going to happen. I've got a book about it.

A slight pause.

In the *Threads* it said everything would start in the oilfields but in my book it says that it starts in Yugoslavia.

John *looks round. He exits.* **Kelly** *thinks. He goes to the video recorder. He fiddles around with it until eventually the tape ejects. He sees that it is* The Jazz Singer *and thinks.* **John** *enters.*

John   Mum's coming back in when she's finished smoking.

Kelly   What?

A slight pause.

John   I said I'd make us breakfast, Dodo.

Kelly   I'm not hungry, John.

John *clocks the tape and* **Kelly** *puts it in the box with the records.* **John** *goes to the video and looks through the tapes.*

Kelly   I told you, we've not got *Star Wars*.

John *finds one, turns the TV on and puts a video in.*

Kelly   I think it's broken, John-boy.

He presses 'play'. An episode from the first series of Only Fools and Horses – *'The Second Time Around' – plays.* **John** *sits on the sofa.* **Alice** *enters and watches* **Kelly**. **Kelly** *sits on the sofa next to* **John**. *They watch for a couple of minutes.* **Alice** *watches too.*

John   Come on, Dad.

Kelly *is restless and stands.* **John** *eventually laughs at a joke.*

John   Come and watch it with me, Dad. Don't you like *Only Fools and Horses* any more? I thought it was your favourite?

Kelly *sits with* **John**. *A minute passes.*

John *leans his head in* **Kelly***'s lap. Another minute passes.*

They laugh. **Alice** *sits at the table.* **Kelly** *strokes* **John***'s hair. They watch, occasionally laughing, for at least five minutes, perhaps longer.* **Alice** *has enough and goes to switch the TV off.*

Kelly   You dare and I'll kick it all the way down the garden. I'm not joking.

Alice *sits in the armchair. They are quiet. They watch for another minute.*

Kelly   I've got to go and stay with your nan for a while.

Pause.

John *stands, he switches off the TV and looks at both his parents in turn.*

John   I wasn't in the shed. I was in the carton.

A slight pause.

I heard everything you said in your row last night.

Alice *and* **Kelly** *are upset.*

John   I'm not upset. I was last night. But everyone was upset last night.

John *switches the TV back on.* Only Fools and Horses *still plays.* **John** *sits back down on the sofa and puts his head in his father's lap. Silence except for the TV.*

Kelly *wipes his eyes and* **John** *kisses him on his cheek.*

Kelly   I'm sorry.

John   Don't be a wally.

Pause.

Alice   John? John, come here, please, son. Come here.

John   In a minute.

Alice   John, I'm upset.

Pause.

Kelly   Go and give your mother a cuddle, she's upset.

John *goes to her.*

Alice   Come here.

John   I'm too old to sit on your lap any more.

He awkwardly holds her hand for a minute and then returns to the TV, which he switches off.

Can I show you my stuff?

Kelly   I need to get my things together, son.

John   I'm not upset any more. Why are you?

Kelly   It's not simple like that.

Alice   Let him show you.

Kelly *nods.* **John** *kneels by the map.*

John   The Russian armies will come into West Germany like this.

John *moves the tanks and the soldiers.*

And the NATO armies will be really trying hard. It'll be bad because after three days there will be too many of them. And our ones will release the chemicals and the germs.

A slight pause.

The Russian soldiers' faces will be twisted and yellow. And so will our soldiers'.

A slight pause.

There'll be bombs going off in different places. Planted by
the Russian spies. To make everyone panic. So that the
people say to Mrs Thatcher to stop the war.

A slight pause.

But Mrs Thatcher won't stop the war, will she? If I was
setting a bomb off in Romford I'd plant it in the Wimpy.

A slight pause.

There won't much electric.

A slight pause.

And they'll put *Coronation Street* and Del-Boy on the telly all
the time. To cheer everyone up.

A slight pause.

Can you see how many soldiers and tanks they've got
compared to us? There'll be too many of them against ours.

A slight pause.

What happens then is our side will bomb them with our
nuclear bombs. The small ones. To try and smash up all
their armies. And they'll do the same back to us.

He points to the map.

All of this will be useless.

A slight pause.

Then what will happen is the Russians will say that if we
don't stop using our nuclear bombs on their armies they'll
bomb us on one of our cities as a warning, they'll nuke us
good and proper if we don't stop. But we won't stop. And
there'll be a bomb on New York.

A slight pause.

New York will be flat and black. Like if you looked at it
from space. Like the patch down the end of the garden after
Fireworks Night.

A slight pause.

Then we'll nuclear-bomb two of their cities as a warning back and that's when the Russians will launch all their nuclear missiles.

A slight pause.

That's when we'll all die.

A slight pause.

See, it's not poofy. I'm too big for Subbuteo now, anyway.

A slight pause.

I'm not doing my exam any more.

A slight pause.

We can't afford it.

A slight pause.

We can all be together down the market. Can't we? That'll be better?

A slight pause.

Kelly   John, I'm going to your nan's.

John   No, you're not.

Pause.

If we all work together on the stall then you won't need to pay Luigi.

Pause.

We can go on holiday. We've never been on holiday, have we, Mum? We can go to Spain like Michael Eddy and his mum and dad.

Alice   John, stop it.

Kelly   I'll make sure you're all right. I promise you, son.

John   I don't want you to go.

Pause.

I don't want you to go to Nan's.

Kelly   I know.

John   If you go to Nan's I'll never speak to you again.

A slight pause.

I'm not doing my exam. What's wrong with us all being together?

Kelly   Me and your mother can't be together any more.

John   Yes, you can.

Kelly   I'm sorry, son, I can't.

John   Yes, you can, you're not trying.

Pause.

Kelly   Your mother's upset me too much. I've got to go to your nan's.

Alice   Don't you blame it all on me.

Kelly   Well, whose fault is it then, eh? You tell me, babe.

Pause.

John   I'll go and live with Nana.

Pause.

I know you wish I wasn't born.

Alice   That's not true. You're the best thing that happened to us.

John   You said.

Alice   I was upset.

John   So was I.

Pause.

I don't mind. As long as I can take my soldiers.

A slight pause.

As long as I can come and see you every now and again, I don't mind.

A slight pause.

I think I'd like it living with Nana. Dad don't like her smoking. And he don't like her tea, does he? Do you, Dad? I like Nana's tea. I like it milky.

A slight pause.

Kelly   You're not going to Nana's, boy. I want you to stop here with your mother and I want you to do your exam.

John *heads towards the kitchen.*

Kelly   What are you doing?

John   I'm thinking.

John *exits.* **Kelly** *continues with his records.* **Alice** *lights a cigarette. The sound of pots and pans crashing in the kitchen is audible.* **Kelly** *stops.*

Kelly   I'm going to thrash that boy if he doesn't pack it in.

Alice   He's only making breakfast.

Kelly   John! John!

Alice   He doesn't want you to go.

A slight pause.

You win, Kelly. You win.

A slight pause.

Kelly   You can't alter what's happened.

Alice   I know.

A slight pause.

We can try.

A slight pause.

What do you think's going to happen if you piss off?

A slight pause.

It won't only be your life you'll be ruining.

The sound of eggs sizzling in the kitchen drifts in.

Kelly   I can't stay here.

Alice   What do you want me to do? I can't take it back!

A slight pause.

There's nothing you can do to me.

Kelly   I know.

A slight pause.

I don't want to win.

A slight pause.

Alice   So you'd rather piss off and ruin everything we've got?

Kelly   What have we got?

A slight pause.

Alice   You can see what you're doing.

Kelly *explodes with rage.*

Kelly   What do you expect, he's just a boy! He's a boy, he's a boy!

Alice   If you really care about your son, don't you raise your voice again.

A slight pause.

If that's all you can do, then go now, go now. Go on.

Kelly   I'll go when I want.

Kelly *goes to the video, which he disconnects.* **John** *enters.*

John   Sit up at the table, everyone. It's nearly ready.

A slight pause.

You're not taking the video as well, are you, Dad?

Kelly   Have the video!

Alice   Kelly.

Kelly   Have it! Have the lot of it!

He takes money from his pocket, which he throws at her.

Here, buy another one! Buy another one, I don't care!

A slight pause.

John   I don't mind.

A slight pause.

I don't mind, Dad.

A slight pause.

I don't.

John *exits. Pause.*

Alice   Come and sit at the table.

Kelly *thinks and sits at the table.* **John** *enters with ketchup, brown sauce and cutlery which he puts on the dining table. He takes the table mats from the coffee table and sets the dining table. He exits. Pause.*

John *enters with two plates for his parents. Each plate has a fried egg and about half a dozen custard cream biscuits. He puts them in front of his mum and dad.*

John   You can start without me.

John *exits. They look at their breakfast. Pause.*

John *enters with his plate, which has more custard creams. He sits down and dips a biscuit in his egg yolk.*

Kelly   Is this a wind-up?

John   No.

Kelly   I'm not in the mood, boy.

John   It's not.

A slight pause.

It's happy food.

He eats. A slight pause.

It's nice.

Kelly *and* **Alice** *don't know what to do.*

John   Eat it!

A slight pause.

I said, eat it!

A slight pause.

I did it specially for you and neither of you are eating it.
I did it specially!

Kelly *dips a biscuit in his egg yolk and so does* **Alice**. *They eat for some time in silence.* **Kelly** *and* **Alice** *don't feel much like it, but eat, if slowly.*

Alice   It's quite nice, really.

John *stops eating and watches his parents.*

John   Not everyone thinks there's going to be a war.

A slight pause.

I was talking to Luigi about the *Threads*.

A slight pause.

Is I still an handsome wally?

Pause.

Alice   Course you are, love.

Kelly *studies* **Alice**.

John   Luigi said it's nuclear bombs that make the peace.

Pause.

I like Luigi.

Alice   Shut up, John.

A slight pause.

John   I like Luigi.

A slight pause.

I've decided that I can forgive him now.

A slight pause.

Is it wrong to forgive?

A slight pause.

I'll tell him when I see him.

Alice   You won't, you'll keep quiet.

Kelly   No one will be seeing Luigi any more.

Pause.

John   Is that true, Mum? Merm?

Alice *nods.*

John   Will you stay with us until I've done my exam?

Kelly   I don't know.

John   It's always Mum helping me. You need to help me as well. I need to get my scholarship.

Kelly   I don't know, son.

John   You won't have to pay any money.

A slight pause.

Kelly   It doesn't matter about money.

John   When you get a scholarship they give you money towards your uniform as well, don't they, Mum? Merm?

Alice *nods.*

John   If you help me, then I'll come down to the stall every Saturday to help you pack up? I can, can't I, Mum?

A slight pause.

Then you can sack Luigi. I don't mind not going to football. You won't miss Geoff Pike, will you, Mum?

A slight pause.

What book did Miss Brooks say to read next?

Alice   I'll have to look at the list, John.

John   Anyway, I'm starting the fat thing again.

Alice   You're being silly.

John   I haven't been taking it in.

A slight pause.

I've been upset.

A slight pause.

I'm going to start from the beginning. It's better having a fresh start.

Kelly   I know what you're doing, son.

He stands with his plate. Pause.

I've got to finish my packing now, John.

Kelly *collects the other two plates and takes them out.* **John** *thinks, gets up and then takes* David Copperfield *from the bookcase.* **Alice** *rests her head on the table.* **John** *sits on the sofa with his book. Pause.*

Kelly *enters.*

John   Will you come and listen to me read?

Kelly   Go and get ready for school.

John *stands.*

John   Dad?

Kelly   What?

John   I thought you wanted me to do my reading?

Kelly   Go and put your uniform on.

John   Don't you want me any more?

Pause.

Kelly   Don't be silly.

John   I'm doing my exam now.

Kelly   Go and get ready.

John   Why won't you listen to me read?

Kelly   Because then it will be something else afterwards and I won't be able to go.

Alice *turns.*

Alice   I'll pack your stuff.

John   You leave his stuff alone!

Kelly   I can't now, John.

Alice   Please, Kelly.

Kelly   No.

John   I hope you both die of cancer! I hope you rot in hell!

Kelly *is gutted. He hovers, unsure what to do.*

John   Why are you leaving me?

Kelly   I'm not leaving you.

John   You are, you're leaving me.

A slight pause.

I promise I'll pass my exam, I promise I'll come to the stall, I promise you. Please, Dad.

A slight pause.

I promise you I'll do everything you want.

A slight pause.

Please, Dad.

Alice   In God's name, Kelly, can't you see what you're doing to him? If you're going, just go!

John   You can shut up as well, you're a cunt!

Alice *is upset. Pause.*

Kelly   Don't speak like that.

John   You can't tell me anything any more!

Kelly   Don't speak to your mother like that, it's not fair.

John   You said it!

Kelly   Listen to me.

John   I don't want to listen any more!

Kelly   Listen to me.

John   Cunt, cunt, cunt, cunt. Cunt! Cunt, cunt, cunt!

A slight pause.

John *sits down. Long pause.*

Kelly *fetches* **John***'s book and sits down next to him on the sofa. He gives it to* **John***. Pause.*

Kelly   Come on, read a bit and then school. Miss Brooks'll wonder where you are.

John *reads from* David Copperfield.

John   'Whether I shall turn out to be the hero of my own life, or whether that station will be held by anybody else, these pages must show. To begin my life with the . . .'

A slight pause.

Kelly   Go on.

John   I don't want to.

A slight pause.

I didn't mean it.

Kelly   Go on.

John   'To begin my life with the beginning of my life, I record that I was born (as I have been informed and believe) on a Friday, at twelve o'clock at night. It was remarked that the clock began to strike, and I began to cry . . .'

A slight pause.

Kelly   I can't say that word.

John *looks at* **Kelly**.

John   'Simultaneously.'

A slight pause.

Kelly   What you waiting for?

A slight pause.

Alice *moves.*

John   Where you going, Mum?

Alice   I'm going to bed.

John   What are you going to bed for?

Alice   Leave it, John. Leave me alone.

Alice *exits.*

Pause.

John   You're not going as well, are you, Dad?

Pause.

Kelly   Go and put on your uniform and go and say sorry to your mother.

A slight pause.

John   Why? I don't want to go today.

Pause.

Kelly *stands.*

Kelly   Because, if you don't put your uniform on and go to school I'm going to Nana's and I'm never coming back.

A slight pause.

John *nods and smiles. Pause.*

Blackout.

'Pounding' by the Doves plays. **John**, *aged eleven, waits and enjoys the room altering around him.* **John**, *aged twenty-nine, enters. They look at each other for some time.* **John**, *eleven, throws* **John**, *twenty-nine, the book. The song ends. Silence.*

John, *eleven, exits.*

Four

14 February 2003. Evening.

The furniture has been cleared out. The room is nicely decorated, and in addition to the photos from before there's a graduation photo of **John**. *A closed coffin stands in the centre of the room.* **John** *looks at the book. There are four bin bags full of junk and old clothes.* **John** *puts the book down and reaches into one of the black bags. He takes out one of* **Kelly**'*s vests and covers his mouth with it. He is upset. He hears something.*

John   Mum?

A slight pause.

Mum?

Luigi *enters. He has some lilies.*

John   I said I'd do it.

Luigi   John.

John *notices him. Long pause.*

Luigi   Do you remember who I am?

John *nods. A slight pause.*

Luigi   How are you?

John *shakes his head.*

Luigi   I hope you don't mind – I wanted to offer my condolences.

John   You're all right.

Luigi   I'm so very deeply sorry for your loss.

Pause.

Luigi *comes further into the room.*

John   Do you want a drink or something?

Luigi   I'm OK.

John   Are you sure? I can put the kettle on? My mum will want a cup.

Luigi   No.

A slight pause.

When did he – ?

John   Tuesday before last.

Luigi   I heard quite by accident. I – I am so sorry, John. I heard – I would have liked to come tomorrow.

Pause.

Where's your mother?

John   She's out, she couldn't – I said I'd do it.

Luigi   It must be a great shock.

Pause.

John   When you've shared your life with someone for forty-odd years and then they're gone, it's a hard one, eh, mate?

Luigi   I am so terribly sorry.

He looks around.

There's no one to look after my stall tomorrow. Really I feel –

John   He got a lot done, didn't he?

Pause.

You've got a stall, then?

A slight pause.

What's your trade?

Luigi   Skirts, jumpers, that sort of thing.

John   You didn't fancy flogging high heels?

Luigi   No. You look very different.

John   You don't.

Luigi   You're still handsome.

John   Are you married?

Luigi   No.

Pause.

John   I'm sorry.

Luigi   No. Are you?

John   No, no, I'm on my own.

Luigi   I'm sorry.

Pause.

Can I –?

John *nods.* **Luigi** *rests the lilies on the side.*

John   I'm sorry – I've not seen you in nearly twenty
years –

Luigi   Would you like me to go?

A slight pause.

John   Part of me wants to tell you to go.

A slight pause.

Luigi   I regretted very much that I fell out with your dad.
I've never forgotten him.

A slight pause.

This is foolish. I should go.

A slight pause.

I wanted to see you and your mother for a few minutes,
that's all.

A slight pause.

John   They say there's going to be two million marching
in London tomorrow. I would have gone.

Luigi *thinks, then takes from his pocket the little tank* **John** *gave him
when he was eleven.*

John   You kept it.

Luigi   I found it. Yes.

He throws **John** *the tank. Pause.*

This place is looking nice.

John *looks at the tank.*

John   Dad found one when he laid the patio last summer.
He got a lot of work done, didn't he? Paint's not come off
has it?

Luigi   No.

A slight pause.

John   I'm pleased you've come.

Pause.

Luigi   It's cold.

John   The heating is on. Did you shut the door?

Luigi *rests his hand very gently on the coffin. A slight pause.*

John   I couldn't bear it. I got the undertaker to –

Luigi   I understand.

A slight pause.

Can I be straight with you, John?

A slight pause.

I don't know if you know why I left the stall?

A slight pause.

I've always felt very guilty about your dad. I calculated I must have stolen at least five hundred pounds from him.

A slight pause.

John   I know.

Luigi   I've been doing very well. I've got three stalls now.

Pause.

Five hundred pounds now – I don't know. There's two thousand pounds. I heard it is a big funeral and the whole market will come to a standstill tomorrow. I would like very much for you to have this to help –

Luigi *reaches inside his jacket. He takes some money from his wallet and offers it to* **John**.

Pause.

John   We don't need your money.

Luigi   Please.

Pause.

John   I've got to write the eulogy.

Pause.

I've never been able to write until the last minute.

A slight pause.

When I was at university my dissertation was a nightmare. I didn't sleep for three days.

A slight pause.

Luigi   You got your scholarship, then?

John   No, I didn't, no.

Pause.

No, my dad paid every last penny for my school.

Pause.

'Future History as Political Discourse – a Reading of Third World War Fiction.'

A slight pause.

I was fart-arsing around looking at women novelists, but my tutor straightened me out. He said I should write about something that actually interested me. I've always been pretty obsessed. I've got *Civilisation Three* on my PC. You don't know how pleasurable it is nuking Pyongyang when I've had a grim day at work.

Luigi   Please.

Luigi *offers the money again.*

John   I don't want your money.

Pause.

My dissertation was quite good, actually. There were allusions to *Utopia* and *On the Beach* and everything. It was published.

Luigi   Your dad must have been very proud.

John   He was, I think.

Pause.

I don't know if you remember this.

A slight pause.

I'd seen that film, *Threads.* I was freaked out. I thought we were all going to die. I thought the world was going to end. Do you remember?

A slight pause.

I nearly ate Dad's toenail.

Luigi *laughs.*

John   You said, by always threatening each other, Russia and America, that that's what kept the peace.

A slight pause.

I think my dad was the only fella on Romford Market who never made any money out of the eighties.

He laughs and wipes his eyes. **Luigi** *smiles.*

Never got the right gear, did he?

Luigi nods.

John   When you left he was lost. He didn't have anyone to chat up the women. My dad couldn't pull a Christmas cracker, could he?

A slight pause.

Once you left all he got was the old grannies, so he started doing two-ninety-nine slippers.

Luigi   I didn't want to leave, John.

Pause.

Please, I ask for the last time. To me it is a debt of honour.

John I've never had a free meal-ticket in my life. I don't want it.

A slight pause.

I always imagined that you had a secret life in the Mafia. Like *The Godfather.*

Luigi A boy, like me? From Stepney?

John *and* **Luigi** *laugh.*

John I used to dream you were my dad. Being on the stall with you on my own – you never shouted.

A slight pause.

But mostly I've thought you're a cunt.

A slight pause.

I should have given it to my dad. You know, the one he dug up sat on top of the telly for a fortnight. He was proud of it.

A slight pause.

Luigi I know you're angry. Your father was very angry inside. So was your mother.

A slight pause.

I'm very angry now as well.

A slight pause.

But I must tell you that your father never spoke to me in that way.

Pause.

When we said goodbye he gave me a week's wages and shook my hand. That's right.

Long pause.

Your father taught me the greatest lesson of life.

Pause.

I'm sorry that you haven't yet learnt it.

Long pause.

You're a very small man, John.

Long pause.

I hope that your speech goes well tomorrow. I'm sure you'll think of something good to say.

Pause.

If you think it will help your mother feel any better, tell her that I'm deeply sorry for your loss.

Luigi *places the money on top of the coffin.*

John   You don't know the sort of man I am.

Luigi   I don't care, John.

Pause.

John   I must have seemed like a right little weirdo with all my strategy games and my books. I tell you what, I wish I'd spent as much time on girls as I did on books when I was a teenager.

Long pause.

Perhaps, if you'd kept your dirty hands off of my mother and stayed on the stall I'd have taken after you a bit more than my dad.

Pause.

I know. I know, you bastard.

Pause.

That's right.

Pause.

I found out the night I last saw you.

Pause.

I heard Mum and Dad arguing.

Pause.

I thought my whole world had come to an end.

Pause. He is choked.

But I was wrong.

A slight pause.

It happened last Tuesday.

He wipes his eyes.

I can't believe it. I can't believe it. I can't believe it.

He composes himself and notices the money.

Take that money off of there before I brain you, you cheating bastard. How dare you?

Luigi *removes the money from the coffin. He hesitates, unsure what to do.*

John   I've always known. Dad always knew what you'd done to him. It's just that he was a bigger man than you.

Pause.

Luigi   I'm not trying to make excuses for what I did. When I – I was – I was trying to –

John   What?

Long pause.

Luigi   I shouldn't have come.

Long pause.

I wanted to pay my respects. I didn't want to –

Pause.

There is a reason why I kept your little tank. Like a sentimental fool.

Pause.

John   Why?

A slight pause.

Luigi   Your father liked me to –

John   What?

Luigi   I felt like I impressed your father –

John   Go on, say it.

Luigi   When I was –

John   Say it.

Luigi   Pulling the women.

Pause.

John   And that's why you did it?

Luigi   No.

John   If you're trying to say it was my dad's fault you can –

A slight pause.

You bastard.

A slight pause.

I can never forgive you. I can never forgive what you did to my dad.

A slight pause.

And if you'd have had the front to turn up tomorrow I would have spat in your face.

A slight pause.

Luigi   Then what can I do?

A slight pause.

I loved your mum and dad.

John   That's why you're here, is it?

Luigi   No –

John   He's not even cold and you're chasing after my mother, you bastard.

Luigi   I haven't seen your mother in twenty years!

John   If you think she'll be pleased to see you, you've got another think coming.

Luigi   I loved your dad – I loved it here – I loved working for him – all the noise and the fighting and the laughing –

A slight pause.

I loved him like I loved my own father, and I pissed all over him! Don't you think I've regretted the things I did every day for the last twenty years? I had no one until your father gave me a job! I loved him like my own father. I'll tell you the truth now and you'll listen. Not a day has passed since I walked away from your dad that I haven't thought about him.

A slight pause.

You filled my life and because of my own foolish actions I lost it all.

He wipes his eyes. Both of them are breathless and shocked. Long pause.

I don't know what to say, John.

A slight pause.

John   My mum started smoking again. She'd given up because of my dad's asthma, but he never criticised her for it. Forty a day for nigh on twenty year. I always wondered which one of them it would kill first.

A slight pause.

The stupid buggers – stupid, stupid buggers.

Long pause.

He wipes his eyes. A slight pause.

Look at this.

He fishes around in one of the bin bags. He takes out the old Betamax video recorder. A slight pause.

Worth a lot of money now, it's mint. Kitsch value, eh, Lulu?

He puts it down. Long pause.

You know what I was doing an hour – an hour before I heard last Tuesday?

A slight pause.

I was standing outside the station with a 'Not In My Name' banner, and some jumped-up dickhead from the *Romford Recorder* was taking a photo.

A slight pause.

Then Mum rang my mobile and everything changed.

A slight pause.

Compared to the things – to the sacrifices, my mum and dad made, I've –

A slight pause.

I've got a nice flat, but I've never left Romford.

A slight pause.

I've never had a girlfriend to speak of that I've brought home to them.

A slight pause.

I work for an American bank. It means nothing to me – it ultimately achieves nothing other than putting money in the pockets of those arseholes that run the world.

A slight pause.

I thought, I've convinced myself, staying in Romford, I've been there for Mum and Dad. Never getting myself attached to anyone, keeping up my housekeeping even though I've left home, it's all –

A slight pause.

Compared to my mum and dad I'm a –

A slight pause.

Compared to my dad I am – I'm a very small man.

Luigi   Don't talk this way, John, please. I didn't –

John   You know, in thirty-odd years of married life they never had a holiday. I've been all over the world. Thailand; Sydney; Mexico; South Africa; California; Poland. I've been too ashamed to tell my mum and dad the money I earn.

Pause.

My dad never had a pot to piss in and he never went further than Collier Row, but the things he tried to do in his life meant more than anything I've ever done or ever could do in my life.

Luigi   I think your mum and dad would be very upset to hear you talking like this.

Pause.

John   Did you love my mum?

A slight pause.

Even just for a while?

Long pause.

Luigi   I liked your mum.

Pause.

John   My mum didn't love you. She loved Geoff Pike. Even when we signed Frank McAvennie he was still her favourite. That funny beard. I don't think he was trying to

be designer either. We saw him play his last match. Up
at Goodison. They beat us four-nil but we drove up to
Blackpool Sunday morning. Saw the illuminations. Dad
didn't put out. And Mum never smoked all weekend.

A slight pause.

I'm glad she smoked.

A slight pause.

There's more meaning in my mum smoking than there is in
a thousand banners.

A slight pause.

In a way my dad won. She was very hard on herself over
what happened. She became very quiet.

A slight pause.

But she still resisted. My dad understood that. My dad
wasn't a bad man. He was a good man.

Pause.

It's the people that want to win that I worry about. Dad
wasn't like that.

A slight pause.

Americans don't understand that, do they?

A slight pause.

There's still time for Armageddon with the bunch that are
in charge now, eh, Luigi?

A slight pause.

When it finally kicks off in Iraq I hope they get those
unfeeling bastards.

A slight pause.

But they'll all be safe. They'll all be deep underground. Or
miles up in the sky nice and safe in their government planes.

A slight pause.

They'll be all right. It'll be decent folk like my mum dying of smallpox when the Arabs get their own back.

A slight pause.

The house has been so quiet. I can't tell you.

Pause.

My dad had to work hard. He put out seven days a week until the day he died to pay for my education – to get the house nice for Mum. And they were still penniless.

A slight pause.

Mum was very quiet. Everything changed. No one complained about anything. I cried in my room when the letter came that said I hadn't got a scholarship. No one said anything. We all just got on with it.

A slight pause.

Dad was frightened my education would take me away from him – and in a way it did. But he broke his back making sure I had it, because he didn't want me pulling out a barrow at five o'clock in the morning like he had. You've got no idea how hard it's been for them. And I'll tell you another thing, it's a mind-fuck having cream buns after games on Saturday and coming home to a packet of stale crisps and a slice of toast for dinner because that's all there is in the cupboard.

A slight pause.

I'd drive a tank through every one of those schools if I had my way. I'd wipe them off of the face of the planet.

Pause.

Luigi   Your father always knew?

John *nods. Pause.*

John   I've spent all this time thinking it was worth it – At least we had each other – telling myself at least things were settled, but I –

A slight pause.

You said, by always threatening each other, Russia and America, that that's what kept the peace.

A slight pause.

That's what I thought Mum and Dad were like – screaming and shouting, always saying they were going, then the endless not-speaking –

Luigi   John –

John   You promised me – I've never forgotten it.

Luigi   I didn't promise you anything –

John   But a fucking Cold War's no better than a hot one, is it? Is it?

Pause.

I got a first. Mum and Dad loved it – seeing me graduate. Apparently I was borderline two-one but my dissertation swung it. My tutor said it was brilliant. It all sort of fitted together in my head. Mum and Dad, and the world. Always pushing each other –

A slight pause.

It's how I made sense of the sacrifices they made for me, for my education. I realised that. I knew I was trying to –

He looks at the graduation photo.

They loved it.

A slight pause.

You did say to me – I haven't imagined that.

Luigi   I don't remember, John.

346   M.A.D.

Long pause.

John   I've always blamed you. I've been kicking against the world – For years I thought that was the night I grew up – When you – But when I heard – When I heard my dad – I couldn't – I couldn't – Seeing you now – Him gone – Seeing you tonight, I can't any more –

Luigi   What can I do? How can I help you? Please tell me.

John   You can't. Leave me be.

Long pause.

Luigi   How – ? How did your father – ? Was it – ?

John *studies* **Luigi**. *A slight pause.*

John   An eighty-six hit him on London Road. He'd stopped off for a bottle of cream soda and some custard creams on the way home and he didn't look where he was going.

Pause.

He didn't know a thing about it.

Pause.

Mum was distraught.

Pause.

The doctor tried to be kind. He told us my dad's left testicle was the size of a tennis ball. And from the look of him he had cancer in his lungs as well. Said, maybe the bus driver had done him a favour.

Pause.

Mum didn't know anything about it.

Pause.

He was that sort of fella, wasn't he?

Pause.

The doctor was trying to be kind, but he didn't know us, did he?

Pause.

I don't know what to say.

Pause.

I can't stand there and say nothing.

Pause.

You know what really pisses me off? Really genuinely angers me?

Pause.

I feel all I've got left are clichés. It's like falling in love except it's worse because it's someone I've known all my life.

A slight pause.

A first, I got a first. And I can't even celebrate the life of the person I loved more than anything –

Pause.

The church is going to be full up. I think the whole of Romford Market's going to be in St Edward's tomorrow. And even if I could find the words I can't kid myself he's listening somewhere, because he's not –

He tries very hard not to crack.

He's gone and he's never coming back.

Long pause. He wipes his eyes.

Mum will be back. She started to clear his stuff out. She found a Valentine's card. She hadn't had one off him in twenty-five years.

A slight pause.

At least he won't see us relegated.

Pause.

Why didn't I let him go?

Long pause.

He was never happy.

A slight pause.

He's gone now, hasn't he? And I can't tell him I'm sorry.

John *finally cries. Long pause.*

Luigi   John –

Pause.

John   You don't know.

Pause.

Luigi   It doesn't matter whether your father can hear you or not tomorrow. It's the best thing you can do for him.

A slight pause.

Don't you think if you can speak from the heart in front of all those people, it will make a huge difference to you?

John   I can't do it.

Long pause.

Luigi   Your dad gave me a job after he caught me trying to pinch a pair of slingbacks for a lady.

Pause.

I told him the truth. I was broke. He joked with me about it. He said I had one chance and not to wear it out.

Pause.

He said I had more front than Selfridges. I like that expression.

Pause.

He always talked about you and your mother. And I was very jealous.

Pause.

The women who came to your father's stall loved him. He couldn't see it. He asked about their lives. He talked about you and your mother. He liked to talk about taking you to the football and bringing you the Walnut Whip. When I asked him why he was faithful he would always say this: 'Why would I go up the road for a cheeseburger when I can have steak at home?'

He smiles.

When the mongrel dog died – Do you remember the mongrel dog – the scavenger?

John *shakes his head.*

Luigi   Another trader found the dog in the yard. Your dad stopped him throwing him in the dustcart. And he buried the dog himself.

John   I don't need this sentimental crap.

Luigi *thinks. Pause.*

Luigi   Your father was silly. But I liked it very much that he was silly.

A slight pause.

He loved that you called him Dodo.

John   Please –

A slight pause.

Luigi   You won't learn anything unless you listen.

Pause.

Then your father, he converted me to liking the Chas 'n' Dave, which I have to say, I have never forgiven him for.

A slight pause.

When I asked him why he didn't follow a better football team, it's the only time he ever got annoyed with me.

John   Please, Luigi –

Long pause.

Luigi   John, your father didn't want to go. He loved your mum. He loved you.

Long pause.

You can say all these things better than me.

John   I –

Pause.

Luigi   You have to do it.

Pause.

I know that part of you must hate me.

Pause.

But my intentions coming here tonight were honourable. I apologise, John. My heart is full of shame.

Pause.

John   I'm sorry.

A slight pause.

Luigi   I don't think I can see your mother now.

Pause.

Will you tell her I came, and that I send my most sincere condolences?

John *nods. A slight pause.*

John *takes the tank and throws it to* **Luigi**. **Luigi** *looks at it and then very gently places it at the centre of the coffin. A slight pause.*

John   You know where we are.

A slight pause.

Luigi   Let's not part on a lie.

A slight pause.

John *reaches towards* **Luigi**.

Luigi   No.

A slight pause.

I like that you planned to march in London tomorrow.

A slight pause.

You can feel like nothing gets better and the world doesn't move on.

A slight pause.

Good luck, John-boy.

John *moves towards* **Luigi**.

Luigi   I mean to go.

A slight pause.

John   Luigi, I –

Luigi   No.

John *and* **Luigi** *look at each other. Silence.*

Luigi *nods, rather formally this time, and moves to go. He pauses for a moment and then exits. Pause.*

John *spots the tank. He slowly approaches the coffin and reaches for it, but he can't touch it. His hand trembles above it. Pause.*

He closes his eyes and gently lowers his hand until it rests beside the tank on the coffin.

Fade.

10821165R00198

Printed in Great Britain
by Amazon